Does God Believe in Human Rights?

STUDIES IN RELIGION, SECULAR BELIEFS AND HUMAN RIGHTS

VOLUME 5

Does God Believe in Human Rights?

Essays on Religion and Human Rights

Edited by

Nazila Ghanea
Alan Stephens
Raphael Walden

MARTINUS
NIJHOFF
PUBLISHERS

LEIDEN • BOSTON
2007

A C.I.P. record for this book is available from the Library of Congress.

Printed on acid-free paper

ISSN 1871-7829
ISBN-13: 978 90 04 15254 0
ISBN-10: 90 04 15254 7

Koninklijke Brill NV incorporates the imprints Brill, Hotei Publishers, IDC Publishers, Martinus Nijhoff Publishers and VSP.

http://www.brill.nl

Designed and digitally typeset by BooKraft@googlemail.com

Printed and bound in The Netherlands.

CONTENTS

PREFACE

It is important that we constantly analyse the relationship between human rights and religion and keep reminding ourselves of our obligation to be aware of the diversity of the views represented in this book. The moral values created by many faiths have been among the foundations upon which societies have based their attitudes. These values have not only been successful in creating a feeling of identity, but have also laid down very clear moral codes on which their adherents, and others, have based their lives.

It is particularly sad that, in spite of the existence of these moral codes, distilled by people throughout the ages, intolerance, bigotry and disregard for those of different beliefs seem to be undergoing a resurgence. The human rights developments of the nineteenth century, which played such a great role in emancipating people from serfdom, enabled societies to alter and to respect their poorest members through complex forms of social welfare, irrespective of faith-led institutions. Both human rights and religion have been catalysts for the improvement of man's welfare, and attempts to underpin this through the United Nations Declaration of Human Rights in 1948, and through regional and universal human rights covenants, have succeeded in making people judge their conduct against new, non-religious benchmarks. Despite this, we see many appalling failures from one side of the globe to the other. The debates summarised in these papers will hopefully contribute to a better understanding of the complexities of the problems confronting us all.

Religion may create a feeling of tension in the human heart; the believer may be filled with anxiety because of the remoteness of God and a longing for His proximity. There may be a conflict between human rights and religion, but we should rejoice in the spiritual conflict which perhaps fortifies this.

We need to broaden and better structure the dialogue between faiths – even between those that do not appear to be mutually compatible – in order to distil principles that will protect human beings and give them dignity where this is lacking. It is, of course, important that we do not give a platform to those who wish to destroy or suppress others. Human rights may have to face limitations if societies are to remain intact. We fervently hope that the debates which we have tried to promote through our meetings and conferences, such as those highlighted in this volume, will help to create something that may ultimately strengthen our spiritual understanding of the apparently incomprehensible.

A book of lectures written at the end of the nineteenth century by Thomas Masaryk, first president of Czechoslovakia, was published in Prague in 1938. In these lectures, he emphasised the danger inherent in compromise: in the end it affected all principles. Thus, it should only be accepted on matters of minor importance. If a principle were endangered, then a compromise should be morally impossible. There were really very few occasions, he stated, in which insignificant matters only were at stake. Compromise, for him, most frequently meant that a party gave in; and thus originated the ethical and political dilettantism so common today.

The necessity for religion in society is to prevent a fall into chaos. Hume, Kant, Compte, Herbert Spencer and Smetana each appealed to atheism or agnosticism but were, in the end, forced to fall back on more or less religious concepts. In his book *After Virtue* (London: Duckworth, 1985), Alastair Macintyre highlighted why the eighteenth century enlightenment project failed. All the philosophers were deeply influenced by their own religious backgrounds, which they claimed were relatively unimportant but which, to a marked extent, contributed to the foundations on which much of their argumentation was based. Of course, Kant denied that morality was based on human nature. Kierkegaard no longer attempted to justify morality, yet his account has precisely the same structure as that shared by the accounts of Kant, Hume and Diderot. If we look at the framework of theistic beliefs, whether Jewish, through Maimonides, Christian, through Aquinas, or Islamic, through Ibn Rushd, they were all influenced by non-theological sources. The fall of man in the biblical sense, on the other hand, was one of the first arguments for the frailty of human conduct. Here the rights of man were perhaps biblically highlighted when God asked Adam why he had stolen from the tree and Adam was entitled to reason and defend himself!

Finally, I would like to express my appreciation to the Shoresh Charitable Trust for their support of this project.

—Clemens N. Nathan

FOREWORD

THE GENESIS OF THIS COLLECTION is in a colloquium of the same name held on 28 February 2005 by the Clemens Nathan Research Centre, the University of London Institute of Commonwealth Studies and Martinus Nijhoff Publishers. Presenters at the conference were invited to 'tackle head-on the question of whether there is an irreconcilable conflict between religious principles, teachings and laws and international and regional human-rights systems that have developed in the period since 1945. Where there is such a conflict, who should give ground? Should religions always be expected to find ways to interpret their teachings so as to conform to the current human-rights system? Or should existing human-rights standards allow for sufficient flexibility to take on board religious sensitivities?' Presenters largely rose to this challenge, and their responses and observations are shared with you in the chapters that follow.

The essays in this collection are revised versions of the papers that were delivered at that conference. In presenting this volume, we would like to express our deep appreciation to the authors for the trouble they have taken in delivering the original papers, as well as in revising and preparing them for publication. We would also like to express our thanks to Martinus Nijhoff Publishers, and especially to Lindy Melman, for their continued interest particularly in the field of religion and human rights.

The following is a brief summary of the essays included in this volume.

1. Richard Harries, 'The Complimentarity between Secular and Religious Perspectives of Human Rights'

Despite numerous suspicions surrounding the relationship between religion and human rights, Harries challenges the notion that human rights is fundamentally a secular concept. He does this through a historical assessment. He argues, from a Christian perspective, that rights are grounded in the dignity of human beings – all of whom enjoy free will. Since God made human beings in his own image, He too respects the worth and dignity of humanity. Human rights is therefore necessary to protect the value of each person. The basis of human rights from this perspective is thus rooted in human dignity. Human rights is necessary because human dignity is too often denied in practice.

This religious perspective, Harries suggests, complements the secular perspective on human rights – which calls for valuing human beings in themselves and for themselves. Whilst through the ages some Christians have called for the need to sacrifice or waive rights, Harries challenges this position. Though a person may feel the compassion or charity to waive his *own* rights, he argues, one cannot waive the rights of *others* without the risk of reinforcing politically oppressive rule.

Human rights constitutes a dynamic historical process that is legally enshrined. However, rights are also grounded in values and in a moral perspective. Just as human rights are evolving, the full implications of our moral values need to be worked out over time too. In this way, moral insights grounded in a religious perspective come to be realised and turned into law. Harries gives a number of examples of where religion has played such a role in promoting the rights of the most vulnerable not out of charity but as a basic and necessary requirement of justice.

2. Roger Ruston, 'Religious Truths and Human Coexistence'

Ruston argues that the tensions between the secular regime of human rights and the conduct of particular religious traditions puts both states and religious bodies to the test and requires reflection and response. Ruston, drawing on the Catholic tradition, puts forward the hypothesis that human rights can only be *fully* understood as originating from a theological perspective of human beings as creatures of God. This is the position of natural justice, that of our common humanity, of being created in the image of God and being part of a global common good. This position also holds that we have obligations or duties towards those outside our own religious tradition because of our common humanity. He argues that Catholicism and other religious traditions uphold an irreducible minimum of duties and respect we owe to other persons that cannot be overridden even by any supposed divine commands seeming to suggest otherwise. If all religious believers accepted this as the true understanding of their religious belief, it would have profound implications. Ruston acknowledges that the particularist claims of religions often obscure this 'truth'. Nevertheless he holds that the biblical position of what he refers to as a 'basic equality' would prove almost impossible to support from a secular perspective. The natural law tradition is examined through a number of historical examples, from Thomas Aquinas to Bartolomé de Las Casas and finally John Locke. All three believed that we owe natural duties of benevolence towards other human beings, and that this benevolence is in the nature of true religion. These positions, Ruston argues, also support the overriding duty of the State to prevent the denial of human rights; they further imply, controversially perhaps, that civil authority has the duty to intervene in the conduct of religious bodies that deny basic natural rights to its members. In this way, the secular discourse of human rights can be seen as actually having grown from within a Christian religious tradition in response to reflection on God's presence in the world.

3. Michael Ipgrave, 'Religion in a Democratic Society: Safeguarding Freedom, Acknowledging Identity, Valuing Partnership'

Ipgrave discusses the issues raised by the existence of religious communities within the framework of plural, democratic and secular society. He singles out three issues. First is the safeguarding of religious freedom in public life. Whilst in principle human rights law distinguishes between the *forum internum*, in which religious freedom is absolute, and the *forum externum*, where it may sometimes be subject to derogation, in practice, Ipgrave argues, derogation from the latter may impinge on the former both in public life and within religious communities. On the one hand, there is the pressure for aspects of religious life to be privatised; on the other, religious beliefs are made public in assessing candidates for public office. The second issue is recognition of religious identity as a constitutive strand of self-understanding and hence of citizenship. This is particularly significant where members of religious communities feel vulnerable and disadvantaged. Whilst there is the temptation to extend legislation in the field of racial discrimination to cater also for religious discrimination, Ipgrave identifies a number of criteria by which the two identities should be recognised as being different. Thirdly and finally, he discusses forms of partnership between religious communities and public authorities. He explores the forms this has taken in the UK and problematises these various relationships, focusing particularly on consultation and service delivery.

4. Javaid Rehman, 'Conflicting Values or Misplaced Interpretations? Examining the Inevitability of a Clash between "Religions" and "Human Rights"'

Despite the widely held position that a clash between religion and human rights is inevitable, Rehman argues for the critical role of interpretation both of religion and human rights. With sensitive interpretation, he argues, there are numerous possibilities of a rapprochement between religions and human rights. He explores these possibilities using the example of Islam and the way Sharia can be used to support rights. He counters positions that believe Islam to be a religion of violence and aggression, whilst acknowledging the need to understand problematic concepts such as *jihad* and the status of minorities. He does so within the historical context of revelation, with consideration of all relevant verses in the Qur'an and also the practice of the Prophet Muhammad. A range of possible interpretations can be given to key Islamic concepts, a fact that insular, myopic and archaic views of the Sharia try to inhibit. Both human rights law and religious law are malleable, and allow for sympathetic readings such that they support one another. Rehman argues that interpretations of the Sharia that fully support modern human rights law are both necessary and timely.

5. Norman Solomon, 'Religion and Human Rights with Special Reference to Judaism'

Solomon digs below the assertion that religion is against human rights. It is the followers of religion interpreting a holy text through an authoritative teacher, then applying it through judges that implement decisions that are accepted by the religious community, that brings about the context for religion having a negative impact on human rights. However, the religious community concerned will assert that these interpretations and laws have been divinely guided and are absolute, and therefore need to be distinguished from mere human law. This gives rise to the dilemmas of authority and of rights. Solomon explores these dilemmas in relation to the Jewish tradition. The dilemma of authority is that if the ultimate authority in religion is God, then what should be the relationship with legitimate government? And in the case of rights, which source of authority is to be obeyed? The rights Solomon explores are those of life, in relation to the Biblical sanction of capital punishment; liberty, in relation to slaves; thought, speech and conscience in relation to blasphemers, idolaters and other believers; and the equality of women with men and equality before the law – that we may be equal before God but we are not necessarily equal before the law. In all these potential clashes with human rights, Solomon's question is who should give way to whom? He asks to what extent disagreements about these issues between the Jewish tradition and modern human rights cause real difficulty today. He concludes that it is the attachment of believers to tradition and doctrine rather than people that ultimately causes clashes, not religion or God.

6. Avrom Sherr, 'Religion and Human Rights: Redressing the Balance'

Sherr outlines the strong similarities between types of religious obligations and human rights in the sense that both comprise sets of ideals that are constantly developing and being interpreted in relation to particular contexts. This can make religious beliefs and human rights competitors in terms of their regulatory systems, which moves Sherr to his key question of whether there are any themes or rules developing which can help us identify whether religions should trump human rights, or vice versa, in particular situations. He examines this question within a Jewish framework.

The questions of slavery, murder and women's rights form part of this examination from within a religious framework. From within a human rights framework, the question is to what extent human rights is culturally contextual and to what extent it is culturally imperialistic. To what extent can human rights accommodate culture and religion and in which situations should human rights prevail over the practice of particular religious traditions? Sherr teases out some thought-provoking questions and puts forward the need for a balancing of rights. He concludes that at present there is not enough jurisprudence examining tensions between religious practice and human rights to allow us to draw out rules for deciding which should trump the other, but some themes assisting in the making of such decisions are emerging.

7. Melanie Phillips, 'Human Rights and Its Destruction of Right and Wrong'

Phillips asserts that modern human rights are in direct conflict with religion and are replacing Judeo-Christian values with godless secular values that are destroying society. The fundamental distinction between human rights and religions such as Judaism and Christianity is that these are religions of duties, duties to God and to man, because humanity is made in the image of God. Duties are prior to rights; so, for example, human freedom is predicated on constraints on human behaviour. In contrast, human rights has put freedoms first and created a culture of entitlement. Human rights, to Phillips, is anti-democratic in its attempts to overrule different cultures that are rooted in religious principles. This puts the vision of the society implicit in human rights and that envisioned by religious cultures fundamentally at odds with one another. To Phillips, the precondition for the flourishing of society is that we all accept that we have duties to each other, as opposed to being set up against one another as different victim groups demanding duty-less rights, which is the human rights position according to this author. Human rights has become a demand for freedom from all authority that might constrain the liberty of the individual and an engine for a culture of extreme individualism. In its promotion of equal entitlements, human rights has effectively destroyed discrimination between all moral judgements and between right and wrong, leading to what Phillips terms 'identicality' rather than equality. She concludes that religion emphasises duties, not rights, and is actually crucial to securing rights to life and liberty, whereas secular human rights culture is actually threatening them.

8. John Barnabas Leith, 'A More Constructive Encounter: A Bahá'í View of Religion and Human Rights'

In this chapter, John Barnabas Leith elaborates the clear theological foundations and commitment of the Bahá'í Faith to universal human-rights values. He draws on both the Bahá'í sacred writings and the practice of the Bahá'í International Community, a UN non-governmental organisation, in support of his position. Bahá'í sacred writings are centrally concerned with questions of good governance and judicial, social and economic justice. This is rooted, at least in part, in the concern that all individuals should be allowed to develop their qualities and capacities for their own good and the good of society as a whole. It is further developed, Leith argues, in the principle of the oneness of humankind which lies at the core of Bahá'í teachings. This has wide-ranging implications for societal justice, from the abandonment of prejudice to the embracing of diversity. Each and every human being, in Bahá'í perspective, is worthy of moral protection and the holder of inalienable human rights; each human being is a trust of the whole of humankind. These principles are explored further in relation to the freedom of all individuals to investigate reality for themselves, the freedom of religion and belief, human dignity, and in the development of a peaceful and united global civilisation. These principles are then examined in relation to a number of Bahá'í human rights activities – particularly the defence of the human rights of the Bahá'ís in Iran.

9. Paul Weller, '"Human Rights", "Religion" and the "Secular": Variant Configurations of Religion(s), State(s) and Society(ies)'

Both religion and human rights have a plurality of meanings associated with them whether in theory or practice. Furthermore, the relationships between them are many and various. Many religions have been reluctant to extend religious freedom to others, but some have come to the position of pragmatically accepting its desirability. Many religions have questions concerning the rights–duties tension in human rights. Many have also prioritised those human rights that they accept as deriving from religion over those that do not – for example regarding gender roles and sexual orientation. The nostalgia of some religions for an age in which they were dominant socially and politically is problematic to Weller, as such dominance has often threatened human rights.

Weller's central argument is that a critical understanding of and engagement with the 'secular' is central to the question of the relationship between religion and human rights. Some claim that the secular spirit enables religious coexistence; however, secularism – like religion – has expressed itself in a number of different historical forms and should also be situated within the context of the debate about religion and human rights. Weller examines a range of different kinds of secular states; the constitutional, legal and practical consequences that follow from each of these models; and the implications of each of these for the relationship between religion and human rights. Weller then identifies four basic patterns of the secular, citing as examples the USA, France, the Netherlands and India. All in all he argues that in examining the relationships between religions and human rights, we should not neglect the question of the relationship between secular models and human rights. Secularism emerged in many social contexts as a reaction to particular dominant national religions, and some of these models are now worthy of contemporary review. In conclusion, Weller's point is that the secular dimension is a highly pertinent, but often invisible, dimension to the discussion about religion and human rights and is thus worthy of greater consideration.

10. Dennis de Jong, 'Freedom of Religion and Belief in the Light of Recent Challenges: Needs, Clashes and Solutions'

Dennis de Jong begins his chapter with an examination of the context wherein religion finds itself: secularisation, decolonisation, the relationship between religion and state identity, and the impacts of cultural globalisation. All of these impact the role of religion in society. Can human rights itself be reduced to an aspect of cultural harmonisation? De Jong answers in the negative and expands on how the relationship between international human rights law and religions or beliefs is a complicated one, serving sometimes to advance them and at other times to limit them – for example, by liberating religious minorities or restricting religious practice. Human-rights law upholds non-discrimination on the basis of religion or belief, requires free access to information about competing religions or beliefs, forbids coercion in matters of religion or belief, allows the right of individuals to convert to another religion or belief, and prohibits religiously inspired violence. Human rights further upholds non-discrimination on the basis of sex, which sometimes runs counter to religious positions or practice, and it forbids incitement to religious or other hatred. De Jong suggests that governments need to recognise the importance of religion or belief in meeting people's spiritual needs, adopt a non-discriminatory approach to religions or beliefs, strike a balance between the rights of the adherents of clashing beliefs (in part by promoting dialogue between them), and promote debate on the interpretations that can emerge from different readings of religious precepts. These methods, de Jong believes, would allow governments not only to avoid undue restrictions on religion or belief – and clashes between religions, beliefs and human rights – but to actually recognise the significance of religions or beliefs for their societies.

11. Conor Gearty, 'Triumphalism and Respect for Diversity'

Gearty draws a parallel between the claims of universality of human rights and religion, a claim that sometimes becomes a universalist triumphalism that contains elements of cultural imperialism. However, religion and belief both share some deference, but not a surrender, to the local. Another commonality is that both, at their core, share a commitment to the dignity of the individual and of others. To Gearty, human rights requires one to imagine the situation of individuals beyond one's own sphere and empathise with it – a requirement and compassion that is almost religious.

Beyond these commonalities, however, are the challenges both, but especially religion, have with post-modernism. Both have to not only deal with difference but engender a respect for difference. Human rights is concerned with creating a society in which everyone is given the chance to personally flourish. Religion needs to better accommodate such a respect of diversity.

12. Nazila Ghanea, '"Phobias" and "Isms": Recognition of Difference or the Slippery Slope of Particularisms?'

Ghanea questions the utility of the typology of language that has emerged in the UN for the racial and religious discrimination suffered by various groups – Christianophobia and Islamophobia being added to the existing category of anti-Semitism. She argues that these are not special rights uncovering new areas where human rights violations were going unnoticed.

The way these terms are being used is actually divisive and particularistic, distracting attention away from the wider scourge of religious or racial hatred and discrimination. They would be much better identified together rather than separated at the international level, in order not to dilute the fight against hate and discrimination. Separation downgrades this wider concern into a sectarian matter and dismembers the possibility of a unified mobilisation of the international community against it. At the regional or national levels, however, separate identification may serve the sharper purpose of being able to bring about legislation and policies to tackle them effectively.

Existing international instruments already deal with racial and religious hatred, hate speech, incitement and non-discrimination; these are clearly sufficient in accounting for the hatreds of Islamophobia, Christianophobia and anti-Semitism.

Ghanea concludes that this separation of language is not victim-centred; the creation of these new 'global victims' does not serve to alleviate their plight. It detracts from the fact that these areas of discrimination are already well catered for at the level of principle at the international level. Attention needs to be given, instead, to ensuring enjoyment of freedom from discrimination and hatred.

13. Peter Cumper, 'Inciting Religious Hatred: Balancing Free Speech and Religious Sensibilities in a Multi-Faith Society'

Cumper examines where the line should be drawn regarding freedom of expression from the perspective of religious communities with regard to criticism, offence and provoking hatred. Attacks on religious figures and beliefs can provoke outrage, unrest and violence, as a number of cases have demonstrated. So how, for example, should the rights of artists to offend faith groups be balanced against the rights of faith groups to be protected from such attacks? Cumper believes that human rights norms offer little guidance, as they recognise both freedom of expression and of religion. He explores this issue from within a UK context, with regard to the attempt to bring about new legislation on incitement to religious hatred, which runs the risk of eroding freedom of expression. Freedom of expression is clearly not an absolute right, but how will the proposed Racial and Religious Hatred Bill come to be interpreted once it is brought into law? Problems surround how broadly or narrowly religious hatred will come to be defined, how a distinction will be drawn between attacks on faith communities (which will be outlawed) and on religious doctrines (which will not be protected), and how incitement to hatred will be differentiated from legitimate free speech. Cumper questions the position of those who assume that this bill would enhance good community relations, that an analogy can actually be drawn between religion and race in the context of incitement to hatred, and that religious speech itself will be sufficiently safeguarded through the European Convention on Human

Rights. Overall, Cumper suggests that this bill will not be as benign as has been suggested by government officials and carries real risks and challenges within it.

14. Frederik Harhoff, 'Theoretical and Institutional Framework: The Soft Spot where Human Rights End and God Begins'

Frederik Harhoff begins with the position that human rights and religion are interrelated in that they both address the substance of the good life. Religion and human rights have impacted one another normatively, but these norms are subject to different standards of interpretation and apply differently depending on whether they are being considered in the context of one or the other. Taking the position that what human rights and religion share is their normative function, Harhoff then assumes a hierarchy between the two with religion as the overarching framework within which human rights operates within a much narrower legal context. He argues that religious doctrine has played an important role in the development of human rights and has brought to it the charitable impulse and non-consumerist attitude to the demand for rights. In examining what role human rights could play in the development of religion, he argues that the universality of human rights may provide a transformative global framework whereby religions come to be interpreted in a manner consistent with fundamental rights. Nevertheless, he admits that differences remain between the frameworks, interpretation, monitoring and enforcement of norms – depending on whether they are being examined from a religious or human rights perspective. Furthermore, the transformation of a norm from a religious one to a legal one may strongly impact its quality, insofar as it needs particular conditions to make it amenable to practical application. Therefore, the norms and values which appear to be common to religion and human rights, he asserts, exist in a polycentric environment, whereby they acquire different and possibly even irreconcilable meanings.

—The Editors
July 2006

INTRODUCTION

Does God Believe in Human Rights? A reflection

Malcolm D. Evans

THE PURPOSE OF this edited collection is to reflect on the question 'Does God believe in human rights?' It is, of course, a rather presumptuous question to ask, and one which I am not particularly well placed to answer. Indeed, the most sensible response might be to decline to enter into a debate on this topic at all. However, with a subtle reformulation it is possible to devise a question that can be reflected upon, and that might also cast some light on whatever answer to the larger question might some day be vouchsafed to us. The problems posed by that larger question are manifest, the most obvious being 'what do we mean by God?' and 'what do we mean by human rights?' I am not a theologian, and I have nothing to say on the first of these questions. My experience as an international lawyer working in the area of human-rights protection does, however, permit me to observe that any answer that is given to that question – what do we mean by God? – is unlikely to remain unchallenged by those who seek to answer the second question – what do we mean by human rights? – which is almost as problematic. The reason for this is that many human-rights lawyers have developed what can best be described as a quasi-transcendental approach to their own calling, and have little difficulty in failing to discern the divine in that which does not accord with their own revelation. And herein lies the crux of the difficulty we have to face up to: we are seeking to probe the interrelationship between two of the most controversial ideas with which humankind wrestles.

The tense is deliberate. I am not about to embark on a history of religious consciousness, since it is hardly necessary to do so in order to make a case in support of the proposition that the search for God, or the search for an absence of God, has been, and remains, a force in human affairs. Like gravity, it must be acknowledged as a force to be engaged with, irrespective of whether we choose to bow to it, or seek to harness it, or, indeed, overcome it. The case is perhaps less clear as regards 'human rights,' since this expression has only entered our collective consciousness as a distinct concept in relatively recent times.[1] Nevertheless, humankind has always been interested in the subject matter of human rights (or the lack of human rights), albeit that the concern has not been couched in these terms. For we are, in essence, considering the manner in which individuals and groups of individuals may be treated, or their needs and treatment by others be responded to, by those who are in a position of authority over them.

Both religion and law seek to influence and direct the conduct of individuals, communities and societies, and so it is not surprising that the treatment of others is a central concern of both. It is, then, hardly surprising that there has always been a very close relationship between law and religion: our idea of law is, arguably, religious in origins if not in nature, and it has also been argued that human rights are themselves 'ineliminably religious' in nature.[2] The difference lies in the manner in which the concern for the treatment of others is understood and articulated by believers.[3]

If the focus of one's religious understanding is on humankind's individual or collective relationship with a / the deity(ies), the manner in which individuals are treated by each other is, to be blunt, little more than a by-product of that primary relationship. The influence of religious belief upon relations between individuals can be at any point on the spectrum from the wholly benign (e.g. sacrificial self-giving and service to others) to the utterly malign (e.g. ritual human sacrifice), depending on what (one thinks) the tastes of one's god actually are. Approached in this fashion, one cannot really speak of 'good' or 'bad' religion, just different religions. The role of the individual is fixed – a static actor whose role is

1 For an excellent account, stressing the novelty of the concept from a legal perspective, see A. W. H. Simpson, *Human Rights and the End of Empire* (Oxford: OUP, 2001).

2 See M. Perry, *The Idea of Human Rights* (Oxford: OUP, 1998), Chapter 1, arguing that this flows from the inescapable reality that the idea of the human person as 'sacred' – foundational to human rights thinking – is itself inescapably religious.

3 The manner in which ideas are presented matters. It has, for example, always struck me that the much vaunted 'Golden Rule' is little different in substance from the much derided *lex talionis*. The difference lies in the manner in which the idea is presented, the former in the language of responsibility and restraint, the latter in the language of revenge. The practical implications of adopting one approach rather than the other are, of course, enormous.

to respond to the demands placed upon him by the tenets of his belief. One might question the demands that one's religion places upon believers, but the call of the religious is to comply, not complain.

If, on the other hand, the focus of one's religious understanding is on the deity's relationship with individuals, with believers and with humankind in general, then religious believers are not *merely* believers but also become part of the subject matter of that religious belief: we assume a place within a broader scheme of relationships which in their totality add to the description and definition of that belief system. How we perceive ourselves to be affected by the outworking of religious belief and practice becomes a criterion by which we can determine our response. This is so irrespective of our understanding of the content and consequences of beliefs which might (indeed, must) change over time. Not only do we have beliefs, we have a mission and a methodology. We also have an evaluative tool since, as subjects of the system, we have been granted status.

As an international lawyer, I cannot fail to notice parallels with the evolution of my own discipline as regards its engagement with individuals and with human rights.[4] International law emerged in its current form in the sixteenth century, largely separating itself from theology and ideas of governance based on notions of divine order. It has since undergone a number of transformations but has become rigidly focussed on the law between peoples, '*inter-gentes*', and, as '*gentes*' crystallised into states, the law between nations: 'inter-national' law. It is true that we are now witnessing many challenges to this approach, with the 'state-centric' model under pressure from many quarters. Although often presented as a consequence of 'globalisation', this term might better be seen as a conceptual catchall which embraces many of the more incremental steps toward the fragmentation of the State as the legitimising vehicle for global discourse. Examples might include the recognition of national liberation movements, such as the Palestine Liberation Organization, as voice-bearers of peoples in states the legitimacy of which they seek to deny; in the

4 I am also alive to the possibility that it is in fact because I am an international lawyer that I see matters pertaining to religion in this fashion. An outstanding general account of the (re)engagement of international law with human rights from a conceptual perspective remains P. Sieghart, *The Lawful Rights of Mankind* (Oxford: OUP, 1985). For an excellent contemporary account see C. Tomuschat, *Human Rights: Between Idealism and Realism* (Oxford: OUP, 2003).

inclusion of 'non state actors' in the development of international law (such as NGOs); in the influence of international organisations such as the European Union, the WTO, the IMF, the World Bank and, indeed, the UN itself, all of which, though rooted in States, develop and pursue their own institutional policies and practices which frequently transcend their intergovernmental origins. Indeed, despite concerns to the contrary, we live in a multilateral age in which unilateral action taken outside the context of the political global commons is increasingly challenged and its legitimacy called into question.[5]

Nevertheless, it is difficult to deny that the basic paradigm remains dominant,[6] and although not forgotten, the manner in which this international legal system treated individuals was secondary to its primary function of facilitating co-existence between sovereign entities. The manner in which states treated those individuals who were subject to their exclusive jurisdiction was, by and large, a matter of little concern. There were, of course, exceptions, such as the extensive body of law concerning the treatment of individuals caught up in international armed conflict and, particularly following the end of the First World War, concern for the treatment of national minorities.[7] The experiences of the Second World War changed this, and gave birth to the 'modern' human rights era in which individuals have increasingly been regarded as subjects of the international legal order, and the manner in which individuals are treated by states under international law has become a touchstone by which to judge not only the states themselves, but the very system

5 For example, how else can one explain the quixotic fixation with the need for a 'second' Security Council resolution before the launching of hostilities against Iraq in 2003? For general discussion of this issue see, *inter alia*, D. McGoldrick, *From '9–11' to the Iraq War 2003* (Oxford: Hart, 2004), Chapter 4 and, in more iconoclastic terms, P. Sands, *Lawless World: America and the Making and Breaking of Global Rules* (London: Allen Lane, 2005), Chapter 8.

6 See Alston who forcefully points out that the very language of 'non-state actors' points to the centrality of the State in contemporary legal thinking. See his editor's introduction in P. Alston (ed.), *Non State Actors and International Law* (Oxford: OUP, 2005). Warbrick has concluded that 'international law is mainly to do with States and, where it is to do with something else, it is because States have chosen to make it so' (C. Warbrick, 'States and Recognition in International Law', in M. Evans (ed.), *International Law* (2nd edn, Oxford: OUP, 2006), 218).

7 For good contemporary examinations from both a legal and historical perspective see, e.g. P. Thornberry, *International Law and the Rights of Minorities* (Oxford: OUP, 1991); T. Musgrave, *Self Determination and National Minorities* (Oxford: OUP, 1997).

of international law itself. Respect for the canon of human rights (and democracy) has become a benchmark of legitimacy, and states are (on the whole) required to proclaim their fidelity to these principles, even if their practice falls lamentably short. It is, then, hardly surprising that one of the most contentious questions international lawyers are called on to address concerns the legitimacy of 'humanitarian intervention', a topic on which much has been written but few conclusions reached: we know it is anathema to the controlling dogmas of the international community – state sovereignty, non-intervention in internal affairs – and we know that the dangers of the abuse of such a right make most human rights activists back away from supporting unilateral action premised on such grounds, rather paradoxically choosing to allow innate distrust of states who seek to act in the name of human rights to triumph over the distaste for those who seek to violate them.[8]

This is not the place to engage in the substance of this debate, which is merely mentioned for illustrative purposes: the essential point is that we are all competent to join in the debate. Once again, then, the manner in which we, as subjects of that concern, perceive ourselves to be affected by the outworking of international human rights thinking becomes a criterion by which we can determine our response to that framework, irrespective of our understanding of the content and consequences of international human rights thinking which might (indeed, must) change over time. Not only do we have a mission and a methodology, we also have an evaluative tool, since, as subjects of the system, we have been granted status.

But we have more than that: we have a variety of evaluative tools (as the preceding paragraphs are constructed to suggest). We can ask ourselves which sets of tools serve our perceptions of our own needs best: we can choose. Reducing this to its basics (and speaking as an international lawyer), it is as if both 'God' and 'Human Rights' can be seen as items on an '*à la carte*' menu for addressing our needs as human beings living in society. Must I choose? How do I choose? Do the flavours blend? Shall I have one? Shall I have the other? Shall I have both? Or am I on

8 For an excellent collection of writing summing up the trends in the voluminous literature see J. Holzgrefe and R. Koehane, *Humanitarian Intervention: Ethical, Legal and Political Dilemmas* (Cambridge: CUP, 2003).

a diet, and have neither? It is only within the context[9] of these questions that the general question posed at the outset – does God believe in human rights? – seems to make much sense to me. Taken in this context, the question points us to the dilemma of conflicting values and invites a response. Yet I still think there are grounds for questioning whether this question ought to be engaged with at all, enticing though it is. The difficulty is that *as a question* it yields too much ground. What happens if the answer is 'no'? Will it be God or human rights that will be taken off the menu? That is the real question that needs to be answered, but which we are rarely prepared to address. Even if there is a choice *to be* made, is there a choice that *can be* made? The truth of the matter is it seems we are already dining *table d'hôte.*

It might be disappointing to discover that we are not as free as we might wish to determine the precepts undergirding our systems of governance, but it is hardly surprising. Outside of the 'revolutionary moment', our choices in this regard are revealed in the pattern of incremental change. Issue by issue, the *grundnorm* mutates. For example, Christianity remains deeply entrenched in the structure and psyche of this country, long after much of the regulatory and legislative reflection of this has been modulated or abrogated. The symbolic significance of the 1998 Human Rights Act should not be lost sight of here: it can be seen as a moment in which a new approach to answering questions of high significance within the domestic legal systems came to be recognised – so fully encapsulated in the title of Francesca Klug's book about the Human Rights Act, *Values for a Godless Age* (Harmondsworth: Penguin Books, 2000). Of course, this age was not – nor is it – any more or less godless than any other. The underlying question, potentially prejudged by that title, is whether there is a dissonance here. Is there a choice, or is there simply a lack of mutual understanding?

I must confess that I have long been surprised by the reluctance of many religious folk to accept the difficulties posed by the ascendancy of human rights. Do human rights and religion clash? Do they present very real – and very difficult – choices? Of course they do; why wouldn't they? Some proponents of human rights go as far as seeing human rights

9 In the original draft of this paper, this was written as 'contest'. I am not sure if this was merely a typographical error.

thinking as being *of necessity* in opposition to that of religion.[10] But it is not necessary to go this far in order to identify the causes of conflict. At the most basic level, it bears repeating that freedom of religion is itself a human right, and human rights come into conflict with each other as a matter of course: my freedom of expression might, for example, conflict with your right to a private life, and so on. Human rights activists and advocates have no difficulty living with this reality: indeed, it is the stuff of life! The very structures within which human rights standards are articulated presuppose the inevitability of a conflict of values. Indeed, the entire business of human rights as a methodology of governance involves testing out the appropriateness of the manner in which conflicts of interests and of values have been resolved by the state.

If any confirmation were needed, one need look no further than the very structure of the legally binding human rights instruments, all of which adopt a common approach, exemplified by Article 9 of the European Convention on Human Rights which provides:

> (1) Everyone has the right to freedom of thought, conscience and religion; this right includes freedom to change his religion or belief and freedom, either alone or in community with others and in public or private, to manifest his religion or belief, in worship, teaching, practice or observance.
>
> (2) Freedom to manifest one's religion shall be subject only to such limitations as are prescribed by law and are necessary in a democratic society in the interests of public safety, for the protection of public order, health or morals, or for the protection of the rights and freedoms of others.

This is a classic human rights formulation. It sets out what appears to be a very clear right – that everyone enjoys the freedom of thought, conscience and religion. This is generally referred to as the '*forum internum*', the sphere of inner belief which is inviolable, but which permits little more (if anything) than the freedom of believing what one wishes. When

10 e.g. G. Robinson, *Crimes against Humanity* (Harmondsworth: Allen Lane, 1999), 383, who includes churches alongside armies and states as 'traditional enemies' of human rights, and K. Booth, 'Three Tyrannies', in T. Dunne and N. Wheeler, *Human Rights in Global Context* (Cambridge: CUP, 1999), 54, where religion is linked to the tyranny of culturalism and traditionalism, from which they need emancipating.

it comes to doing something on the basis of one's beliefs, it is protected only to the extent that it is a 'manifestation' in one of the forms specified (and the European Court of Human Rights has not wavered from the view, first expressed by the European Commission on Human Rights back in 1981, that not all actions motivated by a belief are protected forms of manifestations of that belief).[11] Even should these hurdles be passed, even a protected form of manifestation may be trenched upon by the State provided that its actions are prescribed by law, are necessary in a democratic society for the safeguarding of the interests set out in Article 9(2) and are a proportionate response. In assessing the legitimacy of the interference, the state is accorded a not inconsiderable margin of appreciation.[12] I reiterate these well known points simply in order to stress that *of course* there will be clashes between the practice of religion and the application of a human rights framework: the human rights framework itself mandates that this be so. Thus when religious believers seek to act in accordance with the dictates of their conscience –for example, by refusing to sell contraceptives in pharmacies in France – and the legitimacy of the response of the authorities is called into question, of course there will be questions concerning the extent to which human rights thinking protects the freedom of believers to manifest their beliefs in the manner in which they run their business.[13] When teachers wish to wear headscarves whilst teaching, or students to wear headscarves whilst being taught, and the state, acting in the name of the rights and freedoms of others, seeks to prevent them from doing so, there is a clash of values.[14] Why pretend it can be otherwise?

Why do people find it so difficult to accept this reality? Doubtless this question has numerous answers, but I am sure that many within

11 The *locus classicus* of this remains the decision of the Commission in *Arrowsmith* v. *UK* Application 7050/75, (1978) 19 DR 5.

12 See, for example, *Wingrove* v. *UK*, 25 November 1996, *ECHR* 1996-V; *Murphy* v. *Ireland*, Judgement, 10 July 2003, *ECHR* 2003-IX; 38 *EHRR* (2004) 13 and, for a recent example, *IA* v. *Turkey* Application 42571/98, Judgement of 13 September 2005.

13 *Pichon* v. *France*, Application 49854/99, Decision of 2 October 2001, and see [2002] *EHRLR* 408–9.

14 *Dahlab* (a teacher) v. *Switzerland*, Application 42393/98, Decision of 15 February 2001, *ECHR* 2001-V. *Leyla Sahin* v. *Turkey*, Application 44774/98, Judgement of 10 November 2005. For the similar issue before the Courts in England and Wales see *Begum* v. *Denbigh High School*, [2006] UKHL 16 (22 March 2006).

religious traditions feel uneasy about being identified as an 'opponent' of human rights and therefore seek to understand either human rights or their application in a manner which is more acceptable – or comfortable. This easily becomes an exercise in evaluating one's beliefs in the context of human rights thinking and re-interpreting them accordingly. This then easily spills over into the exercise of projecting those interpretations which accord with human rights orthodoxy as having greater contemporary relevance and legitimacy. The pressure is then on all concerned to bring the understanding of their religious traditions into conformity with human rights approaches. The result is a cycle of argument in which the triumph of human rights is foreordained.

In short, if we look for the resolution of a conflict between religion and human rights from within the body of human rights law itself, the result is not difficult to predict. And for many religious believers, the real difficulty is this: that the ultimate source of resolution of this inevitable conflict lies within one component of that 'problem' itself. One might say that the human rights paradigm has become judge and jury in its own cause. As I indicated earlier, it is arguably very difficult now to do anything other than 'choose human rights' when one perceives that there is a choice to be made, and the inevitable consequence is that religious believers are invited to re-appraise their religious traditions and values in the light of human rights concepts and approaches. That some lawyers and social scientists should suggest this is one thing: the willingness of theologians and those working within religious tradition to do so is increasingly inexplicable, though the charge of unreasonableness levelled at those who resist doing so is certainly predictable. But religion is not necessarily about reason: it is about belief.

Religious believers might certainly find it easier to believe in human rights – or at least, to allow their beliefs and their practices to be influenced or governed by human rights thinking – if they could be assured that God does indeed believe in human rights. What, exactly, 'belief' entails in this context is not something which I am capable of probing, but I do think it fair to observe that if I *were* to insert myself into the place of the deity and ask myself whether I wished to believe in or espouse human rights, I could hardly fail to observe that freedom of religion and belief has not fared particularly well within the human rights framework. Despite the role of religious belief as one of the wellsprings from which human rights protection flowed in its earliest days, it rapidly became something of a Cinderella within the protective framework.

Despite freedom of worship being one of President Roosevelt's four freedoms (the others being freedom of expression and freedom from want and fear) and its figuring as an 'easy case' for inclusion as Article 18 of the Universal Declaration of Human Rights adopted by the UN General Assembly in December 1948, it remains the only one of the key rights identified that has not been developed into a specialist, legally binding instrument. Although there have been attempts to draft an international convention on religious liberty, these stalled in 1967 after the first article had been drafted. The general view is that it is still premature to return to the exercise. The fact that it is still seen to be so difficult an issue tells us something significant about the relationship between human rights and religious belief.

Indeed, it has been a struggle to get the United Nations to address the issue from the perspective of the freedom of religion and belief at all. Although this is the approach of the principal human rights instruments, in 1981 the United Nations embraced a rather different approach when it adopted its 'Declaration on the Elimination of All Forms of Intolerance and of Discrimination based on Religion or Belief'. While this Declaration now tends to be projected as a summation of UN engagement with the freedom of religion and belief, it was originally more focussed on questions of non-discrimination on the basis of religion or belief, and this was reflected in the title of the mandate of the UN Special Rapporteur, established in 1986 to monitor its implementation.[15] It was the Oslo Coalition, a grouping established in 1998, that led a campaign to change this focus, resulting in a change in the mandate-holder's title to the Special Rapporteur on the Freedom of Religion or Belief, thus highlighting the broader question of freedom of religion and belief and treating it as a primary focus.[16]

Another issue that inevitably continues to circulate around this discussion concerns what, exactly, we consider human rights to be. I have

15 See generally N. Ghanea (ed.), *The Challenge of Religious Discrimination at the Dawn of the New Millennium* (The Hague: Martinus Nijhoff, 2004).

16 See the Oslo Declaration, reproduced in Annex F in T. Lindholm, C. Durham and B. Tahzib-Lie (eds), *Facilitating Freedom of Religion or Belief: A Deskbook* (The Hague: Kluwer, 2004).

been projecting a vision of human rights that I readily acknowledge will not be accepted by everyone. It is a view of human rights as a tool, as a methodology for addressing the tensions that arise within the governance of a society. I see human rights as a means of 'policing' the boundaries between the public and the private space, ensuring that the assertion of the authority of the state does not overreach the bounds of legitimacy. I do not see the international human rights instruments as constituting an ethical code, though they are frequently projected as such. Indeed, the manner in which human rights obligations come into being – a tortuous process of negotiation and political compromise – emphasises their instrumental rather than transcendental qualities. Inevitably, others will understand them differently, yet it is conceptual differences rather than different understandings of substantive content which are likely to be the most acute. Theologians will tend to understand human rights in a different fashion from a domestic lawyer; and a domestic lawyer may well understand them differently from an international lawyer and so on. However, it is worth reminding ourselves that no matter how much mystique is generated around them, human rights instruments are not themselves sacred texts. They are the product of varying inputs, many highly contentious, often largely political, and the subject of intense negotiation. They are not the distillation of any great particular form of wisdom. They are the product of a pragmatic process and have to be engaged with as such, as important statements of how the international community believes it can and should configure itself, but not in any sense as absolutes.[17]

Fortunately, it is not necessary to delve deeply into these issues here. Although it is clear that much does indeed turn on what we think human rights to be, if one is speculating on the acceptability of human rights thinking to God, or to religious believers, then it is more important to dwell on what human rights thinking has to say about God and about religion. For all the complexities of its substantive application, the essence of the human rights approach to God and religion is relatively easy – perhaps surprisingly easy – to discern.[18] Rather than dwell on the

17 For a frank acknowledgement of this see, for example, J. Donnelly, 'Universal Human Rights', in Dunne and Wheeler, *Human Rights in Global Context*, 81–82.

18 For an exploration of the common approach to the freedom of religion in international human rights law see M. Evans, 'Human Rights, Religious Liberty and

difficult question of who, or what, is God, the focus is placed on where God may be found (or ought to be found); to put it in stark language, it is a conception of 'God in a Box'.

Of course, religious believers are often very comfortable with the idea of confining their beliefs to the religious space and not allowing them to spill over in any great measure into their more public lives and public personas. Religious leaders enjoin believers to break out into the world, to engage with it as believers. Should they do so, they will find that they are moving *out* of that private sphere in which human rights law protects most fully the exercise and enjoyment of their religious freedoms, and *into* that public space in which their enjoyment is to be circumscribed to accommodate the broader public good. But can believers truly countenance the existence of a broader public good than that which they espouse? Believers continue to believe in their beliefs, even if and when they accept the limitations imposed by a human rights framework. The greater the constraints, and the longer it takes for the systems of authority which impose and validate those restraints in the name of human rights to do so, the greater the tensions between human rights and religion may become.

This may or may not be inevitable, but it is certainly a reflection of the way we have chosen to structure our political life. A lively legal literature is now emerging around the need to find a *modus vivendi* between religious believers and plural society, but in a sense this says it all.[19] Where does this leave those believers from religions traditions who seek to order their life in the public space in a different way, based around, for example, the very tenets of their faith? Why should they be denied the opportunity to do so? The answer is the need for States to order their affairs in the interests of all within their jurisdiction, rather than in accordance with the views of some, be they majority or minority. Tolerance, respect and pluralism are difficult values to cross swords with.

Yet these values are not neutral: they carry with them a very real set of assumptions concerning the legitimate reach of religion in the public sphere. Even advancing these claims of human rights through the instru-

---

the Universality Debate', in R. O'Dair and A. Lewis, *Law and Religion* (Oxford: OUP, 2001).

19 See, for example, R. Ahdar and I. Leigh, *Religious Freedom in the Liberal State* (Oxford: OUP, 2005).

mentality of international law has the effect of validating the inter-state system, with its rather peculiar and eminently contestable way of conceiving the ordering of human society.[20] Moreover, it is arguable that the entire way in which we conceive of human rights has the effect of privileging certain forms of religious belief. It is clearly more difficult for, let us call them, 'fringe' religions or New Religious Movements to benefit from human rights protections than it is for more mainstream religious traditions. Beyond this, it seems to me that the practical application of human rights approaches to the freedom of religion is structurally biased towards those forms of religious belief that are essentially individualist rather than communitarian in orientation. This is not, perhaps, surprising, since the more communitarian-oriented religious traditions tend to challenge the State's ordering of society in a manner which more individualistically focussed religions do not. It is not an accident that Christianity finds it easier to cohabit plural liberal democracies than some other religious traditions.

These latent tendencies are bared for all to see in judgements from the European Court of Human Rights, which, in response to the challenges of absorbing member states in Central and Eastern Europe, has developed a revised understanding of the role of the State in relation to religion. Rather than focussing on the State's legitimacy in restricting the rights of an individual, it has been increasingly called on to consider cases which concern the manner in which the State engages with the organisation of religious life more generally.[21] It has responded by indicating that the State is to assume the role of 'impartial organiser of religious life' within the State, that is, it is to provide a climate or framework in which all forms of religion may flourish.[22] It is not to take sides, but to stand back from the fray, ensuring that believers of all traditions are respected and respect each other. This is because the Court believes that healthy plural democratic societies *need* religious pluralism (or, perhaps, believes that if there is to be religion in a democratic state, there has to

20 For a radical critique, and a resulting plea for a radical re-conceiving of international society, see P. Allot, *Eunomia* (2nd edn, Oxford: OUP, 2001) and *The Health of Nations* (Cambridge: CUP).

21 See M. Evans, 'Believing in Communities, European Style', in Ghanea, *The Challenge of Religious Discrimination*.

22 See, e.g., *Metropolitan Church of Bessarabia* v. *Moldova*, Judgement of 12 December 2001 [GC], *ECHR* 2001-XII; 35 *EHRR* 3, § 123;

be a plural approach). This approach, however, also marks out the limits of the State's tolerance of religion: anything which can be seen as undermining the democratic state is beyond the limits of toleration. Hence in secular Turkey, headscarves can be banned in publicly funded universities in order to protect the rights and freedoms of others,[23] and political parties which meet electoral success when calling for the implementation of policies inspired by *Shari'ah* law may be outlawed in the name of human rights. It is worth quoting the words of the Grand Chamber of the European Court of Human Rights in the *Refah Partisi* case in full. It said that

> The Court concurs in the Chamber's view that *sharia* is incompatible with the fundamental principles of democracy, as set forth in the Convention . . .
>
> 72. Like the Constitutional Court, the Court considers that *sharia,* which faithfully reflects the dogmas and divine rules laid down by religion, is stable and invariable. Principles such as pluralism in the political sphere or the constant evolution of public freedoms have no place in it. The Court notes that, when read together, the offending statements, which contain explicit references to the introduction of *sharia,* are difficult to reconcile with the fundamental principles of democracy, as conceived in the Convention taken as a whole. It is difficult to declare one's respect for democracy and human rights while at the same time supporting a regime based on *sharia,* which clearly diverges from Convention values, particularly with regard to its criminal law and criminal procedure, its rules on the legal status of women and the way it intervenes in all spheres of private and public life in accordance with religious precepts. . . . In the Court's view, a political party whose actions seem to be aimed at introducing *sharia* in a State party to the Convention can hardly be regarded as an association com-

23 See *Leyla Sahin* v. *Turkey,* n. 14 above. For a detailed exploration of the broader debates surrounding the issue of headscarves and religious symbols see the website <http://www.strasbourgconference.org>, this being the website of a conference held in July 2005 devoted to this topic.

> plying with the democratic ideal that underlies the whole of the Convention.[24]

Such statements from the Court of Human Rights are not likely to encourage those seeking to find space for the expression of faith in the political society of which they form a part. Once again, the human rights approach is to ensure that believers might believe as they wish and that they might be free to practice the rituals of their faith provided that this is compatible with the general public good, but the State is to rise above religion, ordering and policing its practice but not embracing or reflecting particular tenets of belief. Now at one level, who can object to that? The answer is that many religious believers will find this objectionable, and confirmation that human rights thinking does indeed place God – places religion – in a 'box'.

Beyond this, it is also difficult to close one's eyes to the harsh reality that the adoption of such an approach in many countries around the world results in the exact opposite of what it is meant to deliver, producing the very forms of discrimination and intrusion into the freedom of religion and belief that it is entirely meant to protect.[25] It assumes that States are willing or able to put themselves in a position where, in truth, it is almost impossible for them to be – one of complete and utter neutrality. I find it difficult to accept that it is possible to be completely neutral in relation to anything, let alone for something as complex as a State to be neutral as regards something so complex as religion.

There is, in my view, considerable danger in deluding ourselves that things can be other than they are and then looking for the sort of accommodations that have the tendency to avoid rather than confront the issues as they really are. It is also important not to confuse the search for accommodations with solutions. Accommodations are not solutions to a problem, but they may be something which it is necessary to engage with in order to make progress towards a solution. It is likely that one must have accommodations, but they should not be seen as solutions.

---

24 *Refah Partisi* v. *Turkey*, Applications 41340/98, 41342/98, 41343/98, 41344/98, Judgement of 13 February 2003 [GC], *ECHR* 2003-II; 37 *EHRR* 1, § 123.

25 A general perusal of the information disseminated by Forum18 <http://www.forum18.org> or Human Rights Without Frontiers <http://www.hrwf.net> can make for salutary reading. For more general surveys of trends see J. Richardson (ed.), *Regulating Religion* (The Hague: Kluwer'Plenum Publishers, 2004)

They form a vital element in an ongoing process of engagement between different communities and different forms of life, religious and secular.

Dialogue between religions is an excellent idea, but I doubt it should be seen as a tool for addressing the tensions between religions or between religions and human rights, since I am not entirely sure it does. Such dialogue certainly feeds into and greatly benefits and enriches other aspects of religious life and understanding, but as a way of addressing the difficulty between religion and human rights, to the extent that there is one that can be addressed, it is arguably more of a diversion than a means of actually addressing the central issues that need to be focussed on. Indeed, I find it interesting that it is usually said that there needs to be dialogue *between religions* on matters of human rights. Why? A more pressing need is for genuine dialogue *between religion and human rights.*[26] Accommodations viewed from the perspective of human rights can become one-way streets in which religious believers are enjoined to reappraise and recontextualise their own understandings in order to engineer conformity with, or even fidelity to, human rights values, the potential malleability of which is conveniently overlooked. When religious folk are called on to examine themselves in the light of the human rights paradigm, they may find they have much to learn. They might also find that they have much to teach. But whether or not God believes in human rights, God only knows!

26 For a far more sophisticated exploration of similar themes, leading to fascinating conclusions, see T. Lindholm, 'Philosophical and Religious Justifications of Freedom of Religion', in Lindholm, Durham and Tahzib-Lie, *Facilitating Freedom of Religion.* For further reflections by this author on the relationship between human rights, law and religion see M. Evans, 'Law, Religion and Human Rights: Locating the Debate', in P. Edge and G. Harvey (eds), *Law and Religion in Contemporary Society* (Aldershot: Ashgate, 2000).

Section One

Religious Perspectives

CHAPTER 1

The Complimentarity between Secular and Religious Perspectives of Human Rights

Richard Harries

I once offered a lecture entitled 'Christianity and Human Rights' to an organiser of a conference. He immediately came back with the reply, 'Well, it's going to be a very short lecture then.' One could say the same about this volume's title, 'Does God Believe in Human Rights?', because there is a deep suspicion in many people's minds that there really isn't any connection. First of all, there are a number of stories in the Bible that seem to suggest God can do what he likes with Creation – send a flood or destroy millions of people. Then, looking at the great Dooms of medieval English parish churches, one finds most of the human race condemned to eternal torture. In Calvinism, there is the terrible doctrine of 'double predestination', whereby some people are created from the start for eternal Hell, without any choice at all. There are, sadly, some commands in the Bible that suggest that people are entitled to destroy women, children and each other. Allied to that, of course, is the Church's rather poor record in many respects – the Inquisition of the Middle Ages, the persecution of Jews, pogroms and so on. Then there is the widespread sense that if religion does inculcate moral values, it is primarily in the area of moral responsibility and duties, rather than rights. I shall return to this point later. Finally, among these suspicions is the belief that human rights is a fundamentally secular concept which religion has resisted from the outset.

I want to challenge the notion that human rights is a purely secular concept even in its origin. The American Declaration of Independence in 1776 declared, 'All men are created equal and are endowed by their Creator with certain inalienable rights'. Indeed, as we know, the Founding Fathers of the United States and of the Constitution were devoutly, fiercely Christian. Even in France, the 1789 Declaration states that it was made 'in the presence and under the auspices of the Supreme Being'.

Of course, those are not consciously *Christian* statements. Some of

The author was bishop of Oxford between 1987 and 2006. On 30 June 2006 he was ennobled as Lord Harries of Pentregarth.

them are deistic. Nevertheless, there was a very strong religious element in the seventeenth and eighteenth centuries which it is too easy to ignore. I would argue in addition that what we in the modern world try to safeguard by the concept of human rights was safeguarded in other ways through other concepts in the pre-modern world.

From a Christian point of view, rights are grounded first of all in the value of the created order; and that goes for Judaism and Islam as well, of course. I say 'rights' rather than 'human rights' at this stage because it may be that others besides humans – animals, for example – have rights. At any rate, we shall limit ourselves here to focus on human rights.

Christian theologians would not be frightened or ashamed of being counted with the babes and sucklings out of whose mouths unadorned simplicities can come by asserting that *all* human rights in the end are grounded in a sense of the dignity and worth of human beings. Even moral philosophers will, on occasion, admit to something as radical and as unsophisticated as this. Ronald Dworkin writes: 'Anyone who professes to take rights seriously must accept, at the minimum, the vague but powerful idea of human dignity.' He goes on to associate this idea with Kant. One wonders why Kant is singled out rather than the framers of the Old Testament's legal codes, or Jesus, or Aquinas, to suggest a few of the thousands of pre-Kantian alternatives. The worth and dignity of the human person is basic to the Jewish, Christian and Muslim traditions and could be illustrated in hundreds of different ways, of which the pre-eminent is the sense that human beings are made in the image of God, endowed with rationality, choice, a capacity to pray and love, and endowed with a moral consciousness.

I indicated initially that one of the objections or suspicions that linger in people's minds is the idea that if one believes in a creator God, that creator God can do as He likes with His creation. This view was classically expressed by St Paul in his letter to the Romans: 'Man, who art thou that replyest against God? Shall the thing formed say to Him that formed it, "Why hast Thou made me thus?" Hath not the potter power over the clay of the same lump to make one vessel with honour and another with dishonour?'

But even with St Paul's analogy – that a potter is allowed to do what he likes with the pot – the conclusion is not, I suggest, what Paul would have us believe. For the potter hasn't just tossed off the pot – he's worked at it day after day; indeed, aeon after aeon. He's literally sweated blood over it, literally put his heart and soul into it; and the pot that is produced, flawed though it may still be, is infinitely precious to the creator. Or to put it another way: God creates and at once recognises the value of what He has created. Here is the foundation for a consciously Christian – and I would suggest also religious – approach to human rights. God makes man in His own image and respects the value of what He has created. He makes man – makes humanity, I should say – in His own image and respects its worth and dignity. That seems to me the starting-point.

If we were living in a family totally governed by harmony, there would be no need for either parents or children to talk about rights. The value of each person would be fully recognised and respected. The language of human rights is necessary because in the world as it is now this is not the case. Human beings are tortured, imprisoned without trial, discriminated against, kept in permanent poverty and so on, making it necessary to assert rights in order to protect human persons from such cruel and degrading treatment. In short, I would suggest the basis of human rights is not simply human dignity as such, but the fact that this human dignity is so often denied in practice. This second aspect is likewise fundamental to a Christian view, which has always insisted that human life as we know it is deeply flawed. As that great American political Christian thinker Reinhold Niebuhr put it, 'Though Christ is the true norm of every man, every man is also in some sense a crucifier of Christ'. It is from these two truths that the concept of human rights becomes absolutely fundamental and must be safeguarded, not only in relation to other human beings as such, but also in relation to the State and its potentially tyrannical and oppressive power.

Now I believe the theological perspective on human rights *can* respond positively to the distinction Dworkin makes in his discussion of utilitarianism between personal and external preferences, a distinction he believes has not been properly taken into account in other discussions on human rights. Utilitarianism is based on preferences, but these preferences may be personal (for example, a white student may prefer segregation in the old United States because it improved his chances of getting into law school) or external (he dislikes people who are not white and disapproves of social situations when the races mix). The problem according to Dworkin is that in practice – that is, in a democratic society based on the preference of its citizens – it is not possible to differentiate between personal and external preferences, and therefore the likelihood of inequality being built into any system based on a utilitarian understanding, which most political systems are, is bound to be very high, for the system will inevitably reflect not just what citizens want for themselves, but their attitude to others. For this and other reasons, Dworkin champions what he calls a 'strong sense of right'; in his famous phrase, 'they act as political trumps.' 'Individual rights,' he says,

> are political trumps held by individuals. Individuals have rights when for some reason a collective good is not a sufficient justification for denying them what they wish as individuals to have or do, or not a sufficient justification for imposing some loss or injury upon them. If someone has a right to something, then it is wrong for the government to deny it to him, even though it would be in the general interest to do so.

It is that last phrase which seems to me to be crucial. 'If someone has a right to something, then it is wrong for the government to deny it to him, even though it would be in the general interest to do so.' To take a particular contemporary example, it might be argued that it was in the interests of society as a whole for various reasons *not* to provide people suffering from AIDS with adequate antiretroviral drugs. But if we believe that a right to equal healthcare belongs to everybody, then that right would need to override any political or economic considerations the State might bring forward.

Human rights are natural rights, and this leads on to one of the main bases of human rights in traditional Christian and present Catholic theology: that ultimately human rights or natural rights are grounded in natural law. Of course there has been a suspicion from various quarters about the whole concept of natural law. Protestants have been suspicious of it because they believe that, unaided by God's grace, we haven't a real capacity to discern right from wrong. I strongly disagree with that notion. Secondly, philosophers have been very suspicious of it because they feel that one cannot actually give any kind of real meaning to such a concept. Most famously, Jeremy Bentham said that to talk of rights as natural and inalienable is 'nonsense upon stilts.' But, from a Christian perspective, they exist not just as legal rights. For ultimately human rights are grounded in certain values, particularly the value, worth and dignity of individual human beings.

I mentioned at the beginning some of the traditional Christian suspicions of rights, and I indicated that the idea that God, because he is Creator, is free is to do what He wants with His creation is undermined by the fact that God himself recognises and respects the worth of what He has created. When it comes to the question of Christianity and Judaism being religions of duty, of responsibilities, of commandments, of law (a kind of language which seems so very different from the language of human rights), it strikes me that there is not a total opposition between these concepts. This is because when we, as religious people, respond to the command or the law – the Torah – of God to act in particular ways in relation to other human beings, we are enjoined before anything else to open our eyes to them and see them as they are. To take a simple domestic example: a brother and sister may be squabbling, one child treating the other in an unpleasant way. This prompts the parents to lay down the law and say, 'You're to stop teasing your sister or your brother!' However, there may come a point where those children actually see and recognise the worth of their sibling for their own sake. That reinforces the original family command, or law or rule, coming from the parents. The rule and the realisation both have the same effect: they enable people to see others in a different light, which in the case of the family means as the parents see them – children of worth who are not to be treated in that way – and from a religious point of view means as God sees them. It seems to me that one of the things that divine commands do – whether we are talking about the Hebrew Scriptures, or the Koran or the Christian Bible as a whole – is to open our eyes. The commands open our eyes to see people as God sees them, and that in turn has the effect of reinforcing the fundamental moral Torah or moral command that lies at its root. If what God desires is the wellbeing and the flourishing of individual human beings, then when we come to recognise people as being of value in themselves for themselves, this, far from contradicting a religiously based religion of law, actually reinforces it.

What has happened with secular human rights language is that it has focussed on the value of human beings in themselves for themselves – and there is nothing wrong with that. After all, how do we relate to our children? We value them in themselves for themselves. But what I have tried to suggest is that, far from being contradictory of a command or law-based language, these two ways of looking at things actually reinforce one another. I think it is very important to try to resolve this contradiction, because otherwise secular people look at religious scriptures and say, 'Well, this is all about law, about command, about responsibilities; but where does the value of humanity for its own sake come in?' While I may not have suggested the right way forward, I do think such a way must be found.

Thirdly, again trying to deal with suspicions of a religious approach (and this suspicion, I suppose, is particularly true in relation to Christianity), there is the Sermon on the Mount in St Matthew's Gospel that seems to suggest that we should have absolutely no concern for our own rights and should be willing to waive them. There is no doubt that in Christian history some thinkers have taken this view in a way that has reinforced repressive, authoritarian and hierarchical political systems. A classical example was Martin Luther saying to those taking part in the Peasant's Revolt of 1529, 'Suffering, suffering, cross, cross. This and nothing else is the Christian law.' He wanted them simply to 'put up with it' and not express any kind of sense of what we would call 'entitlement.'

Now it seems to me that there is a very basic and simple point to be made here: whilst of course it is entirely open to each one of us as individuals to waive our rights if we feel called through compassion and charity to do so, that's *our* particular vocation. But that is very different from calling on other people to waive *their* rights in the name of religion. I think it is very important not to use the Sermon on the Mount to reinforce oppressive political systems by suggesting that if one were a true Christian, one would not, of course, be worried about things like one's human rights.

Human rights are rights that are established in law. I believe equally strongly, as I have already suggested, that those rights are grounded in values, so the laws must ultimately be grounded in a moral perspective. Actual *talk* about human rights, however, is in the end about what is legally recognised, and because of this question of legal recognition we are involved in a dynamic, historical process. It is as a result of a gradual – much too gradual – process that rights are beginning to be enshrined in declarations, conventions and covenants that go up to make that human body of international human rights law.

We could go right back to the Magna Carta of 1215, but clearly that only involved certain aristocratic classes. We could go back to the Charter of 1354, when Edward III introduced the important concept of due process of law, which was strengthened in the eighteenth and nineteenth centuries, and particularly in the twentieth century. Since World War II there has been the very dramatic expansion of human rights, culminating in the various human rights conventions, and, in the United Kingdom, the incorporation into English law of the European Convention on Human Rights.

I think that it is not only inevitable, but absolutely right and good that we should think in terms of human rights as a dynamic, evolving, historical process. Such a process is made possible because underpinning it are certain moral values. It is in the light of those moral values that people began to work out a little more clearly what the implications of those values are. To take an obvious Christian example: St Paul wrote, 'There is neither Jew nor Greek, there is neither bond nor free, there is neither male nor female and yet all are one in Christ'; but it took something like one thousand eight hundred years for the implications of that to be worked out in relation to slavery; and it took even longer for the implications to be worked out in relation to women; indeed, many will think that the full implications in relation to other people have not yet been thoroughly worked out.

Thus we have an evolving, dynamic, historical process whereby certain fundamental moral insights – moral insights that are grounded in a religious perspective of the universe – are gradually realised and turned into law.

I think one of the areas in which this has happened over the last twenty or thirty years has been the realisation that human rights are not just negative rights. They are not just about stopping people being tortured, or imprisoned without trial and so on. There are also positive rights, and these are enshrined in the UN Declaration on Human Rights as well as the European Convention. People have a basic right to a particular minimum standard of living, to healthcare and so on. Within Christian theology over the last two or three decades this has been a particular emphasis, especially with those Christian theologians regarding themselves as 'liberation theologians'. José Bonino, for instance, has written:

> For the vast majority of the population of the world today, the basic human right is the right to human life, to a human life. The deeper meaning of the violation of formal human rights is the struggle to vindicate these larger masses who claim their right to the means of life, the drive towards universality and the quest of the American and French Revolutions; the aspirations in the UN Declaration finds its historical focus today for us in the struggle of the poor, the economically and socially oppressed for their liberation.

Again, another theologian, the German Jürgen Moltman, has written a number of essays on human rights and has said, 'I think that only with this concrete starting-point in the theology of liberation can universal theories and declarations about the freedom of man be protected from their misuse.' I suspect that that is a whole area which we would want to discuss more. But it seems to me – again, to reiterate the point – that if human rights are legal rights grounded in moral insights, then it is to be expected that those moral insights would continue to unfold in an enlarging understanding and conception of what is involved in truly respecting the worth and dignity of human beings.

Since World War II, the Church has had to work out its understanding of human rights in a number of different contexts. When Communism was in power in the Soviet Union, it had to protect not only individual human rights in practice but the whole Western concept of human rights against a Marxist critique of it. The Marxists critique was, at that time, very critical of the Western liberal understanding of human rights. And since the advent of the liberation theologians in South America, the concept has also been enlarged in order to take a more societal view into account.

The Bible, I think, is a book that not only respects the individual worth and dignity of every human being, but has a particular concern for the most vulnerable members of society. That, I feel, is what enables some of these positive rights to have a particularly biblical undergirding. If you look at some of the writings of the early Church fathers, it is interesting to note that the kind of things they say are what we today would call 'positive human rights.' They saw these not solely in terms of the largesse of those who have for those who have not – a sort of pity and compassion – but as a matter of elemental justice. For them, God had bestowed the goods of the earth on humanity as a whole. All things were, in principle, in common, so to meet someone's need for the basic necessities of life was not an act of charity but of justice. It was rendering to him what was his by right, what was his due. Ambrose, for example, wrote: 'Not from your own do you bestow upon the poor man if you make return from what is his, for what has been given is common for the use of all. The earth belongs to all, not to the rich. Therefore you are paying a debt. You are bestowing what is due.' Chrysostom wrote: 'This is robbery, not to share one's resources'; and Augustine made the same point: 'The superfluous things of the wealthy are the necessities of the poor. When superfluous things are possessed, others' property is dispossessed.'

This is a very interesting perspective. It helps to undergird taking positive human rights seriously. They are no longer simply a matter of charity or largesse, but something belonging to elemental consideration and justice – what is actually due to people.

A moral philosopher once said, 'All ethics is a training in sympathy.' That might sound a little simplistic, but it was actually said by a professional moral philosopher. 'All ethics is a training in sympathy', and I believe that what religion has to offer above all is this ability to open people's eyes and see other human beings as fellow women and men. Bartolomé de las Casas, at the beginning of the sixteenth century, when he went out to the Spanish possessions in what we now call the Caribbean, heard a sermon by a fellow Dominican.[1] Regarding the Indians, who were being so disgracefully treated, the preacher said something very simple: 'Are they not men? Are we not bound to love them?' The challenge is to realise that these creatures in front of you are fellow women and men. Then there is the very powerful statement that Shakespeare puts into Shylock's mouth: 'When we are pricked, do we not bleed? When we are tickled, do we not laugh?' What I would suggest, then, is that above all what religion has to contribute is the capacity to open people's eyes and make them see other people, whoever they are, as fellow human beings. It is because of that fundamental moral grounding that we can look for a continuing development of human rights, entrenched and embodied in legal terms.

---

1 Roger Ruston has written on this in his book *Human Rights and the Image of God* (SCM Press, 2004), which I am looking forward to reading.

CHAPTER 2

Religious Truths and Human Coexistence

Roger Ruston

A QUESTION OF THEOLOGY

The tensions now arising between a secular regime of human rights and the conduct of particular religious traditions presents problems for both states and religious bodies concerning their *raison d'être.* Both sides are put to the test. Whether it is a Spanish religious-education teacher living with a divorced partner, a Church of England priest claiming employment rights, a Sikh playwright claiming freedom of speech, or a Muslim woman marrying the person of her choice, the state has some legitimate interest on behalf of the common good, expressed in its guardianship of individual welfare and liberties. If it turns a blind eye, it can be accused of neglect: much like the police ignoring a 'domestic', always at hand is the parallel of failure to intervene in an abusive family until it is too late.[1] But if the state does intervene, it may be accused of disrespecting freedom of religion – a cornerstone of the tolerant, liberal British society for at least two hundred years. In a corresponding dilemma, the church, mosque, synagogue or gurdwara, while needing to remain faithful to its founders' teachings and its traditions, yet finds them subject to *moral* criticism from outside – an uncomfortable position for a guardian of morality to find itself in. Harsh treatment of the aggrieved or dissenting individual brings condemnation from a wider public and from its own members, who, after all, are citizens too; and denial of what are widely accepted to be basic human rights seems particularly discreditable in our world.

Both the civil authority and the religious body need their own kind of practical wisdom in order to deal justly with these conflicts. Answers

1 Aside from well-publicised cases of women being raped by priests of various religions, 'on a daily basis women find their aspirations quashed by religious leaders . . . meanwhile they look outwards to the state for protection – a state which has historically appeased the unelected religious leaders of our community and left the policing of women in their hands.' (Rahila Gupta, arguing against a religious hatred law, 'Too high a price to pay', *Guardian*, 12 March 2005)

have to come from *within* in each case – through reflection on their purpose with regard to the individual person.[2] What is the religious body for, and what is the State for, when it comes to the welfare of the individual? How do we justify their existence in terms of the human good, and the limits they put upon individual behaviour? About both we have to ask whether, in their relation to the abused or dissenting individual, they are fulfilling their true purpose or frustrating it. In the case of a religious community, this involves reflecting on its theology – including the history of interpretation of its scriptures and founders' words. Only a theology – a discourse about God and God's will – can provide the answers it needs. This applies to any religion and its theology. I do not mean to privilege one over all the rest. In the case of the State it means a reflection on coercive power and its purposes and limits – political power is so easily abused that it is always in need of justification, both in general and in the particular case.[3]

The theological tradition (or family of traditions) from which I speak – Christian, Catholic – has long reflected on the purposes of both the Church and the civil authority. They are conceived as separate realities, both deriving from God's general providence for humankind. At no time can these two distinct realities be simply identified, as if priests alone were competent to rule a people, or as if a secular ruler were to be head of the Church. There has always been dual authority, with different areas of competence. And at no time has the Catholic Church been the only religion in any state, even in nominally Catholic countries such Renaissance Spain or twentieth-century Ireland. There have always been religious minorities, whose members have shared the political body but not the faith of the majority. Within confessional states there have always been 'unbelievers', the 'other'. The secular power – even when it is a 'Christian' one – has a responsibility toward them in fulfilment of its God-given purpose. The question is, just how does this responsibility translate into a respect for their different religious practices and customs? Theological

2 Assuming that both the religion and the State exist for the sake of persons and not the other way round.

3 A principal theme in the political thought of both the early-modern authors I shall consider below: Bartolomé de Las Casas (in his book *The Power of Kings*) and John Lock (in *Two Treatises of Government*).

reflection on this question has been one of the origins of natural-rights ideas in European culture.

To leave out many stages in the argument,[4] I want to claim that questions of *human* rights (as distinct, say from civil or canon law rights) can only be fully understood as originating from within a theological thought-world provided by belief about creation and the familial relationship of human beings as creatures of God. Questions of justice toward strangers – that is, human beings with whom we share no contractual obligation, and no bond of faith, but a common humanity – need to be seen as theological questions. I would go so far as to say that the theological nature of *all* questions of natural justice is exposed in the encounter between strangers across religious, political and cultural boundaries. Christian theologies have traditionally expressed the familial affinity we have with all other human beings in terms of the common possession of the *imago Dei*, the image of God (Genesis 1.26–28).[5] (Needless to say, this approach does not tie me to a literal belief in the six days of creation – it is a moral not a literal interpretation.) It posits a global common good – a common good of human beings in their planetary co-existence. Although this belief comes from *within* my religious tradition, it creates for me obligations towards others who do not share that tradition – towards human beings as such. Precisely as a believer in a creator God (something taught by my particular religion, as well as others), I recognise the work of God in others who are unlike me in all other ways. I have God-given *duties* towards other human beings who do not share my faith – but also toward those who do, and for the same reason. Consequently, there is an irreducible minimum of duties and respect I owe to other persons that cannot be overridden by any supposed divine or Church commands that seem to tell me something different.

Yet the particularist claims of religions often obscure this truth. In my own religious tradition, recalcitrant social customs, misidentified with religious truth, have resulted, for example, in the prolonged toleration of slavery, the subordination of women, and the persecution of religious minorities, especially the Jews. Nevertheless, the image of God doctrine that the biblical religions share delivers a belief in *basic equality* that

4 I have explored this topic in *Human Rights and the Image of God* (London, SCM Press, 2004).

5 As, of course, does rabbinic theology – see below.

would be very difficult, if not impossible, to arrive at by considering only the secular reality of human life, with its multitude of ways in which human beings are ranged against each other on scales of value belonging to different cultures.[6] Whatever religion is professed, wealth, class, skin-colour, lineage, gender and other contingent differences are used to discriminate between persons and put them in hierarchies of dignity and worth. The doctrine of God's image born by every human being has been, and remains in some respects, severely counter-cultural. The fact that Christians themselves have had enormous trouble in putting their own doctrine of basic human equality into practice is evidence for this rather than an argument against it. For many centuries, differences of social status, and then differences of economic status, inhibited any practical (especially political) outcomes of the basic equality that is implied in the image of God doctrine. This is not because Christian doctrine held that such things as slavery or the subordination of women is a dictate of God's will, but because social institutions inherited from the ancient world were so powerfully entrenched in people's minds they appeared to be 'natural', and the commitment to natural freedom and equality present in Christian theology was for a very long time powerless to challenge it. The idea of nature has been a two-edged sword, in that the 'natural order' of things has been used to justify oppressive dualities (male–female; highborn–lowborn; pale–dark; rational–irrational) as well as to unite us in a common humanity. But despite the failure of some religious traditions to realise the implications of their own beliefs about equality, such beliefs are ultimately religious in origin and character.

This leads me to my first historical example of theological reflection

6 'Basic equality' is intended to refer to an equality of status (before God, before the law), not of gifts, powers, desert or other qualities and achievements that differ widely between one person and another. Nor does it refer to equality as an *aim*, although it has served as a motivating basis for this. It is an abstract notion that nowadays we tend to refer to as 'human dignity' or 'a principle of equal concern and respect'. It has its roots in the monotheistic religions, relating to our moral status before God and our chances of happiness in a world to come, but it did not become a factor in the political life of *this* world until it made the leap from theology to political theory in the early-modern period, when it had revolutionary implications, as for example in the religious left wing of the English Revolution. See Jeremy Waldron, *God, Locke and Equality: Christian Foundations in Locke's Political Thought* (Cambridge, 2002), 1–6. Waldron shows that basic equality is a largely unexamined and unacknowledged *theology* underlying much secular, egalitarian political thought.

on rights in relation to religious truth-claims. I am going to give three examples, each from a very different political environment, in order to show the development of a single broad tradition – what I will call the natural law/natural rights tradition.

THOMAS AQUINAS: NATURAL RIGHT IN THE CHRISTIAN COMMONWEALTH

In premodern Catholic Europe, before there was any concept of a global international community of peoples, and long before the advent of the secular state, there were nevertheless pressing questions to be faced by rulers concerning the treatment of religious minorities, that is, persons who did not belong to the religion considered by the dominant culture and political institutions to be the 'true' one. Thus Thomas Aquinas (1225–74) formulated some ground rules regarding the proper treatment of Jews and Muslims in the Christian commonwealth, establishing rudimentary principles of objective natural right, although natural or human rights in our subjective sense was not part of his moral vocabulary. By our standards, the resulting tolerance afforded to Jews, for example, looks parsimonious and unstable. The kind of tolerance that was to be extended to Jewish worship was expressed more in terms of allowing something wrong to happen (i.e. practice of a 'false' religion) for the sake of a greater good – in this case the testimony that Jewish worship is supposed to give to the truth of Christianity.[7] This argument applied only to Jewish worship, of course. As for the worship of other religions, Aquinas observes that it should be tolerated only to avoid a greater evil, such as 'scandal and civil disturbance'. In any case, this is an unsatisfactory, lesser-of-two-evils approach that reflects values now wholly repudiated by the Church.

But thankfully, it was not all that Aquinas had to offer – there was also a question of natural justice. Violating the (supposedly erroneous) conscience of the non-Christian believer – would be, according to Aquinas, wrong in itself. Thus it is wrong, Aquinas wrote, forcibly to baptise the children of Jews or Muslims against their parents' wishes, even though, according to the understanding of the time, they would gain salvation by

7 *Summa Theologiae* 2a 2ae, Q. 10, art. 11, 'Whether the rites of unbelievers ought to be tolerated'.

it, the reason being that when a child is under age, 'if it were to be taken away from its parents' custody, or anything done to it against its parents' wish' this could be 'contrary to natural justice.'[8] Natural justice dictates, according to Aquinas, that it is a father's duty and right to control the upbringing of his children, including the communication of religious belief. Aquinas's actual words show that not even what he thought of as the supreme good of eternal salvation can be allowed to override it: 'no one ought to break the order of the natural law (or 'natural right'), whereby a child is in the custody of its father, in order to rescue it from the danger of everlasting death.'

Of course, the resulting treatment of the Jewish minority fell well short of our modern notion of equal human rights or religious freedom. Nevertheless, although we cannot look for liberal freedoms or any notion of the religiously neutral state in Aquinas, he did make clear that it was simply wrong in principle to exercise any kind of coercion in matters of faith. Faith is essentially an act of free personal choice, and free choice is an attribute of all human persons who, created in God's image and capable of rational conduct, cannot be forced to believe anything against their conscience. All major religions have accepted versions of this obvious truth. In Aquinas's terminology, there is an order of 'nature', to which we all belong, that has rules of its own which must not be violated by 'grace', that is, reasons of religion. Thus the formation of civil society belongs to human nature rather than to the regime of grace; it does not require the communication of religious truths or the holiness of citizens and rulers to make a political society, but without it there is no human good.

In sixteenth-century Spain, the Thomist theologian Domingo de Soto (1497–1563), repeating Aquinas's argument against enforced baptism, used a strikingly modern-sounding expression: it is, he wrote, 'against the natural right of freedom.'[9] According to this theology of nature, much developed from its beginnings in Aquinas, there exists a sphere of the *natural* (i.e. what is *given* independently of human intentions) in which values of human coexistence are to be realised that cannot be overridden

8 *Summa Theologiae* 2a 2ae, Q. 10, art. 12, 'Whether the children of Jews and other unbelievers ought to be baptized against their parents' will.'

9 '*contra naturale ius libertatis*', from Soto's commentary on the Sentences of Peter Lombard, V, q. 1, art. 10, quoted by Jaime Brufau Prats, *La Escuela de Salamanca ante el Descubrimiento del Nuevo Mundo* (Salamanca: Editorial San Esteban, 1989), 115.

by the special teachings of our religion and in which a person's freedom cannot be curtailed simply because they are not believers or because they would gain great benefit by it if it was forced upon them. There was a contrary view expressed in medieval theology, notably by John Duns Scotus, to the effect that enforced conversion might well be a failure with the first generation, but would probably 'take' by the second or third and so result in the salvation of souls, justifying enforcement in the long term. The Thomist tradition denied this type of consequentialism and so became a source from which a theory of inviolable natural rights could be developed. The underlying reason is that God is just as much author of our nature as of our scriptures and our faith. Unbelievers too are made in God's image, share our nature and must be considered brothers and sisters in God's sight – what Jesus, in a famous parable about an unbeliever (whom he must have considered to be in error about religion), called our 'neighbours'.[10] In this sense, neighbours are not members of our community, people who share out beliefs and culture, but outsiders, even those with a history of hostility towards us.

THE SPANISH DOMINICANS: THE GLOBALISATION OF NATURAL RIGHTS

My second example is from a contemporary and friend of Soto, the Spanish missionary bishop, Bartolomé de Las Casas (1484–1566), who fought a long battle for the legal recognition of the natural rights of the American Indians in the face of Spanish conquest. He did not start from a position of an already accepted list of human rights, which did not exist in his day. Yet he was outraged by the ruin of God-given (i.e. natural) lives through the aggressive imposition of Christianity on unwilling and unprepared people. Trained in the theology of Aquinas, he argued that grace does not destroy nature but fulfils it; that if God has a plan for the spread of the Christian gospel to the pagans, it cannot be furthered by violating the requirements of their nature, which itself comes directly from the hands of the Creator. That is to say, religious truth cannot be communicated at the expense of natural rights. For the indigenous peoples of the New World, this meant they had rights to their own lands, their own government, a right to defend themselves against attack, a

10 See Luke 10.29–37 for the story of the good Samaritan; and John 4.22 for Jesus' blunt dismissal of Samaritan religion compared with that of the Jews.

right to practice their own religions until individually convinced of the truth of Christianity, leaving them the freedom to accept it or not accept it. Someone arguing merely on grounds of the lesser evil – that peacefully persuading people to become Christians was a lesser evil than trying to force them – would have to admit that occasionally it would be better to use force in view of the good to be achieved in the long-term (as Scotus had done). Even though – in common with almost every other Christian of his time – Las Casas believed that baptism was essential for salvation, he would have none of that kind of argument, maintaining rather that violation of the 'natural' order was a wrong in itself and contradictory to the purposes of God, whatever the benefits that might be intended.

That is not to say Las Casas leaves us without problems. To us he may seem to err in the direction of the freedom of a religion to impose itself on the individual. Among the 'natural' goods of the American Indians that he recognised were their religious practices. Thus he argued – surprisingly, for someone so attuned to injustice – that human sacrifice should be tolerated on the grounds that its practitioners are worshipping God according to their own conscience, offering the most precious good they have – human life – and that until they are persuaded of their error they should be allowed to get on with it.[11] Both then and now this viewpoint has come in for a lot of criticism. But we have to understand the context – the chief enemy of freedom in Las Casas's world was imperial aggression motivated by the lust for gold (the sixteenth-century equivalent of oil), and he saw what he thought of as 'natural' communities being smashed for this purpose with the pretext of converting them to Christ and Spanish civilisation. His first line of defence was, of course, to defend the existence of the indigenous *communities*, without which the individual Indian was lost and an easy prey to the slaver. He thought that all attempts to stamp out the Indians' 'barbaric' religious practices would result in a disproportionate death-toll among them and the destruction of their way of life, as well as being the pretext for conquest.[12]

Las Casas's contemporaries in the Spanish universities, including the theologian–jurists Francisco de Vitoria and Domingo de Soto, took a

11 See Bartolomé de Las Casas, *In Defense of the Indians*, ed. Stafford Poole (De Kalb: Northern Illinois University Press, 1992) 235–48.

12 As it was, for example, in the self-serving memoirs of Hernán Cortez, the conqueror of Mexico.

different view, believing it was a moral duty to intervene – not in order to put a stop to sin or idolatry, but to save the lives of the victims. War of humanitarian intervention could became a moral duty – always supposing the bad consequences were not out of proportion to the cause. They believed that if the state is right to intervene in its own jurisdiction to correct injustices and to save human lives, even to stop certain kinds of violent religious rites, then it is right to intervene on foreign soil to do the same. It is a consequence of our common humanity – an expression of the global common good. In such cases individual rights to life must be defended against the freedom to practice a religion. In this area at least, posterity has been on the side of Vitoria and Soto rather than Las Casas, and the modern development of international law in such areas as genocide and the treatment of civilians in time of war has followed their lead. What it means for our question is that injustices done to individuals in the name of religion are still injustices, and that the civil authority has a *prima facie* obligation to the international community to put a stop to them, both inside and, if possible, outside its jurisdiction.

JOHN LOCKE: NATURAL RIGHTS IN THE MODERN STATE

My final example – from John Locke's *Letter Concerning Toleration* – may seem to be from a quite different tradition than the one I have been citing so far. Locke (1602–1704), after all, was a Protestant political philosopher normally thought of as the father of Anglo-American political liberalism, who considered the Catholic Church of his time the principal enemy of freedom. Nevertheless, he belongs to the same broad natural law/natural rights tradition that stems from the theology of Aquinas. In political philosophy, Locke is best considered as a natural law theologian, whose theological convictions inform everything he wrote, and it makes no sense to treat him as a secular rationalist.[13] His principal source in this area of Church and State is the Anglican Thomist of the previous century, Richard Hooker (1554–1600). Against the Puritan desire for a single-faith State ruled by the righteous, Hooker argued for a spirit of

13 This change in our understanding of Locke has been argued by a number of eminent Locke scholars in recent years. See, for example, James Tully, *A Discourse on Property: John Locke and his Adversaries* (Cambridge: CUP, 1980); Waldron, *God, Locke and Equality*.

charity and reciprocity between people of different religious persuasions and against any attempt to establish the Kingdom of God on earth in a righteous parliament run by Puritans.[14] It was the first modern argument against theocracy.

In common with the other theologians I have mentioned, Locke believed that we owe natural duties of benevolence toward other human beings, whether or not they belong to our political jurisdiction or religion, in so far as we all belong to what he calls 'this great and natural community' of mankind.[15] It imposes obligations of reciprocity on us all, even before the establishment of a political contract. It is a *theological* perception of our fundamental unity, based again on the text from the book of Genesis (1.26–28) relating our creation in God's image. In Locke's eyes this establishes the basic equality of all human beings, in whom we must acknowledge God's 'workmanship':

> [F]or men being all the workmanship of one omnipotent and infinitely wise Maker; all the servants of one sovereign Master, sent into the world by His order and about His business; they are His property, whose workmanship they are made to last during His, not one another's pleasure. And, being furnished with like faculties, *sharing all in one community of Nature*, there cannot be supposed any such subordination among us that may authorise us to destroy one another, as if we were made for one another's uses, as the inferior ranks of creatures are for ours.[16]

In the *Letter*, it leads him to a radical view of religious toleration. Equality frees us in respect of our natural rights from control by any religious authority, because these natural rights derive from our status as equal works of God, not from our adherence to a belief, even a 'true' one, and not from any subordination to a human superior who claims to stand

14 '[M]y desire therefore to be loved of my equals in nature, as much as possible may be, *imposeth upon me a natural duty of bearing to themward, fully the like affection*; from which relation of equality between ourselves and them, that are as ourselves, what several rules and canons, natural reason hath drawn for direction of life, no man is ignorant.' *Of the Laws of Ecclesiastical Polity*, Bk 1 [Ch. 8], quoted by Locke, *Second Treatise of Government* 2.5 (my italic).

15 *Second Treatise of Government*, § 128, in John Locke, *Two Treatises of Government*, ed. Mark Goldie (London: J. M. Dent, 1993), 179.

16 Ibid. § 6, p. 117 (my italics).

closer to God than we do. 'No private person has any right in any manner to prejudice another person in his civil enjoyments [liberty, property, etc.] because he is of another church or religion . . . This the gospel enjoins, this reason directs, and this that natural fellowship we are born into requires of us.'[17] It was a doctrine that cut both ways where freedom of religion was concerned: the radical autonomy of natural rights prohibited, on the one hand, state intervention in the religious affairs of minorities and nonconformists, and on the other hand it prohibited religious leaders from punishing dissident individuals of their communities in any way that violated their civil freedoms. This included the freedom to change their religion without bodily punishment or loss of goods.

Like his predecessors I have considered, Locke is not content to argue tolerance from the 'lesser evil' approach. On the contrary, his radicalism derives from his perception that it belongs to the *nature of true religion* to be tolerant of difference. An intolerant Church is a failed Church (as he clearly thought the persecuting Anglican Church in the time of Charles II was): 'No peace and security, no, not so much as common friendship, can ever be established or preserved among men so long as this opinion prevails, that dominion is founded in grace and that religion is to be propagated by force of arms.'[18] Of course, he was talking about relationships between religious groups rather than within them but, as I have been arguing, relationships of reciprocity and natural justice must obtain just as much *within* faith communities as between them. Locke was clear that we carry our natural relationships and our natural obligations towards others (as God's 'workmanship' made for his purposes) with us into whatever political commonwealth or church we join ourselves to. The laws and rights internal to the political community or church cannot be allowed to contradict those natural rights and obligations, but must give effect to them.

On the other hand, living in a world that was already marked by a plurality of Christian sects – who had to tolerate one another if there was to be any civil peace – Locke had an acute appreciation of religious freedom that is missing from his Catholic predecessors, knowing as they did only the one 'true' church. Thus, taking the principle of free consent to

17 John Locke, *A Letter Concerning Toleration*, ed. James H. Tully (Indianapolis, Indiana: Hackett, 1983), 31.

18 Ibid. 33.

faith to its logical conclusions in a way that the earlier theologians could not, he maintains that churches are voluntary organisations of people gathered to worship in the way they believe God requires of them. This means that the State (or the 'magistrate') has no powers to intervene in religious matters, since it would come between God and the individual conscience.[19] What he had in mind was rituals and worship, rather than the control of individuals in the religious community. Locke thought that the State should keep out of such things and busy itself only with matters of 'civil rights and worldly goods.' But, he writes, there are limits to what can be tolerated in religion: for example, child-sacrifice or sexual abuse: 'Is the magistrate obliged to tolerate them, because they are committed in a religious assembly? I answer: No. These things are not lawful in the ordinary course of life, nor in any private house; and therefore neither are they so in the worship of God, or in any religious meeting.'[20] A church can sacrifice animals if it thinks God demands it. But it must not infringe the rights of persons whom the state exists to conserve, even when these persons are church members:

> Those things that are prejudicial to the commonwealth of a people in their ordinary use and are, therefore, forbidden by laws, those things ought not to be permitted to Churches in their sacred rights. Only the magistrate ought always to be very careful that he do not misuse his authority to the oppression of any church, under pretence of public good.[21]

Of course, many religious bodies might consider such matters as the special status of women (policed as always by men) or the prohibition of various sexual relationships as being part and parcel of their acceptance by God. Rights, they would say, cannot contradict what is 'right' (according to God's law). For Locke, having as he did a fairly traditional view of social relationships and sexual morality, it was perhaps clear where the harmless beliefs of religious sects ended and the serious infringements of the common good began, in order to mark the boundary between legitimate and illegitimate state intervention. But for us, with our moral as well as religious pluralism, it is not so clear. We have a much broader

19 Ibid. 39.
20 Ibid. 41–2.
21 Ibid. 42.

experience of human diversity – if you like, a much broader understanding of what it means to be made in God's image, in which the free, heterosexual man is not automatically the reference point. Indeed, to see the image of God in people not like us should expand our comprehension of the God-like, rather than reduce everyone to the same model of the human. The latter tendency is coercive, since we already have a model of typical humanity that is based on what we know rather than on what we don't know. It is a closed image, when what we need is an open image, that is, something we know to be a reality when we encounter it in others, but which we cannot finally complete. In truth, we don't know what God is like, and therefore cannot decide beforehand how others should be like God.[22] Jonathan Sacks has pointed out a passage in the Mishnah that gives us another version of the endlessly variable image:

> Again [but a single man was created] to proclaim the greatness of the Holy One, blessed is he; for man stamps many coins with the one seal and they are all like one another; but the King of kings, the Holy One, blessed is he, has stamped every man with the seal of the first man, yet not one of them is like his fellow. Therefore every one must say, For my sake was the world created. (Sanhedrin, 4.5)[23]

Nevertheless, even with a diverse, 'postmodern' view of human nature and its different rationalities, there must be a boundary between legitimate and illegitimate intervention by the civil authority, if only because the image of God is frequently trampled in the name of traditions that are confused with the will of God. Basic equality is ignored, and freedoms of action that are part of what it means to be made in God's image are denied. There must still be areas in which the state ought not to intervene, and areas where – perhaps rarely – it *must* intervene on behalf of its citizens. Thus, while providing defence for religious communities against attacks, the state has to legislate and guard a minimum standard of human welfare, including the capacity for any individual to leave or

22 For an expansion of this argument, see Ruston, *Human Rights and the Image of God*, ch. 16.

23 Jonathan Sacks, 'Jewish–Christian Dialogue: The Ethical Dimension', in *Tradition in an Untraditional Age* (London: Valentine, Mitchell, 1990), 175. I have used the translation of the Mishnah by Herbert Danby (Oxford: OUP, 1933), 338.

marry out of their religious community without suffering physical punishment. Underlying this is a belief in a 'great and natural community' of humankind that imposes on us natural duties toward one another irrespective of other, more particularist beliefs.[24]

CONCLUSION

The early-modern discourse on natural rights I have been speaking of concerns a limited area bounded by the needs of human beings as creatures of God living in communities, and it does not cover the entire areas of benefits and freedoms that nowadays prompt many people to claim their 'human rights' when they feel something is lacking in their lives. For both the Catholic Las Casas and the Protestant Locke, it concerns the areas of physical survival and well-being, including the chance of a happy, educated life, freedom from unjust attack and confiscation of goods, from loss of political liberty and access to a livelihood. It is the denial of such things, the 'ruin of lives', that the state has an overriding duty to prevent – as both the Spanish Catholic and the English Protestant recognised. Hence the duty of the civil authority to intervene in the conduct of a religious body that denies such basic natural goods to any of its members.

The examples I have given of pre-modern and early-modern reasoning about the limits of coercion in matters of religion are meant to suggest a pattern: problems of human survival and co-existence are not solved by the myopic application of a single rule of scriptural commands (confused in all religious traditions at some time with their cultural customs) regardless of the consequences to people's earthly lives. No, they require some deep reflection on the conditions of our common presence in this world as creatures of God – which is what the theology of 'nature' from Aquinas to Locke was attempting to do. So the apparently secular discourse of human rights, far from being something alien imposed on religious life from the outside, has grown from within a religious tradi-

24 Cf. Sacks, 'Jewish–Christian Dialogue': 'If I do not have some moral obligations to those I believe to be categorically in error – if I am not prepared to recognize the image of God in the human being as such, independently of his or my theological commitments – then there is at least a possible line from faith to holocaust.'

tion in response to its deepest insights into God's creative presence in the world. The religious and the secular are still different, yet far more entangled with one another than we, with our tidy categories and thirst for absolutes, normally want to admit. It is God's world, and it is for our benefit that this difference, and this entanglement, continue.

CHAPTER 3

Religion in a Democratic Society: Safeguarding Freedom, Acknowledging Identity, Valuing Partnership

Michael Ipgrave

The democratic societies of contemporary Western Europe, Northern America and other parts of the world are, in differing degrees, marked by both the persistence of communities of religious belief and the diversification of those communities. At the same time, these societies show evidence of large numbers of people with no active participation in, and little sustained identification with, organised religious life. This raises some general questions as to how religious communities function effectively in such situations, for their own good and for the wider good of society. What are people of faith looking for in terms of participation in a democratic and plural society? What problems are created for us by trends towards a secularising framework? What measures are needed to address these problems? Any possible clashes between human rights and religious approaches represent just one sharp focus within a much wider, and more blurred, picture of the status of religion in a democratic society.

In what follows, I shall comment on three concentric bands of increasing mundanity, and decreasing legal clarity, within that wider picture – namely: first, the safeguarding of religious freedom in public life; second, the acknowledgement of religious identity as a dimension of citizenship; and third, the valuing of religious communities as partners with statutory authority in the functioning of civil life. It can be seen immediately how these three aspects depend on one another: the formation of effective partnerships requires an acknowledgement of the partner's identity, which in turn will imply some guarantee of their freedom to maintain and express that identity. Conversely, it could be argued that religious freedom is likely to be most robustly defended in a context where the value of religious communities' contributions to the common good, and the significance of religious belonging to citizens' identity, are most fully appreciated. Nevertheless, the issues raised in each band of questions are of different kinds, and the search for appropriate responses to those issues must be conducted in different areas.

SAFEGUARDING RELIGIOUS FREEDOM

The European Convention on Human Rights states that

> [e]veryone has the right to freedom of thought, conscience and religion; this right includes freedom to change his religion or belief, and freedom, either alone or in community with others and in public or private, to manifest his religion or belief, in worship, teaching, practice and observance.[1]

Human rights jurisprudence has distinguished within these rights between those which apply to the so-called *forum internum,* or private sphere, and those which operate within the *forum externum,* or public world.[2] The latter, involving the manifestation of religion or belief, are held to be susceptible to derogation under conditions defined by the Convention,[3] whereas the former are considered to be absolute. In practice, the boundary between these two *fora* is not always easy to draw, and neither is the distinction between the 'holding' of a religion or belief and its 'manifestation.' On the one hand, if the interiority of the absolute right is emphasised, then that right itself becomes minimal in its content, since – short of invasive mind-altering techniques – it is difficult to see how the integrity of the *forum internum,* at least among adults,[4] could practically be violated: 'Viewed from this angle, one would assume that any intervention from outside is not only illegitimate but impossible.'[5]

1 European Convention on Human Rights and Fundamental Freedoms (4 November 1950), art. 9(1).

2 There is a careful and critical discussion of this distinction in Carolyn Evans, *Freedom of Religion under the European Convention on Human Rights* (Oxford: Oxford University Press, 2001), 72ff.

3 ECHR, art. 9(2).

4 The question of religious freedom as it applies to children – as also the understanding of patterns of children's religious identity – is both immensely significant and highly complex. I have not attempted to make any comments on this specialised area within this general survey.

5 Arcot Krishnaswami (Special Rapporteur of the Sub-Commission on Prevention of Discrimination and Protection of Minorities), *Study of Discrimination in the Matter of Religious Rights and Practices* (1960), cited in Evans, *op. cit.*, p. 68.

On the other hand, most accounts of religion or belief would insist that the genuine holding of a belief leads necessarily to some attempt to express the consequences of that belief, and that restrictions on the manifestation of a religion may therefore have implications of curtailing people's absolute freedom to hold that religion.

These complex interactions can be illustrated from three recent issues raised within Western European democracies: the proposal to delineate spaces within which the symbolic manifestation of religious beliefs is prohibited; the exclusion of persons from public office on the grounds of the implications of their religious beliefs; and the question of granting exemptions from religious discrimination legislation to certain religious organisations. Each of these issues raises questions not only about the acceptance of the religious in a democracy but also about the limits of the secular.

One of the most highly profiled recent examples of the delineation of public spaces within which the manifestation of religion is to be prohibited by statute is provided by the French Law 2004-228, which stipulates that

> Dans les écoles, les collèges et les lycées publics, le port de signes ou tenues par lesquels les élèves manifestent ostensiblement une appartenance religieuse est interdit.[6]

The law has attracted widespread public support in France, as well as significant opposition from religious and civil-liberties groups. It followed the report of the Stasi Commission established by President Jacques Chirac, to investigate the application of the principle of *laïcité*, the separation of Church and State which dates back in its present form in France to 1905.[7] The Commission's report begins by stating that *laïcité* is constitutive of the collective history of modern France, and a value which above all distinguishes the Republic from the pre-revolutionary monarchy; at the same time, *laïcité* is described as a *principe universel*. It is indeed in terms of *laïcité* that the long-running debate in France

6 *Loi encadrant, en application du principe de laïcité, le port de signes ou de tenues manifestant une appartenance religieuse dans les écoles, collèges et lycées publics.*

7 The Stasi Commission was established by President Chirac in July 2003, and published its report in December 2003: *Rapport au Président de la République de la Commission de Réflexion sur l'Application du Principe de Laïcité dans la République.*

over Islamic head-coverings for women (*foulard, voile*) has been principally conducted. Law 2004-228 does not, however, specifically mention Islamic symbols, and the recommendation in the Stasi report on which it is based specifically mentioned Christian and Jewish symbols as well as the *voile*.[8] It should be noted also that the law implicitly draws on the Commission's distinction between symbols which are *ostensible* and those which are *discret*,[9] giving tacit permission for the latter; that it applies only to public primary and secondary schools, not to other public spaces or other educational institutions; and that it requires a 'dialogue' with students before any disciplinary procedures are invoked.[10]

One of the major concerns which led to the Stasi Commission's recommendation was in fact over individuals' freedom of 'manifestation' of their identity. It was felt that girls and young women in some Islamic communities were being pressurised into wearing the *foulard* or *voile* against their will, and it was partly in order to protect their right not to adopt these symbols of faith that the prohibition was introduced. Another factor was an anxiety about what was perceived as the growing separatism of Muslim communities, and consequently the desire to insist that at least within the arena of public schools the visible signs of separate identities should be curtailed.

Nevertheless, as critics of the law have pointed out, it does represent a serious limitation of the freedom to manifest religion within an important set of public spaces. It might be expected that effects of such legislation could be experienced in two possible directions. Among those who agree to enter the *laïc* zone of public schools under the terms prescribed by the law, there would necessarily be an acceptance of a curtailment of the right to manifest religion. On the other hand, those who insist on the requirement of their faith to be manifested in the forms proscribed by law would have to debar themselves from participating in these educational institutions – a course of action which could, paradoxically, lead to an increase in religious separatism rather than to the greater cohesion which the law is designed to promote. Moreover, despite the requirement

8 *Rapport*: 'grande croix, voile ou kippa'.

9 *Rapport*: 'Les tenues et signes religieux interdits sont les signes ostensibles . . . ne sont pas regardés comme des signes manifestant une appartenance religieuse les signes discrets . . .'

10 *Loi 2004-228*: 'une procédure disciplinaire est précédée d'un dialogue avec l'élève'.

for 'dialogue' in individual cases, it is difficult to see what scope there is for religious communities to enter into negotiation over the principle of the law, which is essentially an affirmation of the principle of *laïcité* as requiring a clear derogation from the principle of religious freedom, at least in its aspect of manifestation.

Such an approach points towards a certain 'privatisation' of religion as a condition of its toleration in a plural society: the manifestation of religious identity is, according to this view, to be restricted to non-public areas. By contrast, my second example has seemed to many observers to involve a pushing of the curtailment of religious manifestation even into the private sphere itself, insofar as it concerns the eligibility for public office of a person holding specific religious views. That person is the Italian philosopher and social theorist Rocco Buttiglione, who in October 2004 was nominated by the Italian government as the European Union Commissioner for Justice, Freedom and Security. Buttiglione, a devout Roman Catholic and friend of Pope John Paul II, was vehemently criticised by members of the European Parliament for his views on homosexuality and on the place of women, and eventually withdrew his candidacy, given the likelihood that his inclusion would result in the whole Commission being voted down by the Parliament.

What was particularly remarkable about this episode was that Buttiglione, far from seeking to press on others the implications of his religiously founded ethical views, explicitly appealed to the traditional liberal distinction between the private and the public sphere, pledging that he would not allow his individual attitudes to stand in the way of ensuring freedom from discrimination on the grounds of gender or of sexual orientation. He explained: "I may think that homosexuality is a sin, and this has no effect on politics, unless I say that homosexuality is a crime."[11] However, this distinction was deemed inadequate by his critics, with the president of the European Parliament himself declaring: "It does not seem to me that in this day and age we can have people in charge of justice – especially justice – who think like that."[12]

It is difficult to read this as other than a ruling-out from this post of

11 'Hearings of the Commissioners-designate', on 5 October <http://www.europarl.eu.int/press/audiocom2004/medias/buttiglione>.

12 Josep Borrell MEP, quoted on <http://news.bbc.co.uk/1/hi/world/europe/3736764.stm> (12 October 2004).

any person holding conservative religious views, however careful that person might be to distinguish his private opinions from the public exercise of office. Whether or not somebody should be disqualified from a post on the grounds of their stated policy preferences, in this case the distinction between the absolute right to hold a religious belief in the *forum internum* and possible curtailments of its manifestation in the *forum externum* appears to have been broken down. The sense that this is a clear instance of religious discrimination is strengthened by the fact that the distinction between the two was in this case denied not, as it were, from the inside perspective of religious faith, but from the external intrusion of an ideology which allowed no space for difference of ethical opinion on issues of sexual orientation and gender roles.

Whereas I have argued that the Buttiglione case involves clear discrimination against an individual on the grounds of his religion, my third example is more complex, and focuses on the status of religious communities rather than individuals. Legislation recently introduced into member states of the European Union extends protection from discrimination in employment or occupation to the grounds of religion or belief.[13] That is to say, it is no longer possible in general to refuse to give somebody a job on the grounds of their faith. This development has been broadly welcomed by faith communities in Europe, especially by those, such as Muslims and Christians, who could not previously benefit directly from protection against racial discrimination because of their multi-racial character. However, it does raise a series of questions about the ability of religious communities, or religiously based organisations, themselves to have regard to the religion of individuals in making appointments.

In some instances, the issues are obvious and uncontroversial. It is clearly necessary, for example, for a church to be able to insist that only Christians can be appointed as priests, or for a mosque to require evidence of Islamic faith and practice from those who wish to serve as imams. In such situations, an exemption from the provisions of non-discrimination must be made for the church or mosque; in other words, religiously based groups need to have some freedom themselves to discriminate on the grounds of religion. Beyond these examples, however, disputed areas arise in two directions. One concerns the nature of the

13 The national laws were introduced within the framework of the EU Employment Directive (2000/78/EC), drafted under Article 13 of the EU Treaty.

work being undertaken: is it necessary, for example, that a secretary in a Roman Catholic school be himself or herself a member of the Roman Catholic Church? Different organisations, as they interpret differently the implications of what it means to be a faith-based organisation, will identify broader or narrower ranges of jobs as carrying religious commitment as a genuine occupational requirement. The other, and potentially still more contentious, area of ambiguity concerns the extent to which religious organisations can state or enforce requirements about employees' lifestyles which flow from the organisation's religious ethos. The issues here are particularly acute in the area of sexual orientation, and the possibility of conflict is further heightened by the introduction of legislation prohibiting discrimination on this ground at the same time as that on grounds of religion or belief.

From the point of view of human rights thinking, potential clashes such as this will be conceptualised as issues in the prioritisation of one right over another. Does an employee's right to freedom from discrimination on the grounds of sexual orientation, for example, take precedence over an employer's exemption from the duty not to practice discrimination on the grounds of religion or belief, or vice versa? From the point of view of religious communities themselves, however, the issue will appear rather as one of the exercise of corporate religious freedom. Does a religious community possess the freedom to insist on certain ethical positions in the ordering of its internal life, even if these are at variance with the norms adopted by the rest of society? To put the question in these terms, though, immediately raises the further question: who within the community has the right to determine what those ethical positions are, and should dissentient individuals within the community have access to some protection from the wider legal safeguards afforded by society? In finding a way to discuss these questions together, people of faith and human rights practitioners both need to bear in mind the inherently collective nature of the right to religious freedom: as it is 'either alone or in community with others' that religion or belief is typically manifested,[14] the Convention rights to freedom of religion or belief cannot be adequately conceptualised in individual terms alone.

All three of these issues relating to the exercise of religious freedom

14 ECHR, art. 9(1).

certainly raise questions about the status of religion in the public life of contemporary plural democracies. Are religious commitment and religious expression to be tolerated only within the confines of a privatised interiority – or perhaps not even there – or are they to be affirmed as a contribution to the common good of society as a whole? Is religious belonging to be seen just as an individual option, or is it to be acknowledged as a constituent strand of the identity of communities? But these three examples equally raise questions about the nature of the 'secular'. Is this to be seen essentially as a neutral process for holding the ring between people of different faiths and beliefs (including those with no religious beliefs), or is it in itself a more or less clearly defined philosophical or even religious ideology, with a recognisable historical lineage? To use the words applied by the Stasi Commission's report to *laïcité*, is it just a *valeur républicaine constitutive de notre histoire collective*, or is it also a *principe universel*? There is an urgent need to clarify the ways in which words such as 'freedom' or 'secular' are being used in contemporary debates: *Whose Pluralism? Which Secularity?* we might ask.[15]

ACKNOWLEDGING RELIGIOUS IDENTITY

Lying beyond the principle of safeguarding religious freedom is a wider concern, namely, the acknowledgement of religious identity as a constitutive strand in the self-understanding of both individuals and communities. This is particularly important when members of one religious group or another feel that they are especially vulnerable or disadvantaged. In Western Europe, this has most obviously been true in recent years in relation to the Muslim community.[16] On the one hand, Muslims have felt themselves to be the objects of suspicion, distrust, or occasionally even hatred in Western societies. On the other hand, large sectors of the Muslim community have been among the most economically, educationally and socially deprived parts of those societies. In such circumstances, it is not surprising that there has been pressure in Britain

15 Cf. the seminal study by Alasdair MacIntyre, *Whose Justice? Which Rationality?* (Notre Dame: University of Notre Dame Press, 1988).

16 For evidence of this in the British context, see particularly: Paul Weller, Alice Feldman, Kingsley Purdam et al., *Religious Discrimination in England and Wales* (London: Home Office Research Study 220, 2001), 103ff.

for legal protection to be extended to people specifically on the basis of their religious identity. One example of such protection is of course the legislation mentioned above against discrimination on the grounds of religion or belief in the area of employment or occupation. Another has been the series of proposals to curb hatred directed against members of religious communities. In the English context, it is important to note that the intention of legislation against incitement to religious hatred would be to shift the focus away from a concern to defend the honour of God, as embodied in the blasphemy laws, towards the protection of human religious feelings.

However, the implications of such protective legislation reach beyond the legal realm to raise some profound questions of identity. The very concept of 'religious identity' is a relatively new one within public discourse; its parameters are, as yet, largely undefined. In these circumstances, there is a natural tendency to assimilate it to other dimensions of identity which have been part of legal and social discourse for longer. In particular, in the British context, religious identity has often been described in terms that suggest that it is essentially an extension of ethnic or racial identity. In part, this reflects some of the argumentation through which a consensus was reached that a measure of protection should be afforded to religious identity: existing race relations legislation, it was pointed out, covered members of communities such as Sikhs and Jews, where ethnic and religious identities broadly coincide, but did not apply to the multi-ethnic Muslim (or, indeed, Christian) community.[17] Yet the analysis of religious identity in terms of ethnicity is severely defective, and could distort legal provisions unless refined. In what follows, I shall develop this thesis by pointing to five aspects of religious identity which clearly mark it off from ethnicity; namely, religious identity has the character of being developmental, participatory, associational, voluntary, and controvertible. These five aspects are certainly present in the understanding of religious identity among Christians, and it is the Christian

17 The key judgement is in *Mandla v. Dowell Lee* (1983), stating that 'a cultural tradition of its own . . . often but not necessarily associated with religious observance' is requisite for a group of people to be afforded collective protection under race relations legislation' (text in S. H. Bailey, D. J. Harris and B. L. Jones (eds), *Civil Liberties: Cases and Materials* (4th edn, London: Butterworth, 1995), 639).

sense that will provide my starting point. However, all five can also be discerned, to a greater or lesser degree, within other traditions.

□ *Developmental*

Understood theologically – which means, understood in the terms that a Christian believer would regard as constituting the most important framework of analysis – Christian identity is not a quality possessed by an individual, but rather a description of that person's standing in relation to God. As such, it can be expected to be subject to development, as that relationship develops and grows – an image commonly used in contemporary Christianity is that of a pilgrimage or journey towards communion with God.[18] Moreover, this developmental quality is not only a theological concept; it is clear from psychological and sociological studies that religious identity involves patterns of self-understanding and behaviour which change throughout an individual's life. The developmental character of religious identity is evident at the level of communities also. Many of the current disputes among Christians, for example, can be interpreted as debates over the nature and extent of permissible development within the churches. It may be that a recognition of the importance of adaptability and development is more marked in a Christian approach to religious identity than in some other religions, yet all will acknowledge the need to allow for some degree of movement in the understanding of what constitutes authentic expression of that religion, even if such movement be in principle allowed only in a 'backwards' direction, to re-establish a primordial purity of practice overlaid by later accretions.

In this respect, religious identity differs from ethnic identity, which is by definition a more or less static category given from the moment of birth. This is not a theoretical distinction alone, but has practical consequences, for legislative or other measures of the kind designed to afford protection to people on the basis of their given ethnic identity could possibly be inhibitive of the developmental freedom which religious identity requires. In fact, some of the most significant changes in the Christian churches in recent times have come from being open to changes in the

18 This is, for example, the imagery used in the Vatican II Declaration on Religious Freedom, *Dignitatis Humanae*, cap. 3 – see Austin Flannery Op, ed., *Vatican Council II: The Conciliar and Post-Conciliar Documents* (Dublin: Dominican Publications, 1975).

societies in which they are set; had they been cushioned from the impact of those changes by over-protection, their collective lives might not have developed in ways that could maintain their relevance to their contexts. If the developmental nature of religious identity is not recognised, either at an individual or a community level, then, there is a danger that protective legislation might lead to the distortion or ossification of religious life. Attitudes and practices which relate to one stage or context of development could be captured and enshrined as the unchanging norms to define for all time the expression of a given religion.

□ *Participatory*

A second feature which marks off religious identity from ethnic is the emphasis that it lays on participation in certain recognisable ways of behaving, speaking or thinking, a participation which will be taken up in differing degrees by different individuals. To the extent that it overlaps with culture, ethnicity also admits of some measure of participatory variation – people may be more or less aware of, and more or less demonstratively expressive of, their Irish ethnicity, for example. Nevertheless, it is much more meaningful to speak of varying measures of Islamic commitment, for example, than it is to speak of varying degrees of Irishness, and the former commitment can be measured to some extent through externally identifiable criteria – performance of prayer five times daily, observance of the Ramadan fast, giving of the *zakāt* tax, and so on.

However, it is important to recognise that religious identity, while expressed in varying degrees through participation, cannot be simply reduced to the identifiable evidence of commitment. On the contrary, an individual may have a strong sense of identity in relation to one or another religion while demonstrating very little visible participation in the recognised patterns of manifestation of that religion. This in turn raises challenges in the area of any legislation designed to protect religious identity. It would be possible, for example, to provide legal recognition of an interpretation of a particular religion which sanctioned maximal levels of participation as the norm, and thereby imposed an unfair burden on those whose religious participation was set at a lower outward level, or whose patterns of observance differed in some significant way from the orthodox norm. In such situations, minority groups or individuals within communities should be able to count for the safeguarding of their position on the general rights accorded them by society; if those rights are to be qualified in the case of a given religious identity through an interpretation provided by the religious leadership, then dissentients could find themselves in a vulnerable position.

□ *Associational*

Religious identity is inherently associational. To be a Christian, for example, means to be linked in some way to a visible Christian community. This linkage need not, in terms of religious identity, be as strong a relationship as that involved in active church membership; the links between 'believing' and 'belonging' are notoriously complex, and at times elusive, in modern societies. However, it is fair to say that the more religious identity expresses itself through some manifestation (and so the more acutely the question of legal protection comes into play), the stronger the associational dimension will become. The corollary of this is that protective measures will in some way have to apply not only to individuals but also to communities, or at least to organisations based on religion which concretely embody those communities.

To the extent that ethnicity is linked with particular cultural or linguistic practices, it could be said that some measure of corporate protection should be afforded in the case of ethnically based associations too. Measures to ensure the teaching, learning and public use of minority languages, for example, may give special scope to language-based organisations to discriminate on the grounds of linguistic competence. However, as compared with cultural or linguistic organisations, one of the distinguishing characteristics of religiously based organisations is that they often seek to embody not only distinctive religious identities but also the ethical positions which are held to flow from such identities, and such ethical positions may be at variance from those generally accepted in wider society. Given also that there are likely to be differences of opinion on these questions between different organisations within a given religion, the protection of religious associations is certainly likely to raise some very contentious problems quite unlike those associated with ethnicity issues.

□ *Voluntary*

Religious traditions differ between and within themselves over the extent to which belonging to them is to be understood as a voluntary decision on the part of their adherents. In the case of Christianity, for example, there has been both a considerable stress on the part of the human being in accepting, or rejecting, the invitation to discipleship, and at the same time the conviction on the part of those who have accepted the call that God would say to them: 'You did not choose me, but I chose you' (John 15.16). This theological tension is also modulated by the different social contexts in which discipleship is to be worked out. There is likely to be a stronger sense of the 'givenness' of Christian identity, for example, in a settled rural society where normal entry to the church is through infant baptism, contrasting with a stronger emphasis on the voluntary nature of belief in a rapidly changing and diverse urban environment where adult conversions to the faith are common. In other religious traditions, where religious and ethno-cultural belongings are closely aligned, it may be more difficult to see a voluntary element in religious identity. Even here, though, there will be a recognition that the specifically religious strand of community membership cannot be either coerced or assumed, and there may be some provision, such as the Jewish ceremony of *bar mitzvah* or *bat mitzvah*, for the individual to take upon himself or herself the obligations and privileges of religious life within the givenness of their community belonging.

To the extent that religious identity is seen as voluntary, it can also be seen as mutable, with recognition that a person should be free to transfer his or her religious belonging from one tradition, or one form of one tradition, to another. Such an admission will be made with varying degrees of enthusiasm at different levels of religious life and in different religious traditions. Theologically speaking, almost all Christians would regard conversion away from Christianity as almost always a mistake, and many would say the same about moving away from their own form of Christianity to another denomination. In some religious traditions, there will still be, beyond this, a reluctance to concede that people should have the freedom to move away from the true religion to something else, and a feeling that under a properly constituted legal system this should not be possible. However, in democratic Western societies, freedom to change religion is in fact guaranteed as a human right,[19] so that even religious groups with strong theological and jurisprudential objections to conversion have to recognise pragmatically the mutability of religious identity in every conceivable direction.

In terms of protection, both the voluntary nature and the mutability of religious identity raise issues concerning its protection that distinguish it from the case of ethnicity. It is sometimes suggested that the fact that religious identity is in some measure chosen by individuals implies that it is less deserving of full protection than ethnic identity, which is inescapably given. The argument here seems to be both that if people are experiencing problems because of their religion they only have themselves to blame because they chose to be like that any way, and further that they can always resolve those problems in any case by ceasing to manifest their religious identity, or by changing to another religion. However, both these lines of thinking display a failure to grasp the nature of religious adherence, which is at the same time voluntarily embraced and also experienced as unavoidable because of its absolute and ultimate importance. The challenge will be to find ways of protecting this kind of identity that recognise both its freedom to change and its constitutive significance.

□ *Controvertible*

A fifth aspect of religious identity distinguishing it from ethnicity is that it can be argued against. There is, of course, a sense in which ethnicity too is controvertible: an individual may argue with the ethnic group to which they are assigned, or indeed other members of that group may object to another's inclusion within that ethnicity. These are essentially boundary disputes, and they are to be found in the religious context too, where there may be vigorous disagreement over the rights of certain individuals or organisations to describe themselves as belonging to a particular religion. In the religious case, however, there is also a much deeper level of controvertibility to hand: X may disagree with Y calling himself a Muslim, but Z in turn may disagree with the entire set of beliefs on which both X and Y base their Islamic identity. Insofar as religious identity involves a voluntary element, it might be supposed that

19 ECHR, art. 9(1): 'This right includes freedom to change religion or belief . . .'

controversy of this kind is particularly likely in 'converting' religions, since choosing one way over others (or none) will involve weighing arguments for each and finding others wanting compared to the one chosen. However, controversion of particular religions can also come from those who feel that their religious identity is essentially something given as part of their heritage, and from those with no religious belief at all. Indeed, it is specifically in this dimension of controvertibility that religions most closely resemble other, non-religious, beliefs included under the human rights rubric of 'religion or belief'.

The difficulty of finding appropriate protective measures to accommodate this dimension of religious identity has become apparent in the protracted debate in the United Kingdom over legislation against incitement to religious hatred. The purpose of such a law would precisely be to provide protection from attacks on the grounds of religious identity. The concern raised by many critics of such legislation, both from the religious and the secular worlds, is that this kind of identity is so bound up with certain truth-claims that any robust criticism of those truth-claims will be perceived as an attack on people's religious feelings, and so be prohibited under measures designed to protect the latter. It can be argued that the flourishing of religious identity in fact requires freedom to engage in vigorous criticism of other views, not least since such criticism of others is close to the heart of most of the world's great faiths. Certainly, legal provision in this area will have to be carefully drafted and sensibly implemented to allow for such controversion to continue, if what is to be protected is genuine religious identity and not merely a pallid extension of ethnic identity.

The issue of controvertibility highlights, in a particularly focused fashion, the challenges facing modern democratic societies in understanding, and making protective provision for, the religious identity of citizens. This form of identity cannot be simply assimilated to, or treated as an extension of, ethnic identity; it is a *sui generis* element constitutive at a very deep level of the ways in which individuals and communities understand themselves. Adequate and appropriate provision for its recognition and protection in society must rely on a clear understanding of its special features, and this will involve both a process of education in religious literacy and the development of new dimensions of human rights jurisprudence.

VALUING PARTNERSHIPS WITH RELIGIOUS COMMUNITIES

Beyond the specific legal issues of affirming and safeguarding religious freedom and recognising and protecting religious identity within society, communities of faith, and the organisations which are based in them, are very significant partners in the civil societies of modern democracies. In Western Europe, active participation in religious activities has decreased significantly over the past fifty years, yet the evidence is that people still value the presence of the churches and other faith communities, maintain some sense of identification with them, and expect them to play a part in the life of society. From their own perspective, people of faith feel they have much to contribute to the flourishing of human life in society, and faith-based organisations are often among the leading players in social and community enterprises. There is, of course, a long background in Europe to Christian involvement in these areas; indeed, most of the foundations for today's educational, health and welfare provision were laid through the activities of the historic churches. The social outreach of faith communities more recently established in Europe was in the first place understandably directed towards the members of their own minority communities; recently, however, there have been growing signs of a readiness to engage more widely with other agencies (including churches and other faith groups) in seeking the common good.

In the United Kingdom, the profile of churches and other faith communities as partners in civil society has increasingly been recognised in the past few years by government at both national and local level.[20] From an administrative point of view, the faith communities are particularly valuable in two directions. One is in the task of service delivery: religious organisations provide large and committed networks that can organise social, educational and other welfare projects complementary to those provided by the statutory sector, in ways appropriate to the communities they serve, and often very economically. Alongside this is a second theme, of consultation: because religious groups are based in, and link together, grassroots communities across the country, they can provide

20 See in particular the reports issued by the Local Government Association and the Home Office – respectively, *Faith and Community: A Good Practice Guide for Local Authorities* (2002), and *Working Together: Co-operation between Government and Faith Communities* (2004).

policy makers with informed comment on contemporary issues, on proposed legislation, and on the current state of community relations. As a result, there has been in recent years in the United Kingdom a remarkable burgeoning of consultative structures and partnerships involving churches and other faith communities alongside statutory and other voluntary agencies.

Naturally, these developments have on the whole been welcomed by religious communities, although some anxieties have been voiced over the burden of consultation and partnership which is sometimes being laid on under-resourced organisations and individuals without attention to the enlargement of organisations' capacity to enter into partnerships. In general, the invitation to partnership is seen as a refreshing change from earlier attitudes which tended to marginalise the churches' contribution to social projects, and to relegate religion to a private realm. However, from the experience of faith communities and faith-based organisations entering into partnerships of this kind, it is apparent that there are a number of related issues which will require further attention in order for religion to play its full part in the flourishing of civil societies. Three in particular will be mentioned here: the question of public funding for religious organisations; the identification of the agreed grounds for partnership working; and the limitation of faith communities to certain areas and patterns of partnership.

Given that faith communities are in many places extensively involved in providing the types of services which governments want to see delivered to their citizens, it seems natural to assume that they should receive public funding to assist them in this task. In some areas, notably education, this has been an established principle for some time – in England, the large network of state-funded Christian (and Jewish) schools, mostly Anglican and Roman Catholic, has been expanded to include some Muslim and other faith-schools. In other areas, however, there has been a long-standing suspicion of public funding for religious groups, principally from the side of public authorities but also, to a lesser extent, from some faith groups. The key issue here is that of the kind of activities which can appropriately be funded by public money. It would clearly be wrong for the propagation of a particular religious message, or the performance of particular religious ceremonies, to be supported by public money, especially in the context of delivering services to vulnerable people. From the point of view of religious organisations, though, the delivery of services may well be seen as the expression and outcome of an overarching religious commitment, rather than as a discrete end in itself, and will be naturally accompanied by prayer, worship and the delivery of a religious message. It seems wrong that service delivery of this kind should be disqualified from receiving public funding simply because it is done from a religious motivation and in the context of religious practices. Indeed, such an approach could lead to a faith group either suppressing its religious character or artificially separating out 'community' from 'religious' wings in its organisation, when all that is needed is a clear understanding that public money will not be used directly for specifically religious activities and that recipients of services will neither be required to participate in these religious activities nor be treated unfairly if they do not do so. It does, in fact, seem that a consensus in principle may be reached around some such position as this, but there still remain the challenges both of turning around a culture of mutual suspicion between some faith communities and some public funders, and of working out the detailed application of these principles in different types of partnership.

A second, and related, area fraught with potential for conflict concerns the identification of the grounds on which partnerships involving religious organisations are to be established. A recent report on cooperation between UK government departments and religious organisations alludes to this issue, in characteristically understated terms, when it remarks that

> Departments should be aware that they and faith communities may come to consultations with different sets of philosophical and moral assumptions, adding to complexity and sometimes causing tension. Sufficient time should therefore be given for both sides to meet and remove misunderstandings.[21]

What is at issue here is the gulf between two very different ways of deciding what should be done in a given situation. Public legislators will be quite properly seeking as their first goal a public benefit, as understood in the light of their policy framework. On the other hand, religious organi-

21 *Working Together*, § 2.2.26.

sations will be seeking to discern, in the light of their overall commitment to the vision of ultimate purpose and meaning which lies at the heart of their faith, what they are being summoned to do in a particular situation in obedience to their religious calling. It is easy, but ultimately counter-productive and sometimes even dangerous, to try to press communities of obedience to assent to a premature, or even spurious, consensuality as the basis for working together. Authentic partnerships can only flourish when the very different starting points and methods of religious communities are acknowledged.

Finally, and again flowing from this, faith communities can find themselves frustrated by being limited to certain areas or patterns of partnership only. A consultative body may be established, for example, which provides a useful place for policy makers to hear the views and learn from the experience of religious communities in the area of drug abuse among young people. However, when those same communities wish to go further and share their perspectives on some of the underlying social, economic and attitudinal issues which provide a context within which such abuse develops, this may be judged to be beyond the terms of consultation. More generally, faith communities, while not being in a position to offer detailed policy initiatives, will often wish to commend an overall vision of the way that society should best ensure human flourishing, and to promote the values which can help to reach towards that vision. It can be frustrating for people of faith when 'consultation' appears to leave little space for sharing perspectives of this kind, but rather is restricted to eliciting responses to specific proposals. Again, faith communities, while recognising that they have a major contribution to make to helping people in need, will not want to be restricted to this service mode alone, but will want to add to that immediate pastoral response a wider and deeper prophetic questioning of the social order which generates such situations of need in the first place. Partnerships which constrain their independence to do this will rightly be regarded as an unreasonable diminution of their role. In short, the concept of partnership needs to be opened out to recognise that faith communities are not to be cast in fundamentally passive or responsive roles, but rather encouraged to contribute their values and perspectives as well as their expertise and resources to civil society.

CONCLUSION

Through all three of the concentric circles of safeguarding religious freedom, acknowledging religious identity, and valuing partnership with religious communities, it is evident that religion continues to play a crucially important part in contemporary and diverse democratic societies. It is particularly remarkable to note the way in which the profile of faith in public life is being raised after a period in which it was assumed to be in terminal decline. At the same time, to ensure that people of faith and faith communities can participate as fully and as effectively as possible in civic society, there needs to be an enhanced understanding of the distinctive character of religious freedom, identity and partnerships, and a developing body of jurisprudence, public theory, and social practice to ensure that religious contributions are adequately received for the good of all.

CHAPTER 4

Conflicting Values or Misplaced Interpretations? Examining the Inevitability of a Clash between 'Religions' and 'Human Rights'

Javaid Rehman

1. INTRODUCTION

The debate on the conflict between religions and human rights is both historic and contemporary.[1] This debate has been well-rehearsed, and its facets well documented and examined exhaustively, from theoretical as well as practical perspectives.[2] The inevitability of a clash between religion and human rights is so fervently argued, the breadth of the apparent conflict so profoundly explored, that it appears almost nonsensical to dissent. Religions are perceived as advocating regressive policies, whereas the ideals of human rights are viewed as accommodating and progressive. Amidst this impasse, the present chapter adopts a challenging position – it argues that it is possible, indeed imperative, to reconcile the values of religions with those of human rights law. From a contextual and methodological context, it is argued that over time the meanings provided to 'human rights' and 'religion' have varied greatly; and their interpretations continue to vary. In the contemporary legal and political

I am thankful to Dr Nazila Ghanea and Raphael Walden for their generous invitation to present a paper at a conference organised in London (February 2005), and for their support in developing my arguments as presented in this chapter.

1 See B. G. Tahzib, *Freedom of Religion or Belief: Ensuring Effective International Legal Protection* (The Hague: Martinus Nijhoff Publishers, 1995); E. Benito, *Elimination of All Forms of Intolerance and Discrimination Based on Religion or Belief* (New York: United Nations, 1989); B. Dickson, 'The United Nations and Freedom of Religion', *International and Comparative Law Quarterly*, 44 (1995), 327; R. S. Clark, 'The United Nations and Religious Freedom', *New York University Journal of International Law and Politics*, 11 (1978), 197; D. J. Sullivan, 'Advancing the Freedom of Religion or Belief through the UN Declaration on the Elimination of Religious Intolerance and Discrimination', *American Journal of International Law*, 82 (1988), 487.

2 See R. O'Dair and A. Lewis (eds.), *Law and Religion* (Oxford: OUP, 2001); A. Krishnaswami, *Study of Discrimination in the Matter of Religious Rights and Practices* (UN Publication Sales E. 60.X.IV.2, 1960); Benito, *Elimination of Intolerance*; S. C. Neff, 'An Evolving International Legal Norm of Religious Freedom: Problems and Prospects', *California Western International Law Journal*, 7 (1973) 543.

environment, reconciliation is advocated on the basis that not only do the jurisprudence of 'human rights' and 'religion' retain a strong relationship with each other, but elements of ambiguity contained within these two disciplines also allow for numerous possibilities of rapprochement.

The chapter is divided into four main sections. After this introductory section, the next section, section 2, analyses the complexities within international human rights law. The jurisprudential kaleidoscope of 'human rights' raises profound questions regarding the meaning of 'rights' within the international legal framework.[3] As this discussion elaborates, in addition to the conceptual difficulties, there continue to remain substantial disagreements in formulating a substantive code of human rights. The obstacles in establishing a coherent set of human rights standards in international arenas are examined within section 2.

If the consensus on 'human rights' principles is not readily discernable, religious values are often conspicuous through their apparent rigidity. Section 3 elaborates on the difficulties facing conventional interpretations of religions.

The history of all the major religions is littered with instances of a tragic involvement with acts of violence, aggression and substantial violations of human rights. The world's major religions evoke stresses and strains when confronted with modern day challenges posed by marginalised groups such as homosexuals, religious minorities and indigenous peoples. While insular and rigid interpretations of Christianity, Judaism and Islam sanctify inequalities and advocate violence, Islam and Muslim communities have been under the spotlight particularly since the events of 11 September 2001, and the Madrid, Bali and London bombings.[4] Critics argue that Islam is a religion which engenders discrimination

3 J. Shestack, 'The Jurisprudence of Human Rights' in T. Meron (ed.), *Human Rights in International Law: Legal and Policy Issues* (Oxford: Clarendon Press, 1984), 69–113.

4 See National Commission on Terrorist Attack Upon the United States, *The 9/11 Commission Report: Final Report of the National Commission on Terrorist Attacks Upon the United States* (New York: Norton, 2004); P. Ford, 'Terrorism Web emerges from Madrid bombing' <http://www.csmonitor.com/2004/0322/p01s02-woeu.html> accessed 10 July 2005; J. Aglionby, 'Smiling Bomber to Face Firing Squad for Bali Blasts: Relatives in Court Cheer and Weep – But Fear Execution will Create a Martyr', *The Guardian Unlimited* (8 August, 2003) <http://www.guardian.co.uk/international/story/0,,1014406,00.html> accessed 19 September 2004. For a useful summary of terrorist attacks see B. Davies, *Terrorism: Inside a World Phenomenon* (London: Virgin

and supports violence and terrorism.[5] With its focus upon Islam, section 3 of the chapter elaborates upon the methodological and contextual interpretation of *Sharia*.[6] Through a scheme of contextualisation and comprehension, the central message of Islam is advanced – a message that is not antithetical towards human rights and seeks reconciliation and accommodation. Section 4, the final section, provides a number of concluding observations.

2. THE COMPLEXITIES WITHIN INTERNATIONAL HUMAN RIGHTS

(*a*) *The jurisprudential quagmire*

A simplified construction of 'human rights' – though highly desirable – does not record the conceptual and jurisprudential difficulties inherent in the concept.[7] Establishing a unified jurisprudential base for 'human

Books, 2003) 93–127; BBC, 'London Attacks' <http://news.bbc.co.uk/1/hi/in_depth/uk/2005/london_explosions/default.stm> accessed 10 July 2005.

5 For an analysis of the debate surrounding Islam's relationship with human rights law and norms prohibiting discrimination, violence and terrorism see A. E. Mayer, *Islam and Human Rights: Tradition and Politics* (2nd edn, Boulder, Col.: Westview Press, 1995); A. A. An-Na'im, *Toward an Islamic Reformation: Civil Liberties, Human Rights and International Law* (Syracuse NY: Syracuse University Press, 1990); F. M. Denny, *An Introduction to Islam* (New York: Macmillan, 1994); C. G. Weeramantry, *Islamic Jurisprudence: An International Perspective* (London: Macmillan, 1988); R. Landau, *Islam and the Arabs* (London: George Allen and Unwin, 1958); M. A. Baderin, *International Human Rights and Islamic Law* (Oxford: OUP, 2003); R. Afshari, 'An Essay on Islamic Cultural Relativism in the Discourse of Human Rights', *Human Rights Quarterly*, 16 (1994), 235; P. J. Riga, 'Islamic Law and Modernity: Conflict and Evolution', *American Journal of Jurisprudence*, 36 (1991), 103; J. Entelis, 'International Human Rights: Islam's Friend or Foe? Algeria as an Example of the Compatibility of International Human Rights regarding Women's Equality and Islamic Law', *Fordham International Law Journal*, 20 (1997), 1251; S. S. Ali, *Gender and Human Rights in Islam and International Law: Equal Before Allah, Unequal Before Man?* (The Hague: Kluwer Law International, 2000).

6 Islamic Law. Note that the concept of Sharia is not confined to legal norms but conveys a more holistic picture; the Arabic translation of Sharia is 'the road to the watering place'. R Landau, *Islam and the Arabs* (London: George Allen and Unwin, 1958), 141; A. A. Oba, 'Islamic Law as Customary Law: The Changing Perspective in Nigeria', *International and Comparative Law Quarterly*, 51 (2002), 819; A. R. Doi, *Sharíah: The Islamic Law* (London: Taha Publishers, 1997), 2; L. W. Adamec, *Historical Dictionary of Islam* (Lanham, Maryland and London: The Scarecrow Press, 2001), 241.

7 See A. Cassese, *Human Rights in a Changing World* (Philadelphia: Temple University Press, 1990); K. E. Mahoney and P. Mahoney (eds), *Human Rights in the Twenty-First Century, A Global Challenge* (Dordrecht: Maritnus Nijhoff, 1993); A. H. Robertson and J. G. Merrills, *Human Rights in the World: An Introduction to the Study of*

rights' raises profound moral, ethical, philosophical and legal questions. The genesis of human rights law remains contentious: natural lawyers, positivists, utilitarians and relativists have all laid claims to it. In the development of international human rights law the pervading influence has been that of 'natural law' – a philosophy heavily influenced by Greek mythology and Judeo-Christian scriptures. In its pristine form, natural law relies upon the commandments of God as immutable and unalterable laws of nature. During the seventeenth century, attempts were made to detach natural law from religion per se and associate the concept with reason, logic and rationality. Thus Hugo Grotius, the father of modern international law, envisioned natural law as the 'dictate of right reason which points out that an act, according as it is or is not in conformity with rational nature, has in it a quality of moral baseness or moral necessity'.[8] Notwithstanding that 'reason', 'rationality' and 'just cause' are its cornerstones, natural law theorists fail to articulate a catalogue of rights that is compatible with modern paradigms of human rights. Natural lawyers continue to express misgivings over such controversial issues as abortion, euthanasia and the abolition of capital punishment.

Despite criticisms, alternative theorists – for example those campaigning for utilitarianism or positivism – have themselves failed to comprehensively and coherently provide a rationale for human rights.[9] In their emphasis upon the role of legal systems as administered by sov-

International Protection of Human Rights (4th edn, Manchester: Manchester University Press, 1996); L. Henkin (ed.), *The International Bill of Rights: The Covenant on Civil and Political Rights* (New York: Columbia University Press, 1981); M. S. McDougal, H. D. Lasswell and L.-C. Chen, *Human Rights and World Public Order: The Basic Policies of an International Law of Human Dignity* (New Haven, Conn.: Yale University Press, 1980); D. J. Harris, *Cases and Materials on International Law* (6th edn, London: Sweet and Maxwell, 2004), 654–785; D. Weissbrodt, J. Fitzpatrick and F. Newman, *International Human Rights: Law, Policy and Process* (3rd edn, Cincinnati: Anderson, 2001); H. Steiner and P. Alston, *International Human Rights in Context* (2nd edn, Oxford: Clarendon Press, 2001).

8 H. Grotius, *De Jure Belli ac Pacis,* bk. I, ch. 1, cited in J. Shestack, 'The Jurisprudence of Human Rights', in T. Meron (ed.), *Human Rights in International Law: Legal and Policy Issues* (Oxford: Clarendon Press, 1984), 77.

9 See J. S. Mill, *Utilitarianism* (London: Longman, Green, Reader & Dyer, 1871); J. Austin, *The Province of Jurisprudence Determined* (London: Weinfeld and Nicolson, 1955); J. Bentham, *A Fragment on Government* (Oxford: Basil Blackwell, 1967); H. L. A. Hart, *The Concept of Law* (Oxford: Clarendon Press, 1961); P. Hayden, *The Philosophy of Human Rights* (New York: Paragon House, 2001), 136–62.

ereign States, legal positivists deny an a priori source of rights. For these positivists, there is no legitimacy in the moral argumentation of what law 'ought' to be. As a dictate of the sovereign, laws have to be obeyed regardless of their iniquitous nature or disregard for human rights values.[10]

Amidst the jurisprudential conundrum not only do the sources of human rights provoke dissensions, the nature of the term 'human rights' itself has been profoundly complicated. The usage of the word 'rights', a 'chameleon-hued' term, raises more problems than it aims to address.[11] In his exhaustive analysis, *Fundamental Legal Conceptions as Applied in Judicial Reasoning I*, Professor Wesley Hohfeld advances the position that the word 'rights' has been used to identify the existence of a number of varied relationships. It has sometimes been used in a strict sense, reflecting that the right-holder is entitled to something with a co-relative duty on another person. Equally, the term 'rights' has been used to refer to an immunity from having a legal status altered, or to indicate a privilege to do something, or a power to create and alter legal relationships.[12] The application of Hohfeld's paradigm of 'rights', as has been pointed out by Shestack, raises complex scenarios – its application in international law could be particularly disturbing. Investigating this puzzle, Shestack makes the point that

> some of the civil and political rights [as provided in the International Covenant for Civil and Political Rights] are in the nature

10 See H. McCoubrey and N. White, *Textbook on Jurisprudence* (London: Blackstone Press, 1993), 7–54.

11 'One of the greatest hindrances to the clear understanding, the incisive statement, and the true solution of legal problems frequently arises from the express or tacit assumption that all legal relations may be reduced to "rights" and "duties", and that these latter categories are therefore adequate for the purpose of analyzing even the most complex legal interests . . . for in any closely reasoned problem, whether legal or non-legal, chameleon-hued words are a peril both to clear thought and to lucid expression' (W. Hohfeld, 'Some Fundamental Legal Conceptions as Applied in Judicial Reasoning', in W. Cook (ed.), *Fundamental Legal Conceptions as Applied in Judicial Reasoning: Essays by Wesley Newcomb Hohfeld* (New Haven: Yale University Press, 1923), 35).

12 See Hohfeld, op. cit.; F. Von Prondzynski, *Freedom of Association and Industrial Relations: A Comparative Study* (London: Mansell, 1987), 10; N. E. Simmonds, *Central Issues in Jurisprudence: Justice, Law and Rights* (London: Sweet and Maxwell, 1986), 129–30; J. Rehman, *The Weaknesses in the International Protection of Minority Rights* (The Hague: Kluwer Law International, 2000), 10–14.

> of immunities meaning that governments cannot derogate from them. But are there any absolute rights? Surely the right to life guaranteed by Article 6(1) of the Covenant would seem to be so basic as to be considered absolute. Yet, Article 6(1) only offers protection against 'arbitrary' deprivation of life. What is the effect of this qualification on the nature of the right involved. When we speak of inalienable rights, what do we mean? Do we mean a right to which no exceptions or limitations are valid? Or do we mean a 'prima facie' right with a special burden on the proponent of any defeasance? Or do we mean a principle which must be followed unless some other principle weighty enough to allow abridgement arises? Must considerations which justify an exception be of the same moral category as those that underlie the right?[13]

If uncertainty remains as to the nature of fundamental rights, such as the 'right to life', what are we to make of the rights which are derogable? Are they, in the Hohfeldian scheme, rights in the strict sense, or immunities or privileges? A pertinent example would be the case of the United Kingdom – in the absence of a written constitution with an entrenched bill of rights, there remains the possibility of abridgement of many of the fundamental rights. Fundamental human rights in the British constitutional framework are therefore more in the nature of Hohfeldian liberty than immunity. Further confusion arises in relation to the position of economic, social and cultural rights which do not always carry obligations of immediate implementation and some claim are akin to aspirations or goals. Considering their nature, some don't regard them as 'rights', because it is not always clear on whom lies the duties to implement these 'rights'.[14] Still greater confusion ensues when the so-called 'third generation' rights are bracketed into the category of rights. There are substantial difficulties in attempting to treat such rights as the 'right to self-determination' or the 'right to development' as rights *stricto sensu*,

13 J. Shestack, 'The Jurisprudence of Human Rights', in T. Meron (ed.), above n. 3, 69–113.

14 This aspirational approach is reflected by the terms of the International Covenant on Economic, Social and Cultural Rights; see D. M. Trubeck, 'Economic, Social and Cultural Rights in the Third World: Human Rights Law and Human Needs Programs', in T. Meron (ed.), above n. 3, 213; W. McKean, *Equality and Discrimination under International Law* (Oxford: Clarendon Press, 1983), 103–4.

as well as distinguishing the right-holders from the ones who bear co-relative duties. Who, for example, are holders of the 'right to self-determination' and the 'right to development', and upon whom lies the co-relative duty? Can the 'peoples' in fact be treated as synonymous to the State itself, meaning thereby that the holder of 'rights' and the bearer of 'duties' is the identical identity of the State?

(*b*) *Complexities in the substance of 'human rights'*

If the jurisprudential debate is bewildering and complex, an agreement on the substance of human rights has proved impossible. Diversity and dissensions from religious and cultural relativists continually rupture the finely crafted fabric of international human rights law.[15] These disagreements and divisions pervade the core of human rights, raising troubling and irresolvable questions over fundamental rights such as the right to life and the prohibition on torture. The right to life, as noted earlier, is the quintessential right within the architecture of human rights law: all of the international law instruments without exception vigorously defend this right.[16] Yet it '. . . is one of the more controversial rights, due to the

15 See E. Brems, *Human Rights: Universality and Diversity* (The Hague: Kluwer Law International, 2001); A. D. Renteln, *International Human Rights: Universalism versus Relativism* (Newbury Park: Sage Publications, 1990); A. D. Renteln, 'The Unanswered Challenge of Relativism and Consequences of Human Rights', *Human Rights Quarterly*, 7 (1985), 514; H. Gros-Espiell, 'The Evolving Concept of Human Rights: Western, Socialist and Third World Approaches' in B. G. Ramcharan (ed.), *Human Rights: Thirty Years after the Universal Declaration: Commemorative Volume on the Occasion of the Thirtieth Anniversary of the Universal Declaration of Human Rights* (The Hague: Martinus Nijhoff Publishers, 1979), 41–65; D. Donoho, 'Relativism Versus Universalism in Human Rights: The Search for Meaningful Standards', *Stanford Law Journal*, 27 (1991), 345; A. Eide, 'Making Human Rights Universal: Unfinished Business', *Nordic Journal of Human Rights*, 6 (1988), 51; J. Donnelly, 'Cultural Relativism and Universal Human Rights', *Human Rights Quarterly*, 6 (1984), 400; M. D. Evans, 'Human Rights and the Universality Debate', in R. O'Dair and A. Lewis (eds), above n. 2, 205–26.

16 See Article 3 of the Universal Declaration of Human Rights (adopted 10 December, 1948, UN GA Res. 217 A (III)), (UN Doc. A/810, 1948), 71; Article 2 of the European Convention on Human Rights (Signed at Rome, 4 November 1950; entered into force 3 September 1953. 213 U.N.T.S. 221; E.T.S. 5); Article 1 of the American Declaration of Human Rights; Final Act of the Ninth International Conference of American States, Bogotá, Colombia, 30 March – 2 May 1948, 48. (OEA/Ser/L.V/11.7, (1988), 17); Article 4 of the American Convention on Human Rights (Signed November 1969; entered into force 18 July 1978. O.A.S.T.S. Off. Rec. OEA/Ser.L/V/11.23, doc.21, rev. (1979). 9 I.L.M. (1970) at 673); Article 4 of the African Charter on Human and People's Rights (Adopted on 27 June 1981; entered into force 21 October, 1986. OAU Doc. CAB/LEG/67/3 Rev. 5,

inherent problems in defining its scope at the peripheries – the beginning and the end of life'.[17] There are irresolvable conflicts on the central issues as to when life begins, when it ends, under what circumstances the State is authorised to take life, and what the obligation of the State is in promoting and protecting this right.[18] The International Covenant on Civil and Political Rights, a treaty now ratified by over three-quarters of the international community, demonstrates the problems.[19]

Article 6 of the Covenant protects what it regards as the 'inherent right to life', though this protection extends only so far as 'arbitrary' taking of life is concerned.[20] The Article does not prohibit capital punishment if it is carried out 'in accordance with the law in force [and] a final judgement [is] rendered by a competent court'.[21] Women while pregnant and persons below the age of eighteen are exempt from capital punishment.[22] These restrictions however have not prevented capital punishment being imposed upon minors, and in some instances the verdict of the death penalty is hugely disproportionate to the offences committed. Professor Harris makes the sober observation that the death penalty

> exists for political offences (e.g. treason), military offences (e.g. mutiny), terrorist offences (e.g. hijacking), drug trafficking

21 I.L.M (1982) at 58); Also see General Comments by the Human Rights Committee, General Comment no. 6; General Comment no. 14, *Nuclear Weapons and the Right to Life* (Article 6) (Twenty-third Session, 1984), para. 1.

17 R. K. M. Smith, *Textbook on International Human Rights* (Oxford: Clarendon Press, 2005), 205.

18 See W. P. Gromley, 'The Right to Life and the Rule of Non-Derogability: Peremptory Norms and Jus Cogens', in B. G. Ramcharan (ed.), *The Right to Life in International Law* (Dordrecht: Martinus Nijhoff, 1985), 120–59; S. Joseph, 'The Right to Life', in D. J. Harris and S. Joseph (eds), *The International Covenant on Civil and Political Rights and United Kingdom Law* (Oxford: Clarendon Press, 1995), 153–83; S. Joseph, J. Schultz and M. Castan, *The International Covenant on Civil and Political Rights: Cases and Material and Commentary* (Oxford: Clarendon Press, 2000), 108–243; Y. Dinstein, 'The Right to Life, Physical Integrity and Liberty', in L. Henkin (ed.), *The International Bill of Rights: The Covenant on Civil and Political Rights* (New York: Columbia University Press, 1981), 114–37; P. Sieghart, *The Lawful Rights of Mankind: An Introduction to the International Legal Code of Human Rights* (Oxford: Clarendon Press, 1985).

19 As at 9 June 2005, there are 152 States parties to the Covenant. <http://www .unhchr.ch/pdf/report.pdf.> accessed 1 July 2005.

20 J. Shestack, above n. 3, 71.

21 See Article 6 sections (1) and (2) of the ICCPR.

22 Ibid., section (5).

> offences, ordinary offences (e.g. murder, kidnapping), economic offences (e.g. public corruption) and rape. Some Islamic states make apostasy, adultery, sodomy, drinking liquor, and sex between a Muslim and a non-Muslim capital offences. Are these all 'the most serious crimes'? Consistently with the US Constitution, some US states make juveniles of 16 or 17 liable for death penalty; the US made a reservation when ratifying the [International Covenant on Civil and Political Rights] to safeguard this position in view of Article 6(5).[23]

Apart from capital punishment, there are a number of other thorny issues linked to the right to life. There is nothing in the covenant, indeed in the entirety of international human rights law, to identify the point of creation and expiration of human life; abortion and euthanasia, though pre-eminently critical areas, remain conspicuous due to the absence of consensus. The subjects of abortion and euthanasia are shrouded in legal, moral and societal ambiguities.[24] Article 4 of the American Convention on Human Rights (1969)[25] provides, '[e]very person has the right to have his life respected. This right shall be protected by law and, in general, from the moment of conception. No one shall be arbitrarily deprived of his life.' This provision, no doubt inspired by the Catholic religious ethos of the American continent, has nevertheless failed to resolve the ambiguities over the subject of abortion – the question as to whether abortion is a violation of the Convention has been considered by the Inter-American Commission on Human Rights in a case arising from the United States, which is not a party to the American Convention. After considering the *travaux préparatoires* of the American Declaration, the Commission concluded that abortion of a foetus did not lead to a violation of the Declaration. The Commission also held obiter that the term

23 D. J. Harris, *Cases and Materials on International Law* (5th edn, London: Sweet and Maxwell, 1998), 660–1.

24 H. Biggs, 'Euthanasia and Death with Dignity: Still poised on the Fulcrum of Homicide', *Criminal Law Review*, (1996), 878–8; H. Biggs, *Euthanasia: Death with Dignity and the Law* (Oxford: Hart Publishing, 2001); A. McCall-Smith, 'Euthanasia: The Strength of the Middle Ground', *Medical Law Review*, 7, 194–207; J. Davies, 'Raping and Making Love are Different Concepts: So are Killing and Euthanasia', *Journal Medical Ethics*, 14 (1988), 148–9.

25 Signed November 1969; entered into force 18 July 1978. O.A.S.T.S. Off. Rec. OEA/Ser.L/V/11.23, doc.21, rev. (1979). 9 I.L.M. (1970) 673.

'in general' allowed States the discretion to determine the validity of their respective abortion laws.[26] In the context of European constitutional systems there remain considerable differences.[27] There are outstanding controversies surrounding the subject of abortion over the conflicting rights of the unborn child, the mother and in some cases the father.[28]

If there are irresolvable conflicts over the meaning of a right as fundamental as the 'right to life', it is hardly surprising to find divisions over other important rights, as the right to privacy and freedom of expression.[29] The European human rights jurisprudence is littered with conflicting paradigms of privacy and expression; many examples can be cited of a spectacular shifting of positions by the Strasbourg Court of Human Rights.[30] This introspection over consensus-building in relation

26 See *Baby Boy*, Case No. 2141 (United States), Res. 23/81, OEA/Ser. L/V/II.54, Doc. 9, rev. 1, Oct. 16, 1981. For commentary on the case see D. Shelton, 'Abortion and the Right to Life in the Inter-American System: The Case of "Baby Boy"', *Human Rights Law Journal*, 2 (1981), 309.

27 See J. Keown, 'The Law and Practice of Euthanasia in the Netherlands', *Law Quarterly Review*, 100 (1992), 51–78; J. Griffiths, 'The Regulation of Euthanasia and Related Medical Procedures that Shorten Life in the Netherlands', *Medical Law International*, 1 (1994), 137–58.

28 D. J. Harris, M. O'Boyle and C. Warbrick, *Law of the European Convention on Human Rights* (London: Butterworths, 1995), 41–3; *Open Door Counselling* v. *Ireland*, Judgement of 29 October 1992, Series A, No. 246, 142 NLJ (1696); *Paton* v. *United Kingdom*, App. No. 8416/79 19 DR 244 (1980); *H* v. *Norway*, App. No. 17004/90 (1992) unreported; *Brugggemann and Scheuten* v. FRG, App. No. 6959/75, 10 DR 100 (1977). L. A. Rehof, 'Article 3', in G. Alfredsson and A. Eide (eds), *The Universal Declaration of Human Rights: A Common Standard of Achievement* (The Hague: Martinus Nijhoff, 1999), 97; for a consideration at the international level see P. Alston, 'The Unborn Child and Abortion under the Draft Convention on the Rights of the Child', *Human Rights Quarterly*, 12 (1990), 156.

29 D. McGoldrick, *The Human Rights Committee: Its Role in the Development of the International Covenant on Civil and Political Rights* (Oxford: Clarendon Press, 1991), 459–97; J. P. Humphrey, 'Political and Related Rights', in T. Meron, above n. 3, 171–203; J. Michael, 'Privacy', in D. J. Harris and S. Joseph (eds), *The International Covenant on Civil and Political Rights and United Kingdom Law* (Oxford: Clarendon Press, 1995), 333–53; P. Cumper, 'Freedom of thought, Conscience and Religion', ibid., 355–89; D. Feldman, 'Freedom of Expression', ibid. 391–437; K. Ewing, 'Freedom of Association and Trade Union Rights', ibid., 465–89.

30 See J. Rehman, *International Human Rights Law: A Practical Approach* (Harlow: Longman, 2003), 150–53; I. Karstan, 'Atypical Families and the Human Rights Act: The Rights of Unmarried Fathers, Same Sex Couples and Transsexuals', *European Human Rights Law Review*, 3 (1999), 195; *Dudgeon* v. *United Kingdom*, Judgement of 22 October 1981, Series A. No. 45; *Rees* v. *United Kingdom*, Judgement of 17 October 1986,

to the firmly grounded civil and political rights presents an unfortunate backdrop to other 'lesser' rights: the existence of economic, social and cultural rights and the so-called 'third generation' right continue to be questioned.

(c) *Shifting paradigms and the human rights standards*

The difficulty displayed in formulating human rights standards has brought to light the malleable and amorphous nature of human rights law. Although change is integral to all legal disciplines, the international human rights scenery has been particularly tumultuous. The conservatism of the International Covenant on Civil and Political Rights (1966)[31] and the European Convention on Human Rights (1950)[32] is manifest through the retention of capital punishment and through a disregard for collective group rights.[33] The American Convention on Human Rights, notwithstanding caveats and restrictions, does not expressly prohibit capital punishment. Similarly there are no explicit provisions abolishing the death penalty under the African Charter on Human and Peoples'

Series A, No. 106, paras 42–6; cf. *B* v. *France*, Judgement of 25 March 1992, Series A, No. 232-C, paras 49–62.

31 Adopted at New York, 16 December, 1966; entered into force 23 March 1976. GA Res. 2200A (XXI) UN Doc. A/6316 (1966) 999 U.N.T.S. 171; 6 I.L.M. (1967) 368.

32 Signed at Rome, 4 November 1950; entered into force 3 September 1953. 213 U.N.T.S. 221; E.T.S. 5.

33 The European Convention on Human Rights does not contain any article to protect minority rights. See however the Council of Europe's Framework Convention on the Rights of National Minorities (1994) <http://www.coe.int/T/E/human_rights/minorities/> accessed 10 July 2005, and Council of Europe's European Charter for Regional and Minority Languages, 14 (1992), *Human Rights Law Journal* (1993), 152; for commentary on the protection of minorities in Europe see J. Rehman, 'Autonomy and the Rights of Minorities in Europe', in S. Wheatley and P. Cumper (eds), *Minority Rights in the New Europe* (Hague: Kluwer Law International, 1999), 217–31. Article 27 of the International Covenant on Civil and Political Rights (1966) has come under substantial criticism for adopting an individualistic position in its reference to minority rights. For a discussion of the subject of minority rights and indigenous peoples see Rehman, above n. 30, 297–343.

Rights,[34] the Universal Islamic Declaration on Human Rights (1981)[35] and the more recent Arab Charter of Human Rights.[36]

As noted above, the International Covenant on Civil and Political Rights, European Convention on Human Rights and the American Convention on Human Rights sanction capital punishment, albeit with caveats, restraints and restrictions. It was only in 1989 with the adoption of the second Optional Protocol,[37] in 1983 with the adoption of the sixth Protocol to the European Convention on Human Rights[38] and in 1990 through the adoption of the Additional Protocol to the American Convention to Abolish the Death Penalty[39] that a firm move was made to abolish capital punishment. The nature of these protocols remains controversial, in particular the ICCPR second Optional Protocol, which has not been ratified by nearly three-quarters of the world's states, including powerful ones such as the USA, China, India and almost all member-states of the Organization of the Islamic Conference (OIC).[40]

34 Adopted on 27 June 1981; entered into force 21 October, 1986. OAU Doc. CAB/LEG/67/3 Rev. 5, 21 I.L.M (1982) 58; 7 HRLJ (1986) 403.

35 An Instrument prepared by a number of Islamic states including Egypt, Pakistan and Saudi Arabia under the auspices of the Islamic Council (a private London–based organization, working in conjunction with the Muslim World League, an international non-governmental organization). For an analysis of the Declaration see Mayer, n. 5 above, 22.

36 See Council of the League of Arab States, (102nd session, Resolution 5437, 15 September 1994); Robertson and Merrills, above n. 7, 238–42.

37 Annex to GA Res. 44/128. Reprinted in 29 I.L.M (1990) 1464. See generally W. A. Schabas, *The Abolition of Death Penalty in International Law* (Cambridge: CUP, 2002), 155–210.

38 See Protocol no. 6 to the Convention for the Protection of Human Rights and Fundamental Freedoms Concerning the Abolition of Death Penalty, ETS no. 114. Schabas, above n. 37, 259–309.

39 Protocol to the American Convention on Human Rights to Abolish the Death Penalty, O.A.S.T.S. 73 (1990), adopted 8 June 1990, reprinted in *Basic Documents Pertaining to Human Rights in the Inter-American System*, OEA/Ser.L.V/II.82 doc. 6 rev. 1 at 80 (1992); 29 I.L.M. (1990) 1447.

40 As at 9 June 2005, there are fifty states parties to the Covenant. <http://www.unhchr.ch/pdf/report.pdf.> accessed 1 July 2005. According to Amnesty International's most recent report on China, 'The death penalty continued to be used extensively and arbitrarily, at times as a result of political interference. People were executed for non-violent crimes such as tax fraud and embezzlement as well as drug offences and violent crimes. The authorities continued to keep national statistics on death sentences and executions secret. Based on public reports available, AI estimated that at least 3,400 people had been executed and at least 6,000 sentenced to death by the end of the year,

The divisions over the issue of capital punishment are matched by disagreements on the rights of marginalised communities such as homosexuals, transsexuals, same-sex partners, minorities and indigenous peoples.[41] There is also an ongoing debate over the scope of individual rights such as the right to privacy and family life.[42] The sequence of events in the human rights arena, regretfully, has not always been towards greater recognition of civil liberties. The rise of right-wing conservatism in the United States and global developments since 11 September 2001 have led to a significant curtailment of individual rights: the prohibition on torture and cruel, inhuman and degrading treatment has been violated by the United States in Guantánamo Bay, Iraq and Afghanistan.[43] In the course of the 'global war on terror', states have also vacillated over well-established rights such as the right to liberty and protection against unlawful detention. The United Kingdom entered a reservation to Article 5 of the

---

although the true figures were believed to be much higher.' See Amnesty International, *China – Report 2005* <http://web.amnesty.org/report2005/chn-summary-eng> accessed 6 July 2005. On the contemporary position on death penalty in the USA see <http://www.amnestyusa.org/abolish/index.do> accessed 6 July 2005. For the background of OIC see J. Rehman, *Islamic State Practices, International Law and the Threat from Terrorism: A Critique of the 'Clash of Civilizations' in the New World Order* (Oxford: Hart Publishing, 2005), 27–42;

41 On sexual orientation and discrimination see I. Leigh, 'Clashing Rights, Exemption and Opt-Out: Religious Liberty and "Homophobia"', in R. O'Dair and A. Lewis (eds), above n. 2, 247–273; on same-sex issues see R. Wintemute and M. Andenas (eds), *Legal Recognition of Same-Sex Partnership: A Study of National, European and International Law* (Oxford: Hart Publishing, 2001); R. Wintemute, *Sexual Orientation and Human Rights: The United States Constitution, the European Convention and the Canadian Charter* (Oxford: Clarendon Press, 1997). On the subject of minorities and indigenous peoples there is huge amount of legal literature; for further sources see S. S. Ali and J. Rehman, *Indigenous Peoples and Ethnic Minorities of Pakistan* (London: Routledge/Curzon Press, 2001); P. Thornberry, *International Law and the Rights of Minorities* (Oxford: Clarendon Press, 1991); P. Thornberry, *Minorities and Human Rights Law* (London: Minority Rights Group, 1991); C. Brölmann, R. Lefeber and M. Zieck (eds), *Peoples and Minorities in International Law* (Dordrecht: Martinus Nijhoff, 1993); G. Alfredsson and A. de Zayas, 'Minority Rights: Protection by the United Nations', *Human Rights Law Journal*, 14 (1993), 1; N. Ghanea and A. Xanthaki (eds), *Minorities, Peoples and Self-Determination: Essays in Honour of Patrick Thornberry* (Leiden: Martinus Nijhoff, 2005).

42 See above n. 30 for references and relevant case-law.

43 See P. A. Thomas, 'September 11th and Good Governance', *Northern Ireland Legal Quarterly*, 53 (2002), 389; E. Katselli and S. Shah, 'September 11 and the UK Response', *International and Comparative Law Quarterly*, 52 (2003), 245; also see Rehman, above n. 40, 221–30.

ECHR, and has insisted in continuing with a form of internment which it argues is essential to prevent international terrorists from operating within its national borders.[44] This lack of consistency in establishing firm standards of such fundamental human rights as the right to life, the prohibition of torture and cruel, inhuman and degrading treatment, the right to liberty and protection against unlawful detention demonstrates the fragile nature of human rights law.

3. RELIGION AND HUMAN RIGHTS: REVISITING THE 'INEVITABILITY OF A CLASH' ARGUMENT

□ *The case of Islam*

All religions, beliefs or ideologies are to a certain degree infected with forms of inherent tension and contradictions. A strictly literal interpretation of religious norms would amount to the breaching of fundamental norms of equality and non-discrimination. A promise of eternity, of absolute truth and providence – a hallmark of many of the world religions – has acted as the great determinant of human existence. As Macaulay put it:

> I am in the right and you are wrong. When you are stronger, you ought to tolerate me; for it is your duty to tolerate truth. But when I am stronger, I shall persecute you; for it is my duty to persecute you.[45]

Champions of the monotheistic religions Christianity, Judaism, and Islam often find it difficult to reconcile burgeoning modern values of human rights law. Indeed, at the level of principle, proponents of religious and ideological doctrines purport an inherently discriminatory policy in that

> the question of religion takes international law to the limits of human rights, at least in so far as the law functions in a community of states. It is quite meaningless, for example, to the adherents of a religion to have their beliefs or practices declared to be

44 See J. Rehman, 'Islamophobia after 9/11: International Terrorism, Sharia and Muslim Minorities of Europe – The Case of the United Kingdom', *European Yearbook of Minority Issues*, 3 (2005), 217.

45 T. B. Macaulay, *Cultural and Historical Essays* (London, 1870), 336.

> contrary to 'public morality'. To the believer, religion is morality itself and its transcendental foundation grounds it more firmly in terms of obligation than any secular rival, or the tenets of other religions. All religions are to a greater or lesser extent 'fundamentalist' in character in that they recognise that theirs is the just rule, the correct avenue to truth.[46]

The overpowering nature of religion, however, has also been used as a weapon for generating intolerance, and as an instrument for the persecution and ultimate destruction of religious minorities. Religious intolerance and repression were the great predisposing factors of history.[47] Within the texts of religious scriptures, forms of genocide of religious minorities were sanctioned. The tragic wars of the Middle Ages, the Crusades and the *jihads*, translated these religious ordinances into action rigorously.[48] All of the world's major religions have been subjected to intense scrutiny and wide ranging interpretations. However, in the contemporary political environment, Islam faces the sternest examination regarding its human rights credentials.

(i) *Islam as a religion of violence and aggression*

The debate on the compatibility of Islamic values with those of modern human rights is volatile. Classical Islam is equated with violence and aggression – the concept of *jihad* is considered particularly problematic.[49] Islamic law is also considered to perpetuate gender-based discrimination and violate the rights of minorities.[50] Several Western jurists and

46 P. Thornberry, *International Law and the Rights of Minorities* (Oxford: Clarendon Press, 1991), 324.

47 See B. Whitaker, *Report on the Question of the Prevention and Punishment of the Crime of Genocide*, UN Doc E/CN.4/Sub.2/1985/6, pp. 6–7.

48 L. Kuper, *International Action Against Genocide* (London: Minority Rights Group, 1984), 1; L. Kuper, *Genocide: Its Political Use in the Twentieth Century* (New Haven: Yale University Press, 1981), 12–14; J. Kelsay and J. T. Johnson (eds), *Just War and Jihad: Historical and Theoretical Perspectives on War and Peace in Western and Islamic Traditions* (New York: Greenwood Press, 1991).

49 See S. S. Ali and J. Rehman, 'The Concept of *Jihad* in Islamic International Law', *Journal of Conflict and Security Law*, 10(3) (2005), 321–43.

50 J. Rehman, 'Accommodating Religious Identities in an Islamic State: International Law, Freedom of Religion and the Rights of Religious Minorities', *International Journal on Minority and Group Rights*, 7 (2000), 139; J. Rehman 'Minority Rights and Constitutional Dilemmas of Pakistan' *Netherlands Quarterly of Human Rights*, 19 (2001), 417.

statesmen have adopted a negative stance towards Islam and Islamic civilisations.[51] In engineering the 'clash of civilisations', the chief propagator of the doctrine, Samuel Huntington, has perceived Islam as a violent religion, 'a religion of the sword . . . glorify[ing] military virtues'.[52] He argues that 'the Koran and other statements of Muslim beliefs contain few prohibitions on violence, and a concept of non-violence is absent from Muslim doctrine and practice'.[53] Similar sentiments are echoed by J. L. Payne. Payne contrasts what he perceives as the 'Western view of what religion is and ought to be, namely, a voluntary sphere where coercion has no place' with that of Islam.[54] In the course of this comparison he notes that

> the emphasis on non-violence is not the pattern in the Muslim culture. To the contrary, violence has been a central, accepted element, both in Muslim teaching and in the historical conduct of the religion. For over a thousand years, the religious bias in the Middle Eastern culture has not been to discourage the use of force, but to encourage it.[55]

According to another Western academic, Roda Mushkat,

> Islamic law enjoins Muslims to maintain a state of permanent belligerence with all non-believers, collectively encompassed in

51 In the immediate aftermath of the events of 11 September 2001, the Italian prime minister made the controversial though profound statement that 'we must be aware of the superiority of our civilization, a system that has guaranteed well-being, respect for human rights and – in contrast with Islamic countries – respect for religious and political rights. Islamic civilization is stuck where it was fourteen hundred years ago' (Italian prime minister Silvio Berlusconi, comments made in Berlin, 26 September 2001). These comments have been cited extensively: see A. Palmer, 'Is the West Really Best', *Sunday Telegraph* (London, 30 September 2001), 14; A. Osburn, 'On the Brink of War: Reaction – Scorn Poured on Berlusconi Views – European and Muslim Leaders Express Disgust', *The Guardian* (London, 28 September 2001), 4; 'EU deplores "Dangerous" Islam Jibe', BBC News <http://news.bbc.co.uk/1/hi/world/middle_east/1565664.stm> accessed 9 October 2004.

52 S. P. Huntington, *The Clash of Civilizations and the Remaking of World Order* (London: Simon & Schuster, 1996), 263.

53 A. A. An-Na'im, 'Upholding International Legality against Islamic and American Jihad' in K. Booth and T. Dunne (eds), *Words in Collision: Terror and the Future of Global Order* (New York: Palgrave Macmillan, 2002), 162–71

54 J. L. Payne, *Why Nations Arm* (Oxford: Basil Blackwell, 1989), 121.

55 Ibid. 122.

> the *dar al-harb*, the domain of war. The Muslims are, therefore, under a legal obligation to reduce non-Muslim communities to Islamic rule in order to achieve Islam's ultimate objective, namely the enforcement of God's law (the Sharia) over the entire world. The instrument by which the Islamic state is to carry out that objective is called the *jihad* (popularly known as the 'holy war') and is always just, if waged against the infidels and the enemies of the faith.[56]

The association of Islam with violence and aggression has not only been the preoccupation of Western scholars; several Muslim jurists have taken the position that the classical interpretations of Sharia are incompatible with modern international law and human rights law. Professor Majid Khudduri, a leading academic, has, for instance, emphasised the aggressive nature of *jihad*, propounding its apparent incompatibility with modern norms on the ground of the latter's prohibition on the use of force. According to Khadduri,

> In theory the *dar al-Islam* was always at war with *dar al-harb*. The Muslims were under a legal obligation to reduce the latter to Muslim rule in order to achieve Islam's ultimate objective, namely, the enforcement of God's Law (the *Shari'a*) over the entire world. The instrument by which the Islamic States were to carry out that objective was *jihād* (popularly know as holy war), which was always justifiably waged against the infidels and the enemies of the faith. Thus the *jihād* was the Islam's *bellum justum*.[57]

Professor Abduallahi Ahmed An-Na'im, a Sudanese human rights scholar, expresses his concern in the following manner:

> the term *jihad* can also refer to religiously sanctioned aggressive war to propagate or 'defend' the faith. What is problematic about this latter sense of *jihad* is that it involves direct and unregulated violent action in pursuit of political objectives, or self-help

56 R. Mushkat, 'Is War Ever Justifiable? A Comparative Survey', *Loyola of Los Angeles International and Comparative Law Journal*, 9 (1987), 227.

57 M. Khadduri, 'Islam and the Modern Law of Nations', *American Journal of International Law*, 50 (1956), 359.

in redressing perceived injustice, at the risk of harm to innocent bystanders.[58]

These scholars from the world of Islam also highlight the differences and disagreements between classical Islamic legal theory and modern human rights law. The most thorough exposition of the subject matter, it would appear, has been provided by Professor Abdullah Ahmed An-Na'im. In his seminal work, *Toward an Islamic Reformation: Civil Liberties, Human Rights and International Law,* Professor An-Na'im presents a detailed and convincing exposition of the discriminatory nature of what he terms 'pre-modern Sharia'.[59] In advancing his argument, Professor An-Na'im examines the position of women and religious minorities within classical Sharia. As regards religious minorities, he argues that under a strict interpretation of the Sharia human beings are placed within three classifications. First is that of the male Muslim, who holds a predominantly strong, unchallengeable and unassailable position. This category is clearly accorded the highest status. The second category is that of Christians and Jews, who are regarded as the recipients of divine revelations prior to Islam (also known as People of the Book – *ahal-i-kitab*). Jews and Christians ruled by Muslims had the political status of *dhimmis,* being accorded toleration in return for submitting to Muslim rule and accepting a number of conditions governing their conduct. *Dhimmis* had to pay a special capitulations tax known as *jizya,* though they were excluded from high governmental positions. Although generally subject to Sharia law, *dhimmis* were allowed to follow their own rule of personal status, but they were subject to Islamic law in mixed cases in which persons of different faiths were involved, and especially when the other party was a Muslim. The third and final category consisted of the 'non-believers'. It appears that in strict doctrinal terms there was a particular dearth of tolerance for pagan or polytheist minorities. When under conquest their choices were limited: to embrace Islam or perish.[60] In asserting this view of Islam, Khaduri notes that

58 Ibid. 163.

59 An-Na'im, above n. 5.

60 According to Azrt, 'The other class of non-Muslims who were not dhimmis were slaves, the fate of polytheists and idolaters who had been captured as prisoners of war rather than slain in or after battle. They had the choice only of slavery, conversion to Islam or death; no special communal contract allowed them to quietly or even humbly

> no compromise is permitted with those who fail to believe in God; they have either to accept Islam or fight. In several Qura'nic injunctions, the Muslims are under the obligation to 'fight the polytheists wherever ye may find them'; to 'fight those who are near to you of the polytheists, and let them find in you sternness'; and 'when you meet those who misbelieve, strike off their head until you have massacred them . . .' In the Hadith of the Prophet Mohammad he is reported to have declared: 'I am ordered to fight polytheists until they say: "There is no god but Allah."' All the jurists, perhaps without exception, assert polytheism and Islam cannot exist together; the polytheists, who enjoin other gods with Allah, must choose between war or Islam.[61]

(ii) *Contextualising, comprehending and interpreting the central message*

If all Sharia and Islam have to offer to minority communities is death, destruction and discrimination, there would be no point in attempting to reconcile Muslim values with human rights law. Fortunately there are significant possibilities of interpretative flexibility contained within the Sharia that offer versatility and hope. A contextualised, methodological interpretation of Islam and Sharia brings out the central message, which is one of peace, reconciliation and protection of human rights. This approach of a contextualised and methodological analysis of Islam (although a taxing assignment) can nevertheless be illustrated through an examination of the Qur'anic verses, the principal source of the Sharia. Those who advocate that Islam and Sharia are based upon aggression and violence frequently cite the following verse from the Qur'an:

> When the period of four months during which hostilities are suspended expires, without the idolaters having settled the terms of peace with you, resume fighting with them and kill them wherever you find them and make them prisoners and beleaguer them, and lie in wait for them at every place of ambush.[62]

---

practice their religion' (D. E. Azrt, 'The Role of Compulsion in Islamic Conversion: Jihad, Dhimma and Rida', *Buffalo Human Rights Law Review*, 8 (2002), 27.

61 M. Khadduri, *War and Peace in the Law of Islam* (Baltimore: John Hopkins, 1955), 75.

62 Qur'an 9:3–5.

I would submit that this verse, coupled with a number of other injunctions from the Qur'an, does not represent a complete picture of *jihad* within the Sharia. Critics of the Sharia frequently rely on these ordinances to condemn Islam as aggressive, violent and intolerant. However, in doing so they overlook the context in which the verses of the Qur'an were revealed. Islam in its formative phases had to undergo a difficult and uncertain future. The Prophet Muhammad and his followers represented a community facing extermination. Indeed, Muhammad himself was forced to migrate to Medina to avoid persecution and assassination, his migration marking the beginning of the Muslim calendar.[63] It was in the context of persecution, betrayals, attempted humiliation and disregard for kinship and obligations on the part of the Quresh of Mecca that a number of these verses were revealed. Even taking these verses at face value, and comprehending them in their entirety, they do not in fact advocate unconditional aggression and violence. The aforementioned pronouncements are accompanied by a number of caveats and moderating references. For example:

> Warn the disbelievers of a painful chastisement, excepting those of them with who you have a pact and who have not defaulted in any respect, nor supported anyone against you. Carry out the obligations you have assumed towards them till the end of their terms. Surely Allah loves those who are mindful of their obligations. When the period of four months during which hostilities are suspended expires, without the idolaters having settled the terms of peace with you, resume fighting with them and kill them wherever you find them and make them prisoners and beleaguer them, and lie in wait for them at every place of ambush. Then if they repent and observe Prayer and pay the Zakat, leave them alone. Surely Allah is Most Forgiving, Ever Merciful. If any one of the idolaters seeks asylum with thee, grant him asylum so that he may hear the Word of Allah; then convey him to a place of security for him, for they are a people who lack knowledge.[64]

63 Weeramantry, n. 5 above, 4–5; J. Rehman, 'Self-Determination, State Building and the Muhajirs: An International Legal Perspective of the Role of the Indian Muslim Refugees in the Constitutional Development of Pakistan', *Contemporary South Asia*, 3 (1994), 113.

64 *Qur'an* 9:3–6.

In interpreting God's commandments in their proper historical and methodological context, it becomes apparent that there are serious restraints, restrictions and limitations imposed on using force. In the context of freedom of religion, there are similar strong instructions to establish individual autonomy and personal liberties coupled with an egalitarian and just social and legal order. There are also verses within the Qur'an advocating complete freedom of religion. It notes explicitly that 'there is no compulsion in religion. The right direction has become distinct from error.'[65] Similarly, the Qur'an makes the observation, 'Unto you your religion and me my religion.'[66] These are not merely hortatory statements lacking in purpose or meaning. Islamic civilisation at its zenith presented an impressive model of promoting civil rights and protecting the rights of minority communities. Judged by the standards of the time, the practices of Muslim states were a huge advance. In emphasising this egalitarianism and protection of minority rights, one authority makes the point that 'although, like Christianity, Islam was an aggressively universalist religion, it also displayed far more tolerance to followers of other faiths, and particularly Jews and Christians who, like followers of Islam were considered to be "Peoples of the Book". Jewish and Christian communities were, therefore, permitted a large degree of freedom in both religious and civil affairs . . .'[67] It also remains the case that the practices of the Prophet Muhammad and subsequently those of the Muslim rulers (which now form part of the wider code of Islamic law through the Sharia) seriously defy the 'Western images of Muslim conquerors presenting the conquered peoples with the choice of conversion to Islam or the sword.'[68] On the contrary, 'conquered Christians and Jews were allowed to persist in their beliefs because Islamic law opposes compelled conversions.'[69] Commenting on the facts as they prevailed during the prime of Islam, Eaton remarks that

> the rapidity with which Islam spread across the known world of the seventh century was strange enough, but stranger still is the

65 *Qur'an* 2:256.

66 *Qur'an* 109:6.

67 M. D. Evans, *Religious Liberty and International Law in Europe* (Cambridge: CUP, 1997), 59.

68 Mayer, n. 5 above, 126.

69 Ibid. 126–7.

> fact that no rivers flowed with blood, no fields were enriched with the corpses of the vanquished. As warriors the Arabs might have been no better than others of their kind who had ravaged and slaughtered across the peopled lands but, unlike these others, they were on a leash. There were no massacres, no rapes, no cities burned. These men feared God to a degree scarcely imaginable in our time and were in awe of His all-seeking presence, aware of it in the wind and the trees, behind every rock and in every valley. Even in these strange lands there was no place in which they could hide from this presence, and while vast distances beckoned them ever onwards they trod softly on the earth, as they had been commanded to do. There had never been a conquest like this.[70]

In view of these considerations it would be convincing to argue that the *dhimmis*, the *ahl al-kitab*, in fact enjoyed a better status under the jurisdiction of Islam than religious minorities under a Christian state.[71] This contention certainly appears to carry considerable weight during the zenith of Ottoman rule in the Middle East, North Africa and central and eastern Europe. The Ottoman rule, for several centuries, retained a vast empire with adherents of various religions.[72] While religious minorities were not always treated with tolerance, the Ottomans did experiment with a special mechanism for the granting of autonomy through the *millet* system – a system allowing various religious minorities to enjoy a generous measure of autonomy, in social, civil and religious affairs.[73] Professor Van Dyke's comments are valid when, analysing the *millet* system, he notes that 'it was an application of the right of

---

70 G. Eaton, *Islam and the Destiny of Man* (Cambridge: Islamic Text Society, 1994), 29–30.

71 'Despite incidents of discrimination and mistreatment of non-Muslims, it is fair to say that the Muslim world, when judged by the standards of the day, generally showed far greater tolerance and humanity in its treatment of religious minorities than did the Christian West. In particular, the treatment of the Jewish minority in Muslim societies stands out as fair and enlightened when compared with the dismal record of Christian European persecution of Jews over the centuries'. Mayer, n. 5 above, 127–8.

72 H. Inalcik, *The Ottoman Empire: the Classical Age 1300–1600* (London: Phoenix, 1994); P. Mansfield, *The Ottoman Empire and Its Successor* (London: Macmillan, 1973); J. McCarthy, *The Ottoman Peoples and the End of Empire* (London: Hodder and Stoughton, 2000).

73 J. A. Laponce, *The Protection of Minorities* (Berkeley: University of California Press, 1960), 84–5.

self-determination in advance of Woodrow Wilson.'[74] The Ottomans also continued the Islamic practice of granting capitulations to Christians and other Westerners. The capitulations provided a degree of autonomy and self-government including the exercise of civil and criminal jurisdiction over other co-nationals.[75] This latter portrayal of Sharia and Islamic-state practices is radically different from the one noted earlier in this chapter.

In light of these apparently opposing interpretations of freedom of religion and the rights of religious minorities within Islam, critics may point to a confused picture, or they may suggest that Islam is a religion of contradictions and ambiguities. The hypothesis of the present chapter however has been that indetermination and equivocacy within religions (in this case Islam) provides the requisite elements of flexibility to construct a path of reconciliation between religions and human rights. Islamic values can be moulded and accommodated into the framework of modern human rights law.

4. CONCLUDING OBSERVATIONS

This chapter has put forward a number of arguments, advancing the thesis that religious values and human rights are not necessarily mutually incompatible; their overlapping paths do not always lead to a conflict. Among its key arguments, the chapter first adopted the position that there is no single unified meaning to the term 'human rights.' Secondly, it demonstrated that there remain difficulties in ascertaining the substance of human rights; considerable divisions pervade the body of international law on such core rights as the 'right to life.' Thirdly, it pointed towards the inherent contradictions and tensions within all mainstream religions and beliefs; Islam, the focus of this examination, does not prove an exception to this general principle.

---

74 V. Van Dyke, *Human Rights, Ethnicity and Discrimination* (Westport: Greenwood Press, 1985), 74; 'while the [*millet*] system was hardly based on any recognition of "human rights", its application is most compatible with the philosophy of human rights' (J. Packer, 'The Protection of Ethnic and Linguistic Minorities in Europe', in J. Packer and K. Myntti (eds), *The Protection of Ethnic and Linguistic Minorities in Europe* (Turku/Åbo: Åbo Akademi, Institute for Human Rights, Åbo Akademi University, 1993), 42.

75 M. Evans, *Religious Liberty and International Law in Europe* (Cambridge: CUP, 1997), 60.

A study of the Sharia however reveals that there are a range of possible interpretations that could be given to such key concepts as *jihad*, minority rights and fundamental rights. An insular, myopic and archaic view of Sharia is contrary to human rights law. Yet at the same time there is considerable evidence in favour of an interpretation of Sharia in a manner fully according with modern human rights law. Such an exposition is possible through a contextualised and methodological analysis of Sharia and religion itself; the central message of Islam does not advocate aggression and violence of human rights. This latter interpretation of the Sharia provides a real, credible alternative that, in the current climate, must be pursued.

CHAPTER 5

Religion and Human Rights with Special Reference to Judaism

Norman Solomon

In the West, in recent times, religions have been strongly associated with peace and anti-war movements of all kinds. Yet history demonstrates that the same religions, not least Christianity, have often urged people in the name of God to engage in persecution, aggressive war and other barbarous acts, such as the Crusades, the Inquisition, the excesses of the Spanish conquest of South and Central America and the wars of religion in early modern Europe.

Accordingly, there is a popular perception that there is something inherently contradictory about religions, for while they are tireless in their advocacy of peace, historically they have proved themselves ruthless as well as tireless in their pursuit of war.

This common perception is muddled. There is a category error. Religions, as such, are neither peaceful nor warlike. Religions don't do anything; they are abstractions. It is followers of religion who are tireless in their advocacy of peace, and followers of religion who historically have proved themselves ruthless as well as tireless in the pursuit of war.

This is not a semantic quibble. Between the abstraction and the reality comes the interpretation. If the followers of a religion encourage or engage in discrimination, persecution or warfare, this is not the inevitable consequence of an abstract ideal, or of reading a sacred text. A whole complex of circumstances must be present before such an action can take place. There must be a holy text (written or oral), an apposite interpretation of that text by priests, teachers or the like, and a commitment by that particular religious community to the authority of the priests who are responsible for that interpretation of the text and for its application in specific circumstances.

To spell this out more clearly, for a religious group (community, society, nation) to act as a religious group, five things are necessary:

1. There must be a holy text, written or oral, setting out an objective or prescribing some form of action.
2. There must be interpreters of that text — priests, scribes and the like — who determine what the text means.
3. There must be judges (they may be the priests or scribes) who can determine the application of the text to the situation in question.
4. The jurisdiction of these judges must have been accepted by the religious group as binding authority.
5. Conditions must obtain in which the implementation of the judges' ruling is both practicable and socially acceptable.

Take, as an example, the Inquisition instituted by Pope Gregory IX in 1231 for the apprehension and trial of heretics:

1. Numerous New Testament texts set the objective of faith in Jesus Christ, though none calls for this objective to be pursued by torture and persecution.
2. The texts were interpreted, through Church Councils and the like, in terms of a highly defined Trinitarian doctrine and an exclusive claim to salvation.
3. The church, through Gregory IX, applied the doctrine as a basis for coercion to religious conformity.
4. Western Christians had, by this time, endorsed the Roman papacy as possessing ultimate jurisdiction; even kings ruled under its authority.
5. Heretics such as the Cathari and Waldenses had come to be looked upon as enemies of society, and the Church was in a position to call on the power of the 'secular arm' to enforce its designs for the imposition of doctrinal uniformity.

At first sight this is similar to the process by which any system of law operates:

1. There are laws, statutory or conventional.
2. Scholars and lawyers interpret the laws.
3. Judges apply the laws in specific circumstances.
4. The legislators and officers of the law have public endorsement.
5. The law is backed by the power of the state and the will of the people.

However, the religious process differs from the secular process by being set in a metaphysical reference frame, or system of belief.

The followers of religion assert that the texts and their interpretation are the word, not of the priests themselves, or of mere convention, but of God. God is the legislator, and as well as issuing the laws He has issued, or somehow guided, their interpretation. God's law must be obeyed in preference to any merely human system of law; the priests may owe a duty to Caesar, but Caesar, too, is obliged to obey God, and even to fight His wars for Him.

A secular system of law may likewise be set in a metaphysical reference frame; precisely this has been done by philosophers from Plato to Kant and Hegel, though nowadays it is more common to root law in non-metaphysical ethics, including social doctrines. But the metaphysics of the philosophers differs from that of the theologians in that in principle it remains open to question, and to revision. The Word of God, on the other hand, is not in principle open to question, nor may it be revised by any human agency; it is absolute.

This creates dilemmas for the citizen, for secular government, and for the religious authorities:

- The citizen wants to do right by Caesar and by God, but Caesar and God's representatives may issue conflicting orders. The citizen's conscience, moreover, may tell him that one or other or both are wrong.
- Secular government, which by definition rejects claims to infallible knowledge of God's will, must oppose the claim of any religious authority to impose its norms on the public at large. Where a religious community appears to deny individual rights and liberties to its followers, secular government may find cause to intervene in the affairs of the religious community.
- The religious authorities, because they lay claim to special knowledge of right and wrong, seek to control the behaviour of their adherents, and possibly of society at large; this may well bring them into conflict with public law as defined and administered by the state.

Those are the dilemmas with which I shall be concerned in this paper, and I shall illustrate it with reference to the UN Universal Declaration of Human Rights. I shall draw religious material from the Jewish tradition, since that it is my own, but almost everything I have to say is equally applicable within other religious traditions.

1. AUTHORITY

The first dilemma is a dilemma of authority. The source of religious authority is clear; the ultimate authority is God. In practice, unless you are a prophet like Moses, you cannot tap into this authority directly, so you must turn to the guardians of God's word, or revelation, the Torah. In ancient Israel the priests were guardians of the Word, and formed the final court of appeal, but in rabbinic Judaism the rabbis assumed this role, and the Sanhedrin, if and when such a body functioned, would have been the final court of appeal. In theory, God is the source of law; but in practice, his role is implemented by priests or rabbis, which leaves it open to question whether they have correctly determined the divine will.

The mere fact of having their own system of law, whether or not it was of divine origin, generated conflict when Jews lived under someone else's jurisdiction, as they have done through most of their history. The classic solution was devised in the third century by Samuel of Nehardea, under the Sasanian emperor Shapur I. His ruling that 'the law of the state is law'[1] recognised the right of legitimate government to control land tenure and impose reasonable taxes; this ingenious compromise, while acknowledging Sasanian overlordship, left the Jewish authorities free to administer all religious matters, including family law, as well as internal commercial dealings and criminal behaviour.

However, it was ultimately the Jewish religious authorities who confirmed, to their followers, that Shapur's government was 'legitimate government'; this means that Jewish deference to Sasanian commercial law was, from the Jewish point of view, obedience to the law of God. This is analogous to, though not so far-reaching as, the argument by which Luther and other Protestants legitimised the rule of European monarchs in the early modern period; it retains the principle that God's word is supreme, but at the expense of conceding that God commanded us to obey the legitimate secular ruler in certain matters.

1 Babylonian Talmud *Bava Qama* 113a. Even before Samuel, the extent to which external jurisdiction should be recognised had been mooted, for instance in Mishna *Gittin* 2:5.

From where does the Universal Declaration of Human Rights take its authority? Certainly not from God, who is not mentioned in it nor accorded any rights or duties. The Preamble refers to the Charter of the United Nations, and in that we read that 'our respective Governments, through representatives assembled in the City of San Francisco . . . have agreed to the present Charter of the United Nations and do hereby establish an international organization to be known as the United Nations.' It seems, therefore, that the authority of the United Nations derives from that of the individual nations that have acceded to its Charter. However, this merely pushes the problem back one stage further, since we must ask, what is the authority of the individual nations? This question will be answered in terms of current fashionable political philosophies. Usually, nowadays, it will take some form of the democratic argument that the rulers rule as representatives of the people, by the people's consent, and in the people's interest, though this is not in fact true of all member states of the United Nations, even though Article 21.3 of the Universal Declaration states unequivocally, 'The will of the people shall be the basis of the authority of government.'

Evidently then, the authority of the Universal Declaration of Human Rights has ultimately to be traced back to 'the will of the people' expressed through their national governments. The will of the people, religionists will reasonably claim, must surely be subservient to the will of God; to which the secular will retort, 'Certainly. But your claims to know the will of God are highly dubious, they conflict with one another, and frequently conflict with the broad modern consensus on human rights.'

Let us therefore look at specific areas where religious tradition and current doctrines of human rights appear to conflict, and show how in practice the conflict has been or might be resolved.

2. RIGHTS OF LIFE, LIBERTY, AND THE PURSUIT OF HAPPINESS

□ *Life, liberty, and the security of person*

The right to life[2] is set out in Article 3 of the UN Declaration: 'Everyone has the right to life, liberty, and the security of person.'

A basic prima facie right to life, liberty, and the security of person is

2 The classification of rights adopted here conforms in the main to that of Haim H. Cohn, in his valuable *Human Rights in Jewish Law* (New York: KTAV, 1984).

not denied in any Jewish source. However, the right may be forfeited in part or in whole by miscreants; as in any system of law, when courts fine, imprison or inflict physical punishment on lawbreakers they are limiting the lawbreakers' rights. The inalienable right to life is also denied when a nation engages in war. As well as permitting warfare in some circumstances, the Bible mandates capital punishment for a wide array of offences, including idolatry, blasphemy, Sabbath desecration, murder and adultery; that is, the idolater, Sabbath breaker and so on are deemed to have forfeited their right to life.

The UN Declaration does not outlaw capital punishment (though the first Optional Protocol to the International Covenant on Civil and Political Rights does). However, it is certainly with an eye to the Declaration's call for the right to life that Protocol 6, Article 1 of the European Convention on Human Rights declares, 'The death penalty shall be abolished.[3] No one shall be condemned to such penalty or executed.'

It may be categorically stated that no Jewish religious court in Europe or elsewhere today contemplates meting out capital punishment to any offender, or even feels restricted in its operations by not being permitted to do so. The last known case of judicial execution by a Jewish court in Europe took place in Cordoba, Spain, in the early fourteenth century under considerable pressure from the Muslim authorities and with the reluctant approval of the leading rabbi, Asher ben Yehiel, in the Christian North.[4]

But how does this reluctance to inflict capital punishment square with the Bible?

A negative attitude to capital punishment appears in second century Jewish sources: 'A court that executed once in seven years is called murderous; Rabbi Eleazar ben Azariah says once in seventy years; Rabbi Tarphon and Rabbi Akiva say, had we been there no one would ever have been executed; Rabbi Simeon ben Gamaliel says, they would have increased bloodshed in Israel.'[5]

From the Talmud's comments on this statement it appears that one

3 The Convention was signed in Rome on 4 November 1950 and entered into force on 18 May 1954. Protocol 6 was done on 28 April 1983.

4 Rosh, *Responsa* 17:8.

5 Mishna *Makkot* 1:10. Simeon is accusing Tryphon and Akiva of encouraging bloodshed by failing to act firmly against murderers.

of the main concerns was the question of reliability of evidence, and that what we would regard as humanitarian interests also play their part. In addition, there was the question of whether, under Roman rule, Jews were in fact permitted jurisdiction in capital cases, though the Church Father Origen dubiously claimed to have observed that the 'ethnarch'— a descendant of Simeon ben Gamaliel — in his time differed little from a true king, and inflicted capital punishment with the knowledge if not the sanction of the Roman government.[6] Jewish courts in Babylonia, notwithstanding occasional reports of what appear to be extra-judicial executions, did not consider themselves authorised to adjudicate capital offences.[7]

How much of this reluctance to implement the death penalty arose from humanitarian motives and how much was making a virtue of the necessity imposed by a ruling power it is impossible to tell. Whatever the underlying motives, the result is that the Jewish tradition contains ample resources to justify the abandonment of the death penalty notwithstanding its biblical mandate.

There may be some religious Jews who pray for regime change under the rule of Messiah, perhaps not fully realising that this could mean the restoration of capital punishment for Sabbath desecration, homosexual acts and other offences; to forbid them such daydreams would be an infringement of their religious liberty. However, they must not be permitted any attempt to implement such laws, even in the state of Israel, since this would deprive other people of their basic human rights. Indeed, it is reasonable to expect Jewish religious – as well as secular – authorities to accept that citizens are not to be executed for infringements of biblical law; the state law of Israel abolished capital punishment, and had to enact special legislation to execute the notorious war criminal Adolf Eichmann on 31 May 1962.

Has the religious establishment by in effect abolishing capital punishment yielded to libertarian notions on human rights? The religious certainly do not view it that way; in their eyes it is not a surrender, but a correct interpretation of classical sources.

---

6 The claim is put forward to make a theological point in Origen's *Epistula ad Africanus* no. 20.

7 B. *Bava Qama* 84b and parallels.

□ *Of slaves and slavery*

The Bible distinguishes between the Israelite slave and the non-Israelite slave. Jeremiah called for the release of all Israelite slaves, and castigated the people for taking back into slavery those they had released.[8] The condition of slavery, relative to the institution as practised in other ancient societies, was ameliorated in biblical and rabbinic law. This is well expressed by Maimonides (1138–1204), elaborating on the biblical law that a fugitive slave must not be returned to his master (Deuteronomy 23:16):

> The commandment . . . besides manifesting pity, contains a great utility — namely, it makes us acquire this noble moral quality [that is, pity]; namely, it makes us protect and defend those who seek our protection and not deliver them over to those from whom they have fled. It is not enough even to protect those who seek your protection, for you are under another obligation toward him: you must consider his interests, be beneficent toward him, and not pain his heart by speech.[9]

But though ameliorated, slavery was never formally abolished in Jewish religious law. Bondage of Hebrew slaves had ceased by the Talmudic period;[10] ownership of 'foreign' slaves disappeared as an issue when slavery was abolished in the West. Nowadays, no Jewish theologian seeks to justify slavery on the basis of religious law; normal Jewish teaching, even in the most conservative circles, is that the Torah, through its amelioration of slavery, pointed the way to abolition of the institution.

This is a very interesting result, unprecedented in the classical sources. Clearly, 'enlightened' ideas on human equality have brought about a new reading of the sources; religion, that is, has found a way to interpret its teachings so as to conform to the current human rights system.

Would it have been preferable that existing human rights standards allow for sufficient flexibility at the level of application to take on board

8 Jeremiah 34:9 and 12–22.

9 Moses Maimonides, *The Guide of the Perplexed*, Book III:39, tr. Shlomo Pines (Chicago: University of Chicago Press, 1963), vol. 2, 554.

10 B. *Gittin* 65a.

religious sensitivities with regard to slavery? That is, should we regard as acceptable, at least for the time being, the practice of slavery in those societies where it is still endorsed by religious teaching? It seems obvious to me that it would not be acceptable, and that religious teaching in this instance should yield to the standards set by the human rights consensus.

□ *Freedom of thought, speech and conscience*

Article 18 of the Universal Declaration states, 'Everyone has the right to freedom of thought, conscience and religion; this right includes the freedom to change his religion or belief, and freedom, either alone or in community with others and in public or private, to manifest his religion or belief in teaching, practice, worship and observance'. Article 19 establishes a more general freedom of opinion and expression.

This bland call for freedom of expression is modified, in practice, by a number of factors. It cannot be cited, for instance, to legitimise libel or slander, and many states still outlaw blasphemy even if, as in England and Wales, they are unsure what it is. Likewise, states enact laws against incitement to racial or religious hatred, or against missionary activity. Absolute freedom of expression would be intolerable.

Religions, however, go further than banning forms of expression that cause obvious social damage. The Bible is outspoken in its condemnation of idolatry, not only establishing harsh penalties against malefactors, but backing them up with dire threats of divine punishment. The early rabbis attempted to suppress all literature regarded by them as heretical, and enacted laws to humiliate or even harm heretics subject to the limits imposed by foreign jurisdiction, and to the need to avoid inciting retribution against Jews. In later times all available means, including excommunication, were invoked to suppress dissident teachings or beliefs — probably the best known instance of this is the excommunication of Spinoza by the Sephardic rabbinical court of Amsterdam in 1656. Unless dissident teaching can be shown to undermine society, the suppression of such teachings is a denial of the right of freedom of expression; that is why Locke, for instance, in his *Letter on Toleration*, justifies his denial of toleration to Catholics by arguing that they threaten the stability of the state. Yet what one has to ask is whether it is dissidence that threatens the stability of the state, or the suppression of dissidence; otherwise every dictator would be able justify his ruthlessness on the grounds that his enemies threatened stability of government.

Of course, religious leaders – including Orthodox Jews – in Western societies are for the most part vociferous advocates of the principles of freedom of thought and speech. Perhaps they are afraid that in a less tolerant climate they themselves would forfeit that freedom, and perhaps they are right. The question is, would they allow that freedom to others if they had power to deny it?

The late judge Haim Cohn, of the Supreme Court of the State of Israel, approvingly cited these words from a great sixteenth-century rabbi, Judah Loewe (Maharal) of Prague (1525–1609):

> Even if his words spoken are directed against faith and religion, do not tell a man not to speak and suppress his words. Otherwise there will be no clarification in religious matters . . . Thus my opinion is contrary to what some people think. They think that when it is forbidden to speak against religion, religion is strengthened; but it is not so. The elimination of the opinions of those who are opposed to religion undermines religion and weakens it.[11]

This apparently tolerant attitude is belied by Maharal himself, in Part 6 of the same work, when he declares with extreme vehemence that the writings of Rabbi Azariah dei Rossi of Mantua (1511–78), probably the greatest scholar of Hebrew letters during the Italian Renaissance, should be burned.[12]

Even where religious leaders express tolerance for other religions, they are apt to deny that tolerance to those they consider dissidents within their own religion or sect. This is why, for instance, Bahá'ís have been persecuted under Muslim rule, not simply subjected to *dhimmi* status like Jews and Christians; Bahá'ís are regarded as renegades to the True Faith, rather than legitimate 'people of the book'. In an analogous but less violent manner, Reform and Conservative Jews are routinely denigrated by the Orthodox as inauthentic Jews, backsliders from religion who ought not to be allowed the right to voice such heresies, whereas Christians and Muslims (though not Jews who have converted to those

11 Cohn, 128, citing Gordis' translation of *Be'er HaGola*, 1, p. 210.

12 *Be'er HaGola* (Pietrkow, 1910), 125. Maharal does not cite Azariah by name.

religions) are regarded as legitimate followers of other religions to be treated with a certain respect.

Though in most Western democracies this conflict can be kept under control, in Israel, the only Jewish state, it is more serious. There, the Orthodox rabbis have a virtual monopoly, backed by the state, on personal status, including marriage and divorce, and will not readily yield any part of their power to groups they regard as heterodox.

In this case it seems right that religious leaders should be expected to find ways to interpret their teachings so as to conform to the current human rights system, rather than vice versa. Society will not be at peace until the followers of religions are persuaded to live in mutual respect with one another.

3. RIGHTS OF EQUALITY

□ *All men are born equal, but women?*

Article 16.1 states, 'Men and Women of full age, without any limitation due to race, nationality or religion, have the right to marry and to found a family. They are entitled to equal rights as to marriage, during marriage and at its dissolution'; article 16.2 adds, 'Marriage shall be entered into only with the free and full consent of the intending spouses.'

The second point should create no difficulty so far as religious principles are concerned, though there could be conflict with the social customs of some Jewish groups. Free consent to marriage is essential in Jewish law to the validity of the marriage contract; duress invalidates it, though it can be difficult to prove, since most instances of duress arise from pressure of social custom or parental wishes. At any rate, there is no conflict here between human rights doctrine and religious principle.

Jewish tradition does not, however, afford equal rights to women and men 'as to marriage, during marriage and at its dissolution.' Unless specific provision is made to the contrary, men take control on marriage of their wives' property. Though women may sue in the court for divorce, a successful outcome would at best be that the court would order the husband to divorce the wife; if they cannot enforce compliance, the wife has no remedy. This results in the production of *agunot*, a class of women who, so to speak, remain 'chained' to their husbands since they cannot receive permission to remarry.

What should be done? The Orthodox religious authorities refuse to tamper with tradition on the grounds that it is ordained by God. On the other hand, human rights advocates will not abandon such a central principle of sexual equality. Outside Israel a compromise exists, as with so many other instances of conflict between human rights and religious principles. Religious communities are permitted to follow what they regard as their hallowed practices, and public law intervenes only in those instances where an individual suffers obvious personal injustice, as for instance in forced marriages, nowadays virtually unknown in the Jewish community.

The situation in Israel is more difficult, since religious law on personal status is endorsed by the state. An obvious solution to many of the problems would be the institution of civil marriages, but this is currently resisted by much of the Orthodox establishment.

Jewish feminists have argued persuasively that the problem of women's status in Judaism transcends the specific issues of women's legal rights under halakha; it leads to a fundamental theological question about divine revelation being culture-bound. Tamar Ross has articulated this all the more effectively since she writes in defence of a Modern Orthodox position:

> What makes the feminist analysis unique is that the ultimate question it raises does not concern any particular difficulty in the contents of the Torah (be it moral, scientific, or theological). Nor does it concern the accuracy of the historical account of its literary genesis. Highlighting an all-pervasive male bias in the Torah seems to display a more general skepticism regarding divine revelation that is much more profound. What it drives us to ask is, Can any verbal message claiming revelatory status really be divine? Because language itself is shaped by the cultural context in which it is formulated . . . is a divine and eternally valid message at all possible? Can a verbal message transcend its cultural framework? With these questions, the clash between Orthodoxy and historicism is transformed from a dispute over the facts of the matter to a debate over issues of general bias and the ubiquitous traces of cultural relativism . . . Allegorical interpretations of problematic passages in the Torah will not solve anything in this case. The

male bias cannot be limited to specific terms or passages; it is all over the text.[13]

An analogous question might be raised concerning slavery. As we saw above, both Jews and Christians nowadays abhor slavery and condemn it in the name of their traditions, but this requires quite a revolutionary reading of scripture, since neither Hebrew Scriptures nor the New Testament opposes slavery in principle. You can only read scripture as condemning slavery if you are prepared to acknowledge that scripture expresses itself in a culture-bound way, and that it is legitimate to reinterpret it in terms of our own culture.

However, whereas the anti-slavery consensus is strong enough for us to demand the abolition of slavery in any society that still endorses it on religious or other grounds, there may not in practice be a strong enough consensus for a parallel demand to be made for the equalisation of women's status. To some extent, human rights advocates must allow for sufficient flexibility at the level of application to take on board religious sensitivities with regard to the status of women.

This is an unsatisfactory position if you believe that in this instance it is the human rights consensus rather than religious teaching that occupies the moral high ground. It means that a government may not intervene even when the practice of a religious group is to discriminate against women, for instance by excluding them from holding positions of authority, by treating their evidence in court as inferior to that of men, or by subjecting them to social or economic disadvantages.

4. RIGHTS OF JUSTICE

□ *Equality before the law*

The Bible leaves us in no doubt about the equality of all before the law. Perhaps even more powerful than any normative statement is the well-known story of the two prostitutes who burst in upon King Solomon, each claiming that the live child was hers and the dead child the other's (1 Kings 3:16–28). King Solomon's quasi-judicial procedure may be questioned, and has been in the traditional Jewish sources, but no one

13 Tamar Ross, *Expanding the Palace of Torah.* (Waltham MA: Brandeis University Press, 2004), 186.

has faulted him on the principle of easy and equal access to justice for all classes.

Thomas Paine, in *The Rights of Man*, aptly cites a biblical verse as demonstration that 'the equality of man, far from being a modern doctrine, is the oldest upon record': 'So God created man in his image, in the image of God he created him; male and female he created them' (Genesis 1:27).

Rabbinic Judaism is less clear on the point. We are all equal before God (whatever that may mean), but not in all respects before the law. Women, for instance, are unable to give testimony except in limited circumstances; compensation for injury differs between freemen and slaves; while there is no discrimination on the grounds of colour, there is certainly discrimination between those of the 'true faith' and those who reject it. On the positive side, judicial standards and procedural safeguards are impartial, and the prophetic vision of all nations united in peace before God is maintained.

Remedies for traditional discriminations are sometimes to be found within the law; women, for instance, are nowadays heard in the religious courts, and this is justified by the fiction that 'evidence' in the full sense is no longer taken, but the court serves merely as a court of arbitration. Discrimination against slaves or non-believers are of no practical import: there are no slaves, and non-believers do not subject themselves to the rabbinic courts other than for marriage and divorce, on which comment has already been made.

A more fundamental question about the system of halakha is the extent to which it is intended to apply beyond the Jewish community. Early sources envisage the possibility that Jews might govern others, but it is always assumed that the 'others' are idolaters against whom it is legitimate to discriminate, though not to act unjustly.[14] However, this aspect of halakha was not developed, nor was it of practical relevance until the modern state of Israel was established. Israeli law, which is essentially secular, does not itself discriminate on the grounds of colour, race, gender or religion, except, arguably, through the foundational Law of Return that gives Jews a preferential right to citizenship. Most

14 There is a sense in which all discrimination is unjust. The difference here is between discrimination, as for instance in requiring different criteria for evidence, and injustice, as in punishing the innocent.

matters of personal status, however, are delegated to religious courts, whether Jewish, Muslim, Christian or Druze, as in the Ottoman system which preceded the foundation of the state. The secular Supreme Court remains the ultimate court of appeal, but is unlikely to overrule the religious courts where traditional discriminations are applied.

The system of halakha, then, is not in fact applied beyond the Jewish community; non-Jews who are citizens of Israel are governed by secular law for most purposes, and by the law of their own community in personal status. Liberal Jews regard the principles of justice and equity enshrined in biblical and rabbinic laws, though not necessarily the laws themselves, as of universal significance, even though they are expressed in terms of ancient Israelite or Jewish society.

In sum, the judicial system of the state of Israel exhibits a balance between the enlightenment ideal of universal human rights that underlay the foundation of the state on the one hand, and the traditions of the various religious communities on the other. This would probably work better if there were some sort of opt-out for those citizens who are not committed to a religious program, and who often feel that they are subject to discrimination or religious coercion, particularly with the marriage laws. Also, since only those religious courts recognised by the state can act with full authority, groups such as Reform Jews who, on account of Orthodox objections, do not have their own courts to authorise marriages etc., should not be denied the right to have them if they wish.

5. CONCLUSION: WHO SHOULD GIVE WAY TO WHOM?

It is clear that there are areas in which religious demands conflict with universal human rights.

The question, which should yield to which, cannot be solved from within either, since as we showed in the first section there is no agreement as to what constitutes the ultimate authority, the ultimate court of appeal. Religion recognises God, or in practice the rulings of the priests or rabbis, as the ultimate unquestionable authority, whereas secular government relies on a political doctrine about the will of the people. Each system limits the authority of the other.

Solutions to the problems generated by the conflict can nevertheless be approached in a pragmatic fashion, accepting compromise.

On the secular side, it must be acknowledged that some religious groups have laws or principles that they believe to be God-given and therefore non-negotiable. The secular may regard this belief as erroneous or even absurd, but in the interest of peaceful government they may have to go along with it in the hope that the religious will one day become more enlightened. An instance of this is the Orthodox Jewish commitment to what they regard as the divine law that women may not actively divorce men (though they may sue in the courts for divorce); any serious attempt by the secular authorities to force change would most likely stiffen resistance.

At the same time, the needs of those citizens who reject the Orthodox viewpoint must also be respected, and efforts be made to satisfy their legitimate requirements; in the case just mentioned, provision of a civil marriage facility might be appropriate.

There are broader areas where firm secular government will pursue values contrary to religious tradition, for instance in granting equal status to persons of both sexes, all ethnic backgrounds and all religions. This may be regarded as the imposition of a secular faith, but so be it.

From the religious side, accommodation may be reached with the secular in several well-tried ways. Fundamental to this is the acknowledgement that so-called secular values, including universal human rights, are to be found within the religious traditions, and may therefore be viewed not as an imposition from outside but as an internal process of growth leading to new interpretations. This is what has happened with regard to slavery, and in liberal religious circles also with regard to the status of women.

Then there are instances where both the religious and the secular rights-based may pledge allegiance to a particular formula, even though they interpret it differently. For instance, Article 22 sets out a 'right to . . . realization . . . of economic, social and cultural rights . . .' If this is to be understood as the fulfilment of individual potential, some will place the emphasis on economic welfare, freedom of cultural expression and the like, but others will see it in terms of the opportunity for spiritual development, with an eye to eternal life.

The Western-style democracies, including Israel, are at the present time able to manage pragmatically in this way, since their fundamentalist minorities are not very powerful. Other countries, particularly in the Islamic world, are finding it more difficult, and there even exists an Islamic Declaration on Human Rights since, correctly, it is perceived that the UN Declaration does not accord in all respects with Islamic teaching. But I do not see how the United Nations could function at all if it were to recognise alternative, and contradictory, standards in human rights.

So far as Judaism is concerned, the situation is manageable at present, since the number of intransigent Orthodox is containable. Even so, strains are evident, not only with regard to the laws of personal status, but with international situations such as the Israeli withdrawal from Gaza, where some religious and secular nationalist groups (secular nationalism is a debased form of religion) strongly opposed the government.

As to whether God 'believes' in human rights, I have no doubt that He does; unfortunately, his followers often mistakenly think He is more interested in tradition and doctrine than in people. I also think that God believes in secular government; it is He who has most to fear (so to speak) from regimes governed by the reactionary religious.

CHAPTER 6

Religion and Human Rights: Redressing the Balance

Avrom Sherr

INTRODUCTION

I would suggest that there are strong similarities, as others have noted, between types of religious obligation and human rights. Religions comprise sets of beliefs (parts of which may be reduced to writing in the form of regulation) based on cultural, national, spiritual, moral and emotional sources. Human rights comprise sets of ideals (often reduced to writing in the form of regulation) based on rational, cultural, national, spiritual (humanist), moral and emotional sources. Both religious duties and human rights are (at least when brought to book and the subject of decisions) constantly developing, interpreted by representative bodies and reactive to contexts. So the similarity of the compositions and sources of both religious beliefs and human rights often make them competitors –not only in beliefs, but also in corresponding regulatory systems. If so, I would ask: are there any developing themes or rules to help us know which, of religion or human rights, trumps the other, and if so, when? In beginning to ask and answer this question in the following discussion, I intend to reflect by way of example on some issues which are considered to be important within the Jewish religion, and also to reflect briefly on whether there appears to be a Jewish religious approach to human rights. In doing so, I refer to my own religious background, not because it is better or worse than any other, but simply because it is the one I know.

THE PROVENANCE OF HUMAN RIGHTS; FOR EXAMPLE, JEWISH RELIGIOUS TRADITION

Deutscher, when formulating the concept of 'the non-Jewish Jew,' included a comment about the wheels of revolutions often being oiled by Jewish blood. He noted the over-representation of people from culturally or nationally Jewish backgrounds in the lists of those who had brought about changes associated with developments in human rights.[1] If this is true, then is there any provenance for this approach to be found within the religious beliefs and duties set out within the Jewish religion that might have brought about this over-representation?

As a preliminary point, I want to address the 'rights and duties' issue. The Jewish religion itself promotes the concept of duty rather than 'right' in its modern positive form. Duties (as between people; legal actions against the Deity are not very frequent!) may be actionable in rabbinical courts and therefore are equivalent to rights. Some rabbinical writing (and some of the other essays in this volume) contends that rights-based societies engender a sort of 'taker' attitude, whereas duty-based societies encourage a society of 'givers.' But it seems to me, as a lawyer, that if a duty is actionable in law, it does not make any difference whether it is couched in the language of rights or not, since in effect it really becomes a right. One might argue about the degree of exhortatory influence a 'right' might have over a 'duty,' but this would be a largely academic, semantic discussion (and one which already exists in the literature).

What duties of the nature of human rights are referred to within Judaism? A familiar and constant theme relates to the proper treatment of those who are different, alien or strange, as in the verse וְאַתֶּם יְדַעְתֶּם אֶת נֶפֶשׁ הַגֵּר 'for you know the heart of a stranger, since you were strangers in the land of Egypt.'

The Ten Commandments include respect for parents, and forbid murder, adultery, theft, bearing false witness and jealousy. The next set of 'people duties' enumerated in the text of the Torah (the Five Books of Moses) relate to issues of servants – the *eved* (Exodus 21.2). Rabbi Shimshon Refael Hirsch, a German enlightened rabbi of nineteenth-century modernity, asks, Why do the Jewish social laws begin with concepts of servants or slavery? The answer given is that one can determine a society's level of humanity by the way it treats its most vulnerable members.[2] Unlike traditional forms of slavery, the *eved Ivri* (actually a penal system for dealing with criminals who have stolen but cannot repay) is not the chattel of the master, and there are limits in terms of excruciat-

1 Isaac Deutscher, *The Non-Jewish Jew and other essays*, ed. Tamara Deutscher (London: OUP, 1968).

2 Thanks to Paul Taylor's recent '*daf parashah*' for this.

ing, debasing and unnecessary labour he may be asked to perform; the master must treat him properly. For example, if the master only has one pillow it should be given to the servant or *eved*; on his release the master must give him a generous severance payment. The *eved Kanaani* is also protected from inhumane treatment and must be treated with dignity – an unusual demand considering the time and place of the original injunction.

Only after these issues are dealt with does Scripture go on to talk in detail about murder, patricide, matricide, kidnapping, cursing of parents, grievous bodily harm, goring oxen and the *lex talionis* (the principle of an 'eye for an eye', which has been the subject of much misunderstanding throughout the ages though all Jewish explanations refer to monetary compensation only). Relationships between men and women are also heavily legislated for. Though many areas do not come up to modern levels of safeguard, many go beyond. On the basis of this example it would appear true to say that what we know today as 'human rights' may well derive from such 'natural rights' or 'natural law', and human rights may therefore have some affinity to religion or a religious basis. A religious source, background or basis may well have given rise to ideals similar or equivalent to human rights at different times in history when religion was more popular.

HUMAN RIGHTS – THE CULTURAL CONTEXT

It is important therefore to note that human rights do not necessarily come from a strictly 'rationalist' tradition. It is clear from a review of different standards throughout the world – certainly in relation to regulation, let alone the actual performance of human rights – that rationalism is not the only factor in their existence and in their detail. It is fairly clear then that human rights are not in fact universal but cultural: what is appropriate to England in 2005 may not be appropriate to the Republic of Ireland in 2005, let alone Iraq or China or Hong Kong. What is sexually appropriate for the Netherlands, Denmark or Germany may not be appropriate for England even if all of those countries are covered by the European Convention. Hence it could be asked: if human rights – like any other legal regulation – are not culturally contextual, could they ever be respected?

THE OTHER SIDE OF THE COIN

However it could also be asked (and this is the interesting dichotomy), if human rights are not universal do they have any value at all? Are they as good as the Ten Commandments? If human rights are such a movable feast that they can be changed, or are adjustable, according to context, culture or political need, how important can they really be? It is this dichotomy that lies at the root of the great difficulty addressed in this paper. Since no right is absolute and therefore all rights are relative, what happens when religious duties clash with human rights or, put in another way, the right to practice one's religion clashes with some other human right?

Elsewhere in this volume Norman Solomon talks about the issue of the death penalty, so I will not mention that example, but others that spring to mind are behaviour towards the *metzora* 'leper', leprosy and removal from the congregation; the treatment of the *sotah* 'the suspected adulteress' who is given bitter waters to drink (a little perhaps like the ducking chair for witches in medieval England); the carrying out of stoning as a death penalty; and the physical punishment of *makot* or whipping for certain crimes. None of these, by the way, are in use, but each is theoretically a possibility as a concept. Can these in any way accommodate the human rights of those involved? The answer is already given – none apply nowadays and rabbinical courts may not mete out such punishments.

More interesting is the question put the other way round: can human rights accommodate culture or religion? Examples within the Jewish religion include *brit milah*, 'male circumcision', eight days after birth, *shechitah* – kosher treatment including slaughter of animals, and *get* – divorce in which the man has to give the woman a divorce (she can demand it but he has to be forced if necessary to give it) and the resultant problems of the *agunah* 'the chained woman' when husbands refuse the injunction of the rabbinical court to give their wives a divorce. All of these are areas which currently do operate and areas that have raised questions or even political attempts to organise a ban on them.

How then do we know which rights should prevail, which principle should accommodate the other? Two overriding principles are effective here within the Jewish religion: *dina de-malchuta dina* 'the law of the

State is the law to be obeyed' and *vachai bahem* 'you should live by them' – a wonderful principle. In other words, the rules have to be capable of being obeyed or else need not be obeyed. There are also occasions in the Talmud where the rabbis go back on an edict or stricture because it proves intolerable to those who must observe it.

But beyond the realms of a religion which includes within it the precept of conforming to local rule or custom in certain areas, who is right morally or legally in these problem cases? If a young Nigerian woman has a right not to be forced into having a clitoridectomy, does a little Jewish baby boy have a right not to have a circumcision performed on him? Should animal rights prevent *shechitah* or halal slaughter?

If another right prevails over the right to practise one's religion, then human rights may be more universal than previously suggested, but they will also be subject to cultural imperialism. Human rights are usually there to defend the underdog, but in these situations who becomes the 'victim' of whom?

Dworkin suggests models for how to deal with these competing rights.[3] The first model involves balancing individual rights against other social goals. The second holds that one should err on the side of individual rights instead of balancing. The argument against the one is the argument in favour of the other. Dworkin also identifies what he regards as the grounds of fundamental rights.

In an interesting recent lecture on 'Working against Racism: The View from Geneva,'[4] Professor Patrick Thornberry talked about homogenising universalism versus differentiating universalism, equality in diversity versus equality in standardisation, the possibility of preservation of culture, and the mistake of heterophobic application of human rights. Like Dworkin's approach, this begins to give us some leeway in answering the question of competing rights. But we still do not know rationally whether *brit milah* is right and clitoridectomy is not.

So which are 'good' or 'acceptable' cultural/religious traditions and which are not, and why? What is wrong with the *hijab*, the *kippah*, modesty of dress, the cross of a dominant culture or the Star of David/ Red Crescent of a minority culture? What is right, for example, about arranged marriages that is wrong with forced marriages, and what is

3 Dworkin, *Taking Rights Seriously*.

4 Held at Senate House, University of London, in December 2004.

better about serial monogamy than parallel partners? How should society decide what is acceptable here and now or there and then? And how should we decide what is not acceptable? In other words, what level of cultural imperialism do human rights imply?

THE QUEBECOIS SUCCAH STORY – A CASE IN POINT

There have been few cases which actually address these issues in any direct way; one is that of the Quebecois *Succot.* A *succah* is a booth erected for eight days in September or October as part of the Jewish festival of *Succot.* The religious duty (to God rather than man in this case) is to leave one's house or apartment and live in a temporary dwelling that has the roof open to the stars for a week, to remember the forty years of wandering in the wilderness, and also to get away from the material things of life inside the home.

In general this is not a major problem, since erecting a temporary booth tends not to interfere very much with the rights of others. When planning laws or nuisance laws are invoked the case usually takes too long to get to court to actually deal with the eight-day event. But in this particular case, the co-ownership declaration of a set of apartment dwellers in a condominium in Quebec seemed to prevent them erecting things on their balconies. The management corporation sued, saying they would allow a communal *succah* in the shared gardens but not a set of individual *succot* on each balcony for each family. The case went to the highest constitutional court in Canada before the individual *succot* were allowed. The language of the decision is interesting:

> Freedom of Religion is triggered when a claimant demonstrates that he or she sincerely believes in a practice or belief that has a nexus with religion. Once religious freedom is triggered, a court must then ascertain whether there has been non trivial or non-insubstantial interference with the exercise of the implicated right so as to constitute an infringement of freedom of religion under the Quebec or Canadian Charter. However, even if the claimant successfully demonstrates non trivial interference, religious conduct which would potentially cause harm to or interfere with the rights of others would not automatically be protected. The ulti-

> mate protection of any particular Charter right must be measured in relation to other rights and with a view to the underlying context in which the apparent conflict arises.[5]

So a balancing of rights occurs. There is probably insufficient clarity from this case to help many others but it does begin to assist. Neither we nor the courts need decide what is religion and what is religious belief if one follows this particular example; unfortunately, it does not help us enormously beyond that point. To move forward, we need more cases. Lawyers always like more cases, just like researchers want more money for research. Religious rights are not supreme, though they can indeed trump others in certain circumstances. We do not yet seem to have sufficient jurisprudence on these issues to understand what will be the dominant themes that will assist in making these decisions. In truth they are already made, but politically and not judicially. It will be interesting to see whether the judicial decisions are any better made than the social or political ones.

---

5 *Syndicat Northcrest* v. *Amselem,* [2004] SCJ no. 46, 2004 SCC 47 (the 'Amselem decision').

CHAPTER 7

Human Rights and Its Destruction of Right and Wrong

Melanie Phillips

Do religion and human rights invariably clash? Well, it is certainly true on one level that the Bible is at the core of universal human rights, because they are based essentially on the concept of the dignity of the human person. As the Talmud says, 'If a single person is destroyed, it is as if the whole world is destroyed; and if a single person is saved, it is as if the whole world is saved.' However, I personally believe (and I hope I will persuade you) that *modern* human rights are in direct conflict with religion; furthermore, modern human rights are acting as a solvent on Judeo-Christian values, which they are steadily replacing by a set of secular values tailored for a Godless age, with very damaging effects on our society.

Our society is based on Judeo-Christian values essentially of duty and responsibility. Judaism and Christianity are not fundamentally religions of rights at all. They are religions of duties – duties of the individual to God and duties of man to man, because we are all made in the image of God. Certainly, rights are inferred from those duties, but it is terribly important to realise that religion has it that way round: duty is prior to rights.

This means, for example, that the value and virtue of human freedom is predicated on the need to have constraints on human behaviour. This is one of the paradoxes of freedom. If one doesn't have constraints imposed by moral codes, one ends up with licence and anarchy, which are in fact inimical to freedom. Even liberalism – which was the great revolt against the overweening authority of religion and is the source of contract law and the separation of Church and State and therefore the source of our modern human rights – even liberalism was essentially a moral project based on the difference between right and wrong that took for granted the constraints on human appetites deriving from the religious rules of the Judeo-Christian tradition.

In my view, the modern human rights culture has replaced that set of duties, that essential prior set of duties, by a culture of entitlement, which has had a particularly dramatic effect on our society. This is because human rights make a claim to universality, and, being universal, brook no moral opposition and must have primacy over national cultures and laws. But I would say that they are certainly not universal. They cannot possibly be universal because they conflict. The Human Rights Convention and subsequent Acts contain rights that conflict with each other, requiring arbitration by judges. These judges do not originate from any particular jurisdiction (one thinks of the European Court of Human Rights for example), meaning that the human rights project is actually anti-democratic, superseding individual cultures rooted in religious principles.

Human rights principles are said to be Judeo-Christian, but this is not so except on the most banal level of being rooted in the dignity of the human individual, which is taken as read. Rather, they are particular values imposed on a particular culture under a particular set of circumstances: after the Second World War, in response to experiences of mass slaughter, genocide, and the Holocaust of Fascism and totalitarianism, there was an attempt to find a kind of world faith to fill the spiritual void left by Christianity and the Enlightenment. That kind of religious sense, I feel, underpins the passion with which people espouse the human rights culture and will not brook any opposition to it. But there is a conflict between the vision of a society implicit in the human rights culture and religious cultures. The human rights culture is based primarily on the idea that the individual has to be protected from the State; a democracy assumes that in order to bestow rights upon people there must be a collective power created to bestow those rights. Conversely, religion – and I speak particularly of Judaism about which I know a little – has it the opposite way round. In Judaism – and this may be so for Christianity too – human society is seen as a natural phenomenon, part of the order of Creation; therefore human society comes before, is inherently prior, to any kind of contract. Society is thus based on a set of interlocking duties, the idea of human reciprocity giving rise to the saying by the great Rabbi Hillel, 'What is hateful to you, do not do unto others.' In other words, the precondition for human society flourishing is that we all have duties to each other.

All humans are created in the image of God. It therefore follows that everybody has equal and absolute worth: not rights, worth. Therefore we are actually commanded, 'Love your neighbour as yourself.' This is a commandment, an obligation, from which we derive the right to exist and to flourish. It is imperative to imitate God and act in divine ways towards each other. Therefore the wrongs of murder, for example, are wrongs against God. God does not tolerate the shedding of blood, because, 'in the image of God He created man'; the shedding of blood kills the image of God (putting war to one side for a moment). Similarly, the biblical duty to the stranger, the orphan and the widow is to give them equal care and treatment because we are all created in the image of God. Thus religious culture is fundamentally a culture of obligation.

Modern human rights culture, though, is predicated on the belief that law is needed to protect people from each other. Judaism sees people essentially as not in need of protection from each other; it regards the role of law and government quite differently: to nurture moral character in pursuit of a higher ideal of a better society. That is why people are obligated to help each other. But human rights culture, by contrast, is predicated on the essential need of the individual who makes a claim against society. This divides people into groups which basically threaten each other as they all jostle for their rights: 'My rights contradict your rights, my rights supersede your rights, I'm a bigger victim than you are', and so on. It seems we have created a human rights culture which is, as David Selbourne writes in *The Principle of Duty*, 'a system of duty-less rights.' Although it is said that all rights entail duties, this is again a total misapprehension, because the rights we have created impose a duty on the person who is required to grant the rights. Conversely, in a society based on duty and obligation, the individual doesn't have as his precondition of existence a claim on society to give him his rights, but, as his prior obligation, a set of duties to other people.

This culture of duty-less rights has arisen against a general cultural background of freedom. This desirability of freedom from authoritarianism has been translated into a freedom from absolutely all authority that might constrain the liberty of the individual. It is a society in which the individual's freedom of choice trumps everything else, meaning that every individual is entitled to the same treatment regardless of his personal circumstances or behaviour. He is entitled to his rights simply on account of his existing as a rational being with a conscience. As a result,

I believe our human rights culture has produced a licence for irresponsibility. It has become an engine for a culture of extreme individualism in which people feel obligated to grasp whatever they can, to demand their rights and to satisfy themselves for whatever they want, at any cost. A recent example, completely absurd in my view, is the Prince of Wales being told that he is legally able to marry in a register office, in a civil marriage, notwithstanding that it is a matter of some conflict between lawyers whether the 1836 Marriage Act conflicts with the 1949 Marriage Act. Yet human rights must trump everything: he has an absolute right to marry. Absurd!

Because everyone has equal entitlements, we have effectively destroyed discrimination between right and wrong. The anti-discrimination provisions of human rights culture rest on the premise that no moral distinctions or judgements can be made that draw distinctions between people. In the interests of equality, everyone must be treated in exactly the same way and be entitled to exactly the same outcomes, regardless of their circumstances or behaviour.

It is not so much the principle of equality as what I would call 'identicality' that is in play here. In the principle of 'identicality', the effects of difference are simply denied altogether, meaning that people, whatever they do, are all entitled to claim exactly the same outcomes by right. What was originally a protection from actual oppression has turned into a wish list for personal happiness and personal gratification which, in my view, dissolves obligations. And this has had a number of effects.

It has dissolved the idea of normative sexual behaviour. That is why human rights legislation promotes same-sex unions.

It has destroyed the sanctity of life, because the right to die becomes effectively the right to kill, and especially because, in certain circumstances where people are no longer rational, they are presumed not to have any right to life because they are no longer rational beings.

It has produced the instrumentalisation of life and the commodification of early human life, witness the creation and destruction of embryos in *in vitro* fertilisation and stem cell transfers and cloning.

It encourages victim groups organising to claim their rights on the basis that if they don't have the same thing as everyone else, it must be everyone else's fault, regardless of how they behave. This has given rise to a victim culture in which any apparent disadvantage suffered by any group regarding itself as powerless – principally ethnic or sexual minorities, disabled people or women – can say that that disadvantage is discrimination.

A situation has thus been created where anyone who identifies himself as part of a victim group is beyond reproach. The only people who can ever be guilty are those deemed to be in power over such minorities and victim groups, namely, men, the middle classes, white people, the physically able – we can all add to the list. In other words, mainstream society, whose principle crime is that it is mainstream, is therefore – by definition according to human rights thinking – exclusivist, elitist, racist, sexist and innately oppressive towards any group considering itself to be handicapped by anything. Thus human rights culture has turned into a stick with which to beat the innocent. How can this possibly be a human right? In my view, it's a human wrong.

Human rights have become an attack on mainstream values and on justice itself. For example, a recent human rights ruling held that gypsy families were entitled to override planing law, which they were said by various legal authorities to have clearly broken, because they had an overriding right to family life. In that particular case, I would suggest, human rights law became a solvent of law itself.

The governance of Britain has become increasingly impossible in such areas as immigration and asylum policy. Take the recent key judgement by the Law Lords – the ruling which plunged the government into crisis – that said foreign terrorist suspects could not be locked up without trial. The judges reached this view in part by comparing foreign and British nationals and deciding that, as the former were not being treated in the same way as the latter, this constituted unlawful discrimination. But this is not to compare like with like, because foreign nationals do not have the rights or responsibilities of British citizens. British nationals cannot be deported. They can't move to another country once they are arrested, as these foreign terrorist suspects can. These are two completely different groups, and to say it is discrimination to treat different groups differently is, I think, grotesque. Indeed, we can see the absurd logic being carried to its conclusion in the Home Secretary's current writhings.

But 'identicality' is doing yet deeper damage, because it bars us from making moral judgements, making it an enemy of morality itself, which must by definition discriminate between right and wrong, between truth and lies. Human rights law tears up, when it desires, our moral rules, including the concept of truth itself. That is why, for example, it now has allowed transsexuals to destroy the birth certificate which reveals truthfully the sex into which they were born, and present instead a new birth certificate, solemnly declaring the lie that they were born in the opposite sex. It is not just a case of transsexuals being allowed the right to change their sex: this is not what is being allowed to them. The law has said, 'You are now legally entitled to tell a lie on your birth certificate.' How can there be a human right to tell a lie?

And since this kind of discrimination between right and wrong, truth and lies, lies at the very core of our Judeo-Christian moral codes, identicality in the human rights culture is a principle engine for the destruction of fundamental Western values. That is why those who most lose out under anti-discrimination law tend to be Christians or other defenders of traditional beliefs.

In conclusion, far from expanding human freedom as it purports to do, human rights culture has become instead our society's most powerful means of suppressing it. Far from protecting human life and liberty, it has become a weapon against it. I close with this paradoxical thought: religion – which overwhelmingly emphasises duty, not rights – is crucial for preserving our rights to life and liberty, while the secular human rights culture – which purports to guarantee life and liberty – actually constrains, reduces and even threatens them.

CHAPTER 8

A More Constructive Encounter: A Bahá'í View of Religion and Human Rights

John Barnabas Leith

The rise of human rights as a system of values and ethics commanding respect and motivating action with quasi-religious force was a notable feature of the twentieth century, which was also a time of increasing secularisation and 'privatisation' of religion. The tension between human rights values and religious values has led some to wonder if religion and human rights are compatible. This tension has been reinforced by the emergence in the late twentieth century and early twenty-first century of an increasingly aggressive form of religious extremism which is clearly contemptuous of human rights.

This chapter will explore the relationship between religion and human rights from a Bahá'í perspective and will examine the work of the Bahá'í community in wholeheartedly supporting the theory and practice of universal human rights.

INTRODUCTION

Human rights discourse has a compelling quality at a time when religion no longer holds the centre of the public square. The value placed on human rights and human rights as values seem to have a transcendent quality that compels respect with, in some cases, a quasi-religious force.[1]

In this paper I want to give an example of a religion that has emerged in modern times, which clearly and directly addresses modern concerns and which is wholeheartedly committed to universal human rights. The Bahá'í Faith, which has grown from its initial milieu in the Middle East of the mid and late nineteenth century into a religion with a following in all parts of the world, has very clear theological foundations for its commitment to universal human rights and has long worked to promote

1 Cf. James V. Spickard, 'Human Rights, Religious Conflict and Globalisation: Ultimate Values in a New World Order', *IJMS*, 1/1 (1999), 3–20.

the values that underpin human rights. This paper will adduce evidence from the Bahá'í sacred writings and other sources to demonstrate this commitment and will examine work done by the Bahá'í International Community (BIC) in support of the human rights of the Bahá'ís in Iran and of human rights more generally.

THEOLOGICAL UNDERPINNINGS

Bahá'u'lláh (1817–1892), founder of the Bahá'í Faith, firmly places religion in the public sphere. In his extensive writings (which form a major part of the Bahá'í scriptures) he addresses questions of good governance, of judicial, social, and economic justice, of the environment, of the relationship between science and religion, of social and familial relations, and, importantly in the present context, of the relationship between the individual and society. He envisages a future global society based on a deeply rooted understanding of human oneness in which principles of justice and equity are central to the form of government. This vision is expressed epigrammatically in the emblematic quotation from Bahá'u'lláh's writings: 'The earth is but one country and mankind its citizens.'

There is a close relationship between Bahá'u'lláh's political vision and his teachings about the nature of the individual. Bahá'u'lláh holds that every individual has qualities and capacities that must be released and developed for the good of the individual and, indeed, for the good of society as a whole. The job of government is, amongst other things, to establish conditions under which these capacities can be developed and put to use. This is a key point in understanding the Bahá'í position on human rights.

Human beings are seen as being fundamentally spiritual in nature. Much is said in the Bahá'í scriptures of the importance of developing the intangible, but nonetheless effective, qualities and capacities that are deemed to be spiritual: the virtues, such as truthfulness, trustworthiness and generosity; rationality and the enquiring mind; the capacity to know and love God. Since these qualities and capacities are to be found in each and every individual, and since, according to Bahá'u'lláh, God intends these capacities to be developed, it follows that everyone has the right to a life that will allow this development to take place.

> Regard man as a mine rich in gems of inestimable value. Education alone can cause it to reveal its treasures, and enable mankind to benefit therefrom.[2]

The principle of the oneness of humankind is the core of Bahá'u'lláh's teachings and is seen as foundational to everything else Bahá'u'lláh wanted his followers to accomplish in the public realm. As a result, the oneness of humankind features centrally in Bahá'í statements and actions on human rights.

The language of rights is to be found in the Bahá'í scriptures from a relatively early date. Writing in the last quarter of the nineteenth century, Bahá'u'lláh warned the rulers of the world: 'They that perpetrate tyranny in the world have usurped the rights of the peoples and kindreds of the earth and are sedulously pursuing their selfish inclinations.'[3] The following exhortation by Bahá'u'lláh to his followers does not use the word 'rights,' but clearly foreshadows an important part of what the framers of the Universal Declaration of Human Rights set out to achieve:

> Thou must show forth that which will ensure the peace and the well-being of the miserable and the down-trodden. Gird up the loins of thine endeavour, that perchance thou mayest release the captive from his chains, and enable him to attain unto true liberty.[4]

In addressing the requirements of just governance, Bahá'u'lláh again uses language that human rights workers would recognise, although he goes beyond the normal range of human rights discourse by calling on the ruler (referring to all those with leading roles in government)

> to weigh his own being every day in the balance of equity and justice and then to judge between men and counsel them to do that which would direct their steps unto the path of wisdom and understanding. This is the cornerstone of statesmanship . . . From these words every enlightened man of wisdom will readily per-

2 Bahá'u'lláh, *Tablets of Bahá'u'lláh Revealed after the Kitáb-i-Aqdas* (Wilmette: Bahá'í Publishing Trust, 1978), 162.

3 Ibid. 85.

4 Bahá'u'lláh, *Gleanings from the Writings of Bahá'u'lláh*, (Wilmette: Bahá'í Publishing Trust, 1983), 92.

ceive that which will foster such aims as the welfare, security and protection of mankind and the safety of human lives.[5]

In addition to addressing human rights in general terms, Bahá'u'lláh forbids specific abuses such as slavery and clearly enjoins practices such as freedom of religion and the equality of women and men. He strongly censures two great European powers for persecuting their Jewish populations, and in so doing approves, by implication, the principle of external intervention into the affairs of a sovereign state.

Similar rights and rights-related language is also to be found in the writings of 'Abdu'l-Bahá, eldest son and successor of Bahá'u'lláh as head of the Bahá'í community. For example, in 1912, while on a prolonged visit to North America, 'Abdu'l-Bahá spoke of a day when 'there shall be an equality of rights and prerogatives for all mankind'.[6] In other talks and writings he refers to the rights of labour, equal rights for women, and indeed equal rights for all.

The concept of human rights is, therefore, not at all problematic for the Bahá'í Faith. The values that underpin our modern understanding of human rights are strongly advocated, and Bahá'u'lláh constantly exhorts his readers to practise these values in their daily lives. He even goes so far as to prescribe to those in government that they should daily examine their consciences before presuming to advise or make judgements about or between others.

As stated above, the core spiritual principle in the writings of Bahá'u'lláh and 'Abdu'l-Bahá is summed up in the phrase 'the oneness of humankind'. The Bahá'í account of human rights starts from and expresses this principle. However, the focus on this principle would seem to require some examination.

We may be inclined, in the early twenty-first century, to regard the notion that all human beings are part of one human race as too obvious to be worthy of attention. That Bahá'ís and their institutions take this as the foundation of their work may not be seen as particularly significant or radical. And yet throughout the years when Bahá'u'lláh, 'Abdu'l-Bahá and Shoghi Effendi, 'Abdu'l-Bahá's successor as head of the Bahá'í

5 Bahá'u'lláh, *Tablets*, 166–7.

6 'Abdu'l-Bahá, *The Promulgation of Universal Peace: Talks Delivered by 'Abdu'l-Bahá during His Visit to the United States and Canada in 1912* (rev. ed., Wilmette: Bahá'í Publishing Trust, 1982), 318.

community, were working and writing, theories of racial superiority and extreme forms of nationalism were rampant. Bahá'u'lláh's commitment to human oneness is without qualification. He explicitly removes notions of the 'saved' and the 'unsaved' from his frame of discourse and directs his (and our) attention to the needs of the whole of humankind of whatever ethnic, religious or national background, male and female alike, whether young or old, saint or sinner.

The implications are wide-ranging. Realisation of this principle as the foundation for the Bahá'í conception of a future global order based on justice requires that we abandon all our prejudices and that we fully embrace diversity as the essential complement to oneness – the other side, so to speak, of the oneness 'coin.' This 'unity paradigm' stops diversity being threatening and renders it something to be welcomed as enriching human life. Bahá'ís are particularly fond of a metaphor to be found in the Bahá'í scriptures that compares humankind to the flowers in a garden. The flowers are diverse in kind and character, but the garden is one single place. Diversity is actually essential to unity. Without diversity, unity descends into uniformity – and uniformity, whether in the biosphere or the sociosphere, is a kind of death. But diversity outside the framework of unity leads to division. Unity and diversity are, in the Bahá'í understanding, inextricably linked.

The source of human unity, in Bahá'í theological terms, is the one creator God, whose divine qualities are reflected in the inner reality; it is the capacity of all humans, of whatever race, religion or national origin, to reflect these divine qualities that renders them deserving of moral protection. As Matthew Weinberg writes:

> A Loving Creator exists Who is the Source of all that is. It is not simply because human beings have the capacity for rational choice that they deserve moral protection, as modern philosophic liberalism would claim, but that they are spiritual beings who have the capacity to reflect Divine attributes such as love, creativity, and charity.[7]

The statement presented by the National Spiritual Assembly of the

---

7 Matthew Weinberg, 'The Human Rights Discourse: A Bahá'í Perspective,' in *The Bahá'í World 1996–97* (Bahá'í World Centre), 247–63.

Bahá'ís of the United States to the first session of the UN Commission on Human Rights in February 1947 also makes this point:

> The source of human rights is the endowment of qualities, virtues and powers which God has bestowed upon mankind without discrimination of sex, race, creed or nation. To fulfil the possibilities of this divine endowment is the purpose of human existence.[8]

And here we come to the heart of the matter. The Bahá'í picture of human nature is founded on notions of the divine origin of what constitutes humanity at its very core – although it should be said that the Bahá'í teachings on the relationship of divinity and creation are not simple and are beyond the scope of this paper. Suffice it to say that the Bahá'í scriptures teach that each individual has 'the image of God' 'engraved' on them as the essence of their being:

> O son of man! Veiled in My immemorial being and in the ancient eternity of My essence, I knew My love for thee; therefore I created thee, have engraved on thee Mine image and revealed to thee My beauty.[9]

It is this heritage that makes each human being worthy of moral protection and the subject of inalienable human rights. Furthermore, because humankind is one, each and every human being is a trust of the whole:

> From this basic principle of the unity of the human family is derived virtually all other concepts concerning human rights and freedoms. If the human race is one, any notion that a particular racial or ethnic group is in some way superior to the rest of humanity must be dismissed; society must reorganize its life to give practical expression to the principle of equality between women and men; each and every person must be enabled to 'look into all things with a searching eye' so that truth can be independently ascertained; and all individuals must be given the opportu-

8 Bahá'í International Community, *A Bahá'í Declaration of Human Obligations and Rights*, presented to the first session of the United Nations Commission on Human Rights, Lake Success, NY, USA, February 1947.

9 Bahá'u'lláh, *The Hidden Words* (Wilmette: Bahá'í Publishing Trust, 1985), Arabic No. 3, p. 4.

nity to realize their inherent potential and thereby contribute to 'an ever-advancing civilization.'[10]

Inextricably linked to these conceptions – of the divine origin of what is fundamentally human, of the necessity that divinely conferred talents and capacities must be discovered, trained and brought to bear in meeting human needs, and of human oneness – is the principle that everyone has the capacity, the right and the obligation to investigate reality for themselves. Human beings must be free to discover and know God. In so doing, they discover their own reality. This process of spiritual discovery – of God and of oneself – is of the essence of life:

> For Bahá'ís, the most fundamental of human rights is the right of each individual to investigate reality for himself or herself, and to benefit from the results of this exploration.[11]

> The primary task of the soul will always be to investigate reality, to live in accordance with the truths of which it becomes persuaded and to accord full respect to the efforts of others to do the same.[12]

Clearly the right to follow one's conscience in matters of religion and belief and the right to education are closely connected, and other rights are necessary to make the fulfilment of this right in everyone's lives possible.[13]

However, it may not be at all obvious in a secular frame of reference why the right to investigate reality for oneself assumes such central importance in the Bahá'í universe of discourse. One might well ask, 'Isn't the right to life prior to the right to investigate reality for oneself (and all that follows from that right)?' Clearly Bahá'ís would never deny the importance of the right to life, physical safety, wellbeing and so on. But the Bahá'í frame of reference includes what is considered in Bahá'í theology to be transcendent and intangible; in a word, eternity. At stake is

10 Weinberg, xx.

11 Bahá'í International Community, 'Development, Democracy and Human Rights', statement to the United Nations World Conference on Human Rights, Vienna, June 1993.

12 The Universal House of Justice, *To the World's Religious Leaders*, April 2002.

13 Clearly the right to live, the right to development and the right to adequate housing would be among those required to make it possible for individuals to investigate reality for themselves.

not just what happens to humans in life ante-mortem but what happens, according to Bahá'í beliefs, post mortem. The relationship of the soul to its God can, under certain circumstances, assume greater importance for an individual than physical life itself – and the readiness of Bahá'ís at different times in the history of the community to lose their lives rather than deny their faith bears witness to the importance of the eternal in Bahá'í life and thought. This strong belief has had particular force for the Bahá'ís in Iran and has helped shape the response of the Iranian Bahá'ís to sustained persecution.

A written comment submitted by the Bahá'í International Community to the fiftieth session of the Commission on Human Rights highlights the importance of dignity and the fulfilment of individual potential:

> Recognition of the oneness of humanity gives rise to an elevated concept of human rights, one that includes the assurance of dignity for each person and the realization of each individual's innate potential. This view differs markedly from an approach to human rights that is limited to preventing interference with the individual's freedom of action.[14]

To live a life that is fully human, that allows the individual, regardless of gender, ethnic origin, religion or belief and so on, to develop their capacities and to put them to use for their own benefit and in service of society requires that the individual be free to investigate reality themselves, to follow their conscience, to be educated, to have the necessary physical and psychological well-being, to experiment with their aesthetic and intellectual capacities, and to struggle to cultivate moral and spiritual insights. All of these are inextricably linked. We have God-given capacities, the argument goes; God requires us to develop those capacities, and governments and individuals alike have the duty of ensuring that it is possible to do this.

---

14 Bahá'í International Community, 'Responsibility to Promote Human Rights', written comment on the Draft Declaration on the Right and Responsibility of Individuals, Groups and Organs of Society to Promote and Protect Universally Recognized Human Rights and Freedoms, submitted to the 50th session of the Commission on Human Rights in response to an invitation from Ibrahima Fall, assistant secretary-general for human rights, issued in accordance with resolution 1993/92 of the Commission on Human Rights, Geneva, December 1993.

> In undertaking this search, a search that is for all practical purposes synonymous with the living of a life that can be said to be truly human, every individual needs the assurance that the exercise of the faculties referred to will enjoy access to whatever benefits, protections, and opportunities can reasonably be provided by the society in which he or she lives. These benefits include . . . not only civil and political rights, but also rights in the area of economic, social, and cultural life.[15]

Human dignity is also a key concept in human rights discourse and, indeed, in the Bahá'í approach to human rights. It is another of those intangible but effective qualities of human life. Societies give a high value to the preservation of dignity, particularly for high status individuals. Loss of dignity can have serious negative psychological and social repercussions for individuals, and deliberate deprivation of dignity is one of the more powerful sanctions that can be applied to persons who are deemed to have transgressed. Preservation of the dignity of the vulnerable, notably of the elderly, is a matter of great concern in many societies.

In the Bahá'í view, dignity stems from what Quakers refer to as 'that of God in everyone'. It is the divine in the human that deserves respect, regardless of the person's outer appearance and circumstances. Protection and promotion of human dignity is the responsibility not just of governments but also of individuals and of society *in toto*:

> If, as in the Bahá'í perspective, the realization of human rights involves promoting human dignity, then it becomes apparent that governments alone cannot implement human rights. Legal protections for human rights and freedom from government oppression are unquestionably essential to human dignity. But dignity is fostered fundamentally by the way one is treated by others.[16]

A useful summary of the principles underpinning and governing the Bahá'í approach to human rights is provided by an article on the 'Bahá'í World' website:

---

15 Bahá'í International Community, 'Development, Democracy and Human Rights'.

16 Bahá'í International Community, 'Responsibility to Promote Human Rights'.

> As recognised in 1993 at the World Conference on Human Rights in Vienna, human rights are universal, indivisible and interdependent. Upon reflection, it can be seen that these concepts stem from our underlying sense of oneness and the subconscious recognition that we are all parts of an interrelated whole.
>
> The basic human rights which flow from this principle, as noted, are now widely recognised. They include, of course, the understanding that human rights must be applied irrespective of differences of racial background, ethnic origin, religious belief or national identity. They encompass the equality of women and men. And they comprehend that all individuals worldwide possess the same rights to freedom of investigation, information and religious practice. They also include an understanding that basic social, economic and cultural rights, such as the right to basic necessities such as food, shelter, and health care, also stem from the understanding that the benefits of medicine, science and technology, the products of agriculture, and the knowledge that is imparted by education come from a collective process of evolution that has led to the creation of our present day civilization. The fruits of civilization are the birthright of all, and steps to promote and protect human rights should keep this understanding clearly in the foreground.[17]

The Bahá'í view, then, is that 'human rights are not arbitrary in nature because they are grounded in the universal realities of human experience and embody values presupposed by a wide range of cultures.' The humanness that underlies local cultures is a universal and 'includes a set of potentialities, not wholly determinable, that are actualized differently by every human being.'[18]

> The logical extension of this point is that all human beings are entitled to flourish, if not as a claim on God or nature, then as a claim on each other. This implies a universal obligation to promote collective well-being and suggests that human morality itself must be universal. Human rights can then be regarded as a vehicle

17 'Human Rights' <http://www.bahai.org/article-1-8-0-3.html>.

18 Both quotes from Weinberg, xx.

> for shaping social conditions 'so as to realize the possibilities of human nature.'[19]

As Spickard says:

> the triumph of human rights ideals is not just an intellectual, but a social-structural matter. It involves the creative shaping of a social order that encourages people to value their stake in each other's lives.[20]

This link between human rights and the creation of a social order that allows individuals to fulfil the potentials that the Bahá'í teachings say they have is crucial and motivates what the Bahá'í community does to promote human rights.

BAHÁ'Í HUMAN RIGHTS ACTIVITIES

Having set out the theological underpinnings of the Bahá'í approach to human rights, I now propose to examine some of the activities undertaken by the Bahá'í community in relation to human rights. These activities fall into two broad areas: promotion of universal human rights in general, and work to protect the human rights of Bahá'í communities that suffer human rights abuses or are deprived of their human rights.

The latter area has focussed largely on the situation of the Bahá'ís in Iran and it is this that I shall consider first. I shall do this from the perspective of one who is part of an international team of Bahá'ís involved in defending the human rights of Bahá'ís in Iran and who takes the lead in work with the British government and parliament. I shall briefly outline the history and present situation of the persecution of the Bahá'ís there and then look at how the Bahá'í International Community and leading national Bahá'í communities work to defend the Bahá'ís in Iran.

19 Ibid; Weinberg is quoting Jack Donnelly, *Universal Human Rights: In Theory and Practice* (Ithaca, NY: Cornell University Press, 1989).

20 Spickard, 18.

DEFENCE OF THE HUMAN RIGHTS OF THE BAHÁ'ÍS IN IRAN

Spickard considers that 'the call for human rights has achieved what amounts to near universal veneration. It has become a cultural icon . . .' But, he says, 'There is, of course, a counter-trend':

> The growth of rights-discourse has occurred despite the opposition of some non-Western regimes, who argue that rights language stems from Western philosophic principles and is thus not applicable to other civilisations. For example, Iran has announced that Islamic law requires an interconnection between religion and the state; so Iran represses Bahá'ís, whom it accuses of heresy.[21]

The Bahá'í community in Iran, founded in 1844, has suffered persecution at the hands of both the religious and the civil authorities of that country from very early in its history.[22] Around twenty thousand Bahá'ís are estimated to have died as a result of pogroms in the nineteenth century. The community has continued to be persecuted periodically throughout the twentieth and twenty-first centuries. From time to time oppression of the Bahá'í community has been part of official policy under both the Pahlavi and the Khomeinist regimes.

Under the Islamic government of Ayatollah Khomeini it quickly became clear that the intention of the new Islamic regime was to extirpate the Bahá'í community from its country of origin. Even before Khomeini returned to Tehran he had condemned the Bahá'ís as a political faction:

> In an interview given by the Ayatollah Khomeini to Professor James Cockcroft of Rutgers University in December 1978, the Ayatollah was asked: 'Will there be either religious or political freedom for the Bahá'ís under an Islamic government?' His answer: 'They are a political faction; they are harmful. They will not be accepted.' Professor Cockcroft then asked: 'How about their freedom of religion – religious practice?' The Ayatollah answered: 'No.'[23]

---

21 Ibid. 6.

22 A useful summary of the persecution of the Bahá'ís is to be found in *The Bahá'í Question: Iran's Secret Blueprint for the Destruction of a Religious Community. An Examination of the Persecution of the Bahá'ís of Iran* (New York: Bahá'í International Community, 1999).

23 Ibid. 20.

Once Khomeini had returned to Iran, the Bahá'í community was rapidly engulfed in a flood of attacks by government agencies and the increasingly powerful Shi'ite clergy.

The holiest Bahá'í shrine in Iran was destroyed in 1979. In 1980 the increasingly powerful Shi'ite clergy began to destroy the leadership of the community, presuming that the ordinary Bahá'ís would quickly give way to social pressure to recant their faith.

The Bahá'í International Community and Bahá'í communities across the world moved to protest to the UN and to their national governments about the treatment of the Bahá'ís in Iran.[24] But despite the growing international outcry, ever larger numbers of Bahá'ís were executed.

Bahá'ís arrested in the 1980s, particularly those who had been members of the elected Bahá'í councils, were systematically tortured, and some were subjected to mock executions or made to witness the torture of friends or family members. The purpose of the torture was almost always to try to force Bahá'ís to recant their faith or to confess to supposed crimes or action against state security.

Perhaps the most notorious of the Bahá'í executions was the hanging of ten Bahá'í women in Shiraz on 18 June 1983. The youngest of the ten was only 17; her 'crime' had been teaching Bahá'í children's classes.

In addition to the more florid examples of human rights abuses, the authorities in Iran have consistently attempted to undermine the survival of the entire Bahá'í community. In the wake of the 1979 revolution, Bahá'ís were refused access to primary, secondary and tertiary education; Bahá'ís were dismissed from their jobs, and the pensions of retired Bahá'í civil servants were terminated. The government expropriated as many of the assets of individual Bahá'ís as it could: homes and personal possessions were confiscated, life-savings swept away, community properties transferred to the state, the assets of Bahá'í welfare agencies confiscated. Bahá'í holy places were desecrated and destroyed, and Bahá'í cemeteries razed. Bahá'ís were forced to bury their dead in barren pieces of land without any of the necessary funerary facilities.

In 2004, two significant pieces of Bahá'í heritage were destroyed,

24 The most complete examination of the interaction between the United Nations human rights system and the case of the Bahá'ís in Iran is to be found in Nazila Ghanea, *Human Rights, the UN and the Bahá'ís in Iran*, (Oxford: George Ronald Publisher, and The Hague: Kluwer Law International, 2002).

either with the connivance or at the instigation of the religious authorities;[25] and properties belonging to Bahá'ís continue to be confiscated.[26] Most seriously, Iranian Bahá'í youth are still deprived of access to higher education, unless they deny their faith.

Given the importance placed upon education by the Bahá'í Faith, this deprivation of access to higher education for its most able young people is extremely serious. It is demoralising for the young people concerned and leads to the increasing impoverishment of the Iranian Bahá'í community. The authorities in Iran have also made a number of attempts to close down the Bahá'í Institute for Higher Education, established by the Bahá'ís in Iran in 1987 as a way of harnessing their own resources to educate Bahá'í youth at university level.[27]

The efforts made by the Iranian authorities to prevent young Bahá'ís from receiving education are instances of a long-standing policy of the Islamic Republic of Iran to suppress the development of the Bahá'í community. In his 1993 report to the UN Commission on Human Rights, Reynaldo Galindo Pohl, special representative on Iran, revealed the existence of a secret memorandum drawn up by the Supreme Revolutionary Council in 1991 on 'the Bahá'í question.'[28] The memorandum makes it clear that the Supreme Revolutionary Council considered the Baha'i question at the express instructions of the supreme leader, Ali Khamenei, and it recommends steps to stifle the development of the Bahá'í community in Iran.

The memorandum was approved by Khamenei's own signature. It has never been disavowed, and the policy it sets out remains in force.

To understand why the government of the Islamic Republic of Iran would wish to suppress the Bahá'í community, which made important

---

25 The grave of a significant early Bahá'í, Mulla Muhammad-'Ali Barfurushi (known as Quddus), and a house in Tehran that had belonged to Mirza Buzurg-e-Nuri, the father of Bahá'u'lláh. It was noted in an article in an Iranian newspaper, *Etemaad*, 1 July 2004, that the latter was an important piece of Islamic architectural heritage.

26 In 2003, for example, several Bahá'í families in the village of Katá in the Buyír-Ahmad region of Iran were dispossessed of properties that provided them with income. Information provided by the Bahá'í International Community.

27 Information provided by the Bahá'í International Community in their periodic 'Update: Situation of the Bahá'ís in Iran', February 2005.

28 Summarised by the special representative in Doc.E/CN.4/1993/41, para. 310. A translation into English of the complete memorandum can be found in *The Bahá'í Question*. It can also be found at <http://www.bahai.org/>.

contributions to the social and economic development of the country in the first half of the twentieth century, one has to pay attention to the theological position of the Shi'ite clerical hierarchy. Friedrich Affolter explains that

> In a country with already low religious diversity, a post-Islamic religion such as the Bahá'í Faith (while in itself a tool for making sense of a society in change) was perceived not only as a contradiction of Islamic logic; it also was perceived as a threat to the legitimacy of Khomeinism. It went counter to the interests and emotional needs of the Iranian mullas and their followers. Hence, Bahá'ís were declared heretics, deviants and destructive ideologists who ought to be exterminated. Doing so did not only help to get rid of a perceived threat; in addition, it also strengthened and consolidated 'ties of closeness' within the Shí'i faith community.[29]

Affolter goes on to explain that the current Iranian regime, although 'seeking to create a system . . . capable of enhancing the spiritual and socio-economic liberation of the oppressed', is propagating an authoritarian political culture:

> This time, however, it is based on an assertion of divine legitimacy for an Iranian Shí'i population socialized into subjugation to authority, communal identity, and acceptance of the clergy's claim of the divine right to lead. In this context, scapegoating anything that is perceived as a threat to the clergy's legitimacy becomes a political imperative.[30]

If Affolter's analysis is correct, the persecution of the Bahá'ís is based partly in theology and partly in power politics.

Ghanea's analysis would seem to add weight to this perspective.[31] She considers that her extensive study of the treatment of the Bahá'ís in Iran, which she sees as a test case for the UN's human rights system, has implications for the relationship between religion and the State and for the relationship between religion and human rights.

---

29 Friedrich W. Affolter, 'The Specter of Ideological Genocide: The Bahá'ís of Iran', in *War Crimes, Genocide, and Crimes Against Humanity*, 1/1 (January 2005), 59–89.

30 Ibid. 74–5.

31 Ghanea, 215–16.

> The main question that emerges is that of religious 'oppositional' communities – defined here *not* as those which are politically opposed to the government or those which demand territorial independence or resort to the use of force but those which are *construed* as 'oppositional' by the majority in historical or political mythology. In States where religion (or the absence of religion) is still seen as a factor in relation to national identity, and therefore of loyalty, there have been problematic human rights consequences owing to difference of belief being perceived as a threat. . . . the Bahá'í case in Iran clearly indicates a case where even individual human rights have been made conditional on coercing a particular religious affinity and where members were targeted for legally-sanctioned, systematic and intense persecution.[32]

It would seem clear that the underlying motivation for the breach by the Iranian government of the human rights of the Bahá'ís in Iran over many years is (and has always been) the desire to eliminate a community that is, according to the interpretation of Islam by the Shi'ite clergy, religiously heterodox and ineluctably in conflict with the traditional understanding that there can be no prophet after Muhammad.[33] Religious and civil authorities, whose legitimacy is based on an Islamist ideology, cannot countenance the survival of a community which they see as challenging everything they stand for.

Article 13 of the Iranian Constitution makes it clear that Iranian Zoroastrians, Jews and Christians are the only recognised minority religious groups free to practise their religions within the limits of the law. It follows, therefore, that Bahá'ís are not free so to do, and long experience shows that the Iranian authorities hold the Bahá'ís to be 'unprotected infidels'.

Representatives of the Iranian government have repeatedly and publicly denied that the Bahá'í community is a religious minority at all, let alone the largest religious minority in Iran, a claim made by the Bahá'í International Community and backed by references in a range of UN documents. They have also subjected the Bahá'ís to a range of wholly

32 Ibid. 216.

33 For a discussion from a Bahá'í perspective of the meaning of the phrase 'Seal of the Prophets' see Moojan Momen, *Islam and the Bahá'í Faith* (Oxford: George Ronald Publisher, 2000), 34 ff.

unsustainable accusations: that they were supporters of the Pahlavi regime; that they are agents of Zionism; that they are involved with prostitution, adultery and immorality; and that they are heretics or enemies of Islam. All these accusations have been consistently and effectively refuted by those involved in the defence of the human rights of the Iranian Bahá'ís.

Defence of the rights of the Bahá'ís in Iran has been co-ordinated over many years by the United Nations Offices of the Bahá'í International Community (BIC) in New York and Geneva, with the aim of seeking the full emancipation of the Bahá'í community in Iran to practise their religion freely and publicly.[34]

The whole strategy of the Bahá'í International Community and of Bahá'í National Spiritual Assemblies in support of the BIC is based on arguing from international human rights norms that the abusive treatment of the Bahá'ís in Iran is egregious and that the justifications put forward by the Iranian government for its treatment of the Bahá'í minority are wholly fallacious. Iran as a State Party to all the relevant UN Covenants must protect the human and civil rights of all its citizens. As Professor Abdelfattah Amor, Special Rapporteur on religious intolerance to the 1996 Commission on Human Rights, stated in his report to the Commission:

> The Special Rapporteur deems it important that Iran ... should reconsider its attitude to the Bahá'í Faith, in the interests of freedom of religion or belief, in compliance with its international commitments and teachings to the effect that religion admits of no constraint. Whatever perception certain Iranians may have of the Bahá'í question, it is for the State, which is responsible for all its citizens, to focus on constants rather than variables and consider each individual and each minority, as repositories of rights

34 The affairs of the Bahá'í community throughout the world are governed by elected councils or assemblies at local and national levels. The world governing council of the Bahá'í community is also an elected body and is called the Universal House of Justice. The Bahá'í International Community is an international NGO with consultative rights at ECOSOC; every National Spiritual Assembly or national Bahá'í governing council is an affiliate of the Bahá'í International Community.

> and obligations, to be worthy of respect and attention and to have the right to consideration and protection.[35]

It should be noted that the second sentence of the paragraph cited above is wholly consistent with the principles underpinning the Bahá'í approach to human rights in general, as set out in the first section of this paper.

The full emancipation of the Bahá'í community will be considered by the BIC as achieved once the Iranian government has fully implemented a series of recommendations concerning the situation of the Bahá'ís in Iran made by the Special Rapporteur, who calls on the government of Iran to allow Bahá'ís access to education and employment, the right to citizenship, freedom to bury and honour their dead, freedom of movement, security of the person, re-establishment of the Bahá'í institutions, non-discrimination on grounds of religion and belief, return of community properties, and legal and human-rights training for the judiciary.

It should also be noted that the Bahá'ís do not seek to become a 'recognised' religion under the Iranian Constitution, but seek, rather, 'the right to freedom of thought, conscience and religion' and the 'freedom, either individually or in community with others and in public or private, to manifest [their] religion or belief in worship, observance, practice and teaching,' as set out in the International Covenant on Civil and Political Rights (Article 18), an instrument to which Iran is a State Party.

In other words, the Bahá'í community does not in any way seek exceptional treatment, but works, as a matter of principle fully within the international human rights framework, to win for the Bahá'ís in Iran what should be theirs by right.

PROMOTION OF UNIVERSAL HUMAN RIGHTS

In addition to defending the human rights of the Bahá'ís in Iran (and in other countries when necessary), the Bahá'í community nationally and internationally does a lot of work to promote universal human rights. As

35 Doc.E/CN.4/1996/95/Add.2. BIC has set these recommendations out as a series of benchmarks which can be used to measure progress in the phased implementation of the Special Rapporteur's recommendations. The Special Rapporteur on Religious Intolerance is now known as the Special Rapporteur on Freedom of Religion and

explained towards the beginning of this paper, Bahá'í religious principles are such that the community is bound to make its views known in relevant forums and do what work it can in promoting the principles and practices of human rights.

However, to grasp the nature of the work that the Bahá'í community does in this field it is essential also to understand that any aspect of the Bahá'í teachings must be seen in the context of the whole corpus of Bahá'í scripture. Certain themes appear again and again in Bahá'u'lláh's writings. As already mentioned, unity is an overarching theme in the Bahá'í universe of discourse – everything else is seen in the light of unity. Justice is another, related, central theme – and for Bahá'u'lláh, justice is something that starts with the individual's own investigation of reality and goes on to embrace not only judicial applications of justice, but social and economic justice as well.

The implication for Bahá'í practice is that every element of life is interconnected with every other element. In a particularly powerful passage in his writings, 'Abdu'l-Bahá reminds the Bahá'ís of a saying of Bahá'u'lláh, 'Ye are all the fruits of one tree, the leaves of one branch.' 'Abdu'l-Bahá continues:

> Thus hath He likened this world of being to a single tree, and all its peoples to the leaves thereof, and the blossoms and fruits. It is needful for the bough to blossom, and leaf and fruit to flourish, and upon the interconnection of all parts of the world-tree, dependeth the flourishing of leaf and blossom, and the sweetness of the fruit.
>
> For this reason must all human beings powerfully sustain one another . . . Let them at all times concern themselves with doing a kindly thing for one of their fellows, offering to someone love, consideration, thoughtful help. Let them see no one as their enemy, or as wishing them ill, but think of all humankind as their friends; regarding the alien as an intimate, the stranger as a companion, staying free of prejudice, drawing no lines.

The moral imperative in these lines is one that 'Abdu'l-Bahá lived by;

Belief. The current Special Rapporteur is Mrs Asma Jahangir.

it connects very strongly with how Bahá'ís strive to live and how Bahá'í individuals and institutions work to make human rights a reality.

These themes of human oneness, of equality of treatment for all, of justice in all its forms, are ones that run through the many statements made by the Bahá'í International Community to the UN since 1947. A quick survey of issues addressed by these statements indicates both the range of concerns that the Bahá'í community believes require attention and the way in which the above-mentioned central Bahá'í principles are applied to finding solutions to the world's problems. Issues include human rights, the advancement of women, global prosperity (including care for the environment) and moral development. Much is being done by the Bahá'í community on international, national and local levels, through public statements and practical projects, to develop and promote good practice in all of these areas. The Bahá'í International Community has addressed statements to all the major UN conferences, to the General Assembly and to a wide range of UN commissions and agencies. A small and fairly random sample of statements (in no particular order) includes:

- A Bahá'í Declaration of Human Obligations and Rights – statement by the National Spiritual Assembly of the Bahá'ís of the United States to the first session of the UN Commission on Human Rights, February 1947.
- Human Rights and Extreme Poverty – statement to the UN Sub-Commission on the Prevention of Discrimination and Protection of Minorities, August 1994.
- Responsibility to Promote Human Rights – written comment on the Draft Declaration on the Right and Responsibility of Individuals, Groups and Organs of Society to Promote and Protect Universally Recognised Human Rights and Fundamental Freedoms, December 1993.
- Development, Democracy and Human Rights – statement to the UN World Conference on Human Rights, June 1993.
- Protection of Minorities – written statement presented to the 55th session of the UN Commission on Human Rights.
- Promoting Religious Tolerance – statement to the UN Commission on Human Rights, January 1995.

- The Role of Religion in Promoting the Advancement of Women – written statement to the UN Fourth World Conference on Women, Beijing, September 1995.
- The Right to Education – written statement to the 56th session of the UN Commission on Human Rights, March 2000.
- United Nations Decade on Human Rights Education – written statement to the 53rd session of the UN Commission on Human Rights, March 1997.

In making these and many other statements, the Bahá'í International Community believes that it can help shape the thinking of governments and influential groups and individuals about the principles and practices of human rights. The statements always address the headline issue from a foundation of the central Bahá'í principles outlined above and others that derive from them. They do not – and could not, given the Bahá'í stance on non-involvement in partisan politics – suggest political solutions to these issues, but rather show how the Bahá'í spiritual principles, thoughtfully applied, will create a foundation for a new social order in which the abuses under consideration would no longer happen. For example, the statement on Human Rights and Extreme Poverty shows how the application of spiritual principles will change the nature of society:

> The Baha'i approach to the problem of extreme poverty is based on the application of spiritual principles. The economic relationships of a society reflect the values of its members. Therefore, to transform those relationships, man's character must be transformed. Until justice is valued over greed, the gap between the rich and the poor will continue to widen, and the dream of sustainable economic growth, peace and prosperity will elude our grasp. Sensitizing mankind to the vital role of spiritual values in solving economic problems will, we are convinced, create a new impetus for change.[36]

The emphasis is always on the need for transformation of individuals and society, and the inextricable connection between the two is shown.

36 Bahá'í International Community, *Human Rights and Extreme Poverty*, statement to the UN Sub-Commission on the Prevention of Discrimination and Protection of Minorities, Geneva, August 1994.

And, while legal protections for human rights are understood to be necessary, they are clearly not sufficient. We have a *collective* and pressing responsibility for ensuring that the human rights of every individual are protected and fostered:

> it is impossible to implement human 'rights' without a sense of collective responsibility. Indeed, if the whole of humanity is one interconnected body, then an injury to any member is an injury to the body as a whole. Thus it behooves every individual member of the human family to take action whenever and wherever human rights violations occur.[37]

An examination of the meaning of the concept of 'responsibility' takes us right back to our starting point:

> Yet in the Bahá'í perspective, the concept of 'responsibility' in the context of human rights encompasses the responsibility devolving upon every person, as a divinely-created being, to recognize the essential oneness of the human race and to promote the human rights of others with this motivation.[38]

Bahá'í communities around the world also undertake a wide range of projects to learn in practice how the Bahá'í principles can be applied to human rights (broadly understood) and other concerns. In some countries the Bahá'í community has encouraged governments to introduce human rights education as an essential part of the curriculum:

> As we educate our children to accept diversity as part of the human condition and to extend respect and full human rights to the entire human family, civilization will benefit from an unimaginable wealth of contributions.
>
> In that respect, human rights education could be considered basic education for life in the modern world.[39]

Even the work done by Bahá'ís in many countries to educate and train

---

37 Bahá'í International Community, *Responsibility to Promote Human Rights.*

38 Ibid.

39 Bahá'í International Community, *United Nations Decade on Human Rights Education*, statement to the 53rd session of the UN Commission on Human Rights, Geneva, March 1997.

children, youth, women and men in a wide range of knowledge and skills, from basic literacy to agriculture and village banking, can be understood as a major contribution to human rights by empowering the individuals and communities concerned with a new sense of purpose and dignity to manage their own lives and to interact on a more equal footing with governments and large organisations and businesses. As 'Abdu'l-Bahá commented in *Secret of Divine Civilization*, his seminal work on the creation of well-developed society:

> And the honour and distinction of the individual consist in this, that he among all the world's multitudes should become a source of social good. Is any larger bounty conceivable than this, that an individual, looking within himself, should find that by the confirming grace of God he has become the cause of peace and well-being, of happiness and advantage to his fellow men? No, by the one true God, there is no greater bliss, no more complete delight.[40]

CONCLUSION

From the foregoing it becomes apparent that, far from being in conflict with modern human rights norms, the Bahá'í Faith's foundational principles – to be found in the writings of its founder, Bahá'u'lláh, and of his eldest son and successor as head of the community, 'Abdu'l-Bahá – are entirely congruent with the principles of human rights as found in the Universal Declaration of Human Rights and successive UN human rights covenants. The Bahá'í International Community has consistently and openly supported, through statements and through involvement in the UN human rights system, the development and implementation of international human rights law. National Bahá'í communities and their governing councils have, within the limitations of their resources, reinforced the work of the BIC, working with their respective governments and with partner human rights NGOs to build a culture of human rights across the world.

Regrettably the Bahá'ís have also had to defend the human rights of their co-religionists in Iran (and in some other countries) over a number of years. Working with national governments and with the UN human

40 'Abdu'l-Bahá, *Secret of Divine Civilization*, 2–3.

rights system, the Bahá'í community has developed a considerable level of expertise as an international human rights NGO; its work is widely respected by diplomats and by other human rights NGOs. It has been effective, without resort to violence or to partisan political manoeuvring, in persuading governments to help stay the hand of the oppressor, but this aspect of its work is far from over. Much remains to be done before the Bahá'ís in Iran can be said to be fully emancipated, to be free to manifest their faith in accordance with international law.

The motivating vision of the Bahá'í community is the development of a peaceful and united global civilisation. Promotion of universal human rights is integral to the rest of the work the community does to help make this vision a reality.

Section Two

Models, Tensions and Frameworks

CHAPTER 9

'Human Rights', 'Religion' and the 'Secular': Variant Configurations of Religion(s), State(s) and Society(ies)

Paul Weller

'HUMAN RIGHTS' AND 'RELIGION': TERMS AND RELATIONSHIPS

The relationship between 'human rights' and 'religion' is a multi-faceted one that can be considered in relation to a number of dimensions, including the historical, philosophical, legal and theological, to name but a few.[1] The complexity of this relationship is compounded by the fact that neither 'human rights' nor 'religion' are, in themselves, self-evident or straightforward concepts. For this reason, whenever they are referred to within this chapter, they appear within inverted commas. This is done not in order to 'deconstruct away' the importance or significance of either, but to act as a reminder that, if we are seeking to understand and engage with what is signified by both of these words, there is a need to recognise the plurality of meanings that are associated with them, both in theoretical debate and in terms of historical forms through which they are actualised.[2]

Thus, 'human rights' can be considered either in the sense of the general corpus of thinking that relates to what the French Revolution celebrated as the 'Rights of Man' – *liberté, égalité, fraternité*; in the popular and more generalised contemporary sense of 'human rights' as being to do with matters of equitable treatment in relation to differences of gender, race, religion, age or sexual orientation; or in terms of the specific, limited and precise meanings of 'human rights' found within the vari-

1 For discussions of some of this, see: Janis and Evans, *Religion and International Law*; Runzo, Martin and Sharma, *Human Rights and Responsibilities in the World Religions*; and Ruston, *Human Rights and the Image of God*.

2 It should, though, be acknowledged that there are those who do wish to argue that the category of 'religion' is one that is both an inaccurate and unhelpful construction of realities that would better be described in other ways. See, for example, Fitzgerald, *The Ideology of Religious Studies*. There are also those who seek to question the universal applicability of human rights, on the basis of an extreme relativism and/or as justification for the perpetration of unjust and discriminatory treatment. It is no part of the argument of this paper to give succour or support to such positions.

ous instruments of international law such as the Universal Declaration of Human Rights and the European Convention on Human Rights and Fundamental Freedoms, and/or as incorporated into national law, as in the United Kingdom's Human Rights Act of 1998.

'Religion' has also been understood in a variety of ways in different places and times. Both popularly, and in some legal contexts (for example, historically, in charity law in England and Wales), religion has often been understood as relating to belief in a god or divine being. Such an understanding, however, is restrictive in that it does not embrace the reality of generally accepted world 'religious' traditions such as Buddhism or Jainism that are 'a-theistic', let alone that of some of the so-called 'New Religious Movements', which may not be seen by some as 'religious' at all in the conventional sense.[3]

In terms of etymology, the English word 'religion' derives from the Latin *religare*, which is related to the idea of a 'binding' together. Apart from this etymology, however, there is a wide range of definitions of 'religion' to be found in theological, sociological and anthropological approaches to its study. Among these there is some overlap, but there are also significant differences. Perhaps the best that can be achieved are provisional 'working definitions', one of which the present author has proposed elsewhere, and which is that 'religion' is

> a way of living in which some form of identification (either in a weaker and more general sense, or in a stronger and more specific sense of alignment with particular movements, communities and/or organisational forms) is often (though not always or necessarily) to be found in conjunction with different forms of 'believing' (in various combinations of certain values, ideals and doctrines) and can be expressed through 'practice' (that is related to shared symbols, rituals, observances and ethical orientations).[4]

In addition to the complexity of the individual concepts and historical forms taken by both 'religion' and 'human rights', the *relationships*

3 The terminology 'New Religious Movements' is generally used by scholars in the study of religion to refer in a non-pejorative way to traditions and movements which, in popular and media debate, are often referred to with strongly (negative) evaluative overtones as 'sects' and/or 'cults'.

4 Weller, 'The Dimensions and Dynamics of Religious Discrimination', 66.

between 'human rights' and 'religion' can also be considered in a variety of ways. This can include consideration of the relationship between 'religion' and 'human rights' in terms of the articles that deal with 'religion' as a part of international 'human rights' law, including those clauses that deal with 'religion' itself as a specific 'human right' in terms of (the absolute) freedom of (internal) belief and (the more limited) freedom of its expression that is found in international law.[5]

Historically, of course, many majority religious groupings have been resistant to the emergence of such religious freedom and have only grudgingly and/or pragmatically come to accept an approach to religious diversity based on toleration. At the same time, it should be noted that there have been some religious traditions that have always upheld a commitment to religious freedom, understood not merely as a concession to social and political change, but as a principle of theological anthropology rooted in a particular understanding of the nature of the divine and the human and the relationship between them.[6]

Nevertheless, from the general philosophical perspective of the 'religions', there is at least some degree of tension between a way of thinking and acting that emphasises the 'rights' in 'human rights' and the kind of approach found historically in religious traditions that considers the responsibilities and obligations of human beings as being of equal importance as their rights. Related to this, there are also a set of questions about the emphasis on the 'human' in 'human rights' when 'human rights' are detached from acknowledgement of any rooting of this within the 'ultimate' and the 'unconditioned' that 'religions' claim to be the ultimately necessary foundation and guarantor of the 'human'.

However, as has already been noted with regard to the 'human right'

5 Thus, Article 9 of the European Convention on Human Rights and Fundamental Freedsom states that 'Everyone has the right to freedom of thought, conscience and religion; this right includes freedom to change his religion or belief and freedom, either alone or in community with others and in public or in private, to manifest his religion or belief, in worship, teaching, practice and observance', and that 'Freedom to manifest one's religion or beliefs shall be subject only to such limitations as are prescribed by law and are necessary in a democratic society in the interests of public safety, for the protection of public order, health or morals, or for the protection of the rights or freedoms of others.'

6 For example, for an overview of the Baptist Christian tradition's radical theological commitment to religious freedom and its contemporary relevance see Jordan, *The Development of Religious Toleration*, and Weller, *Time for a Change*.

of religious freedom itself, looked at historically it has appeared to many that 'religions' have often been concerned to prevent the emergence of 'human rights.' But even where there is not explicit opposition and conflict, a series of difficulties can arise in relation to the so-called 'hierarchy of rights' between those 'human rights' deriving from 'religion' as a 'human right,' and other 'human rights.' In particular, these difficulties concern those areas of contemporary 'rights' discourse and movements that have, at least historically, been in tension with the teaching and practice of a range of religious traditions – in other words, especially matters relating to issues of gender roles and equality and the genital sexual expression of gay and lesbian sexual orientation.

It is because of these and other similar tensions that discussions about the relationship between 'religion' and 'human rights' often focus on the problems that arise from 'religion.' Within an overall historical perspective, such a focus – at least within the European context – is, perhaps, understandable. After all, one of the most important aspects of the historical development of the 'human rights' tradition in the European context has been the struggle for the right *not to believe*.[7]

From this perspective, the persistence among some 'religious' people of an apparent nostalgia for the recreation of a pre-modern set of social and political arrangements in which 'religions' are the dominant and integrating force in societies is problematic. This is especially so when it moves beyond nostalgia into specific social and political – and sometimes, tragically, military or terror-based – projects to re-establish the previous dominance of particular 'religious' traditions, such as those found in the Serb Orthodox nationalism in the territories of the Former Federal Republic of Yugoslavia; the attempts of the Hindutva strand of Indian politics to 'Hinduize' the Indian state; and the stance taken locally by such groups as the Taliban in Afghanistan, or globally by radical international 'Islamist' and 'jihadist' movements.

But 'religion' can also be felt to be threatening to 'human rights' when the force exerted does not operate through the expression of direct physical violence, but rather through strong religious teachings and their socialising ethos and effects, as in the perceptions of many in relation

7 Berman, *A History of Atheism in Britain*.

to the Vatican's stance on the use of condoms in the face of the HIV pandemic.

Thus it is not surprising that, from the perspective of many, 'religion' and 'human rights' are, if not opposites, then at least in serious historical and contemporary tension and that, in the relationship between them, 'religion' can often be seen as opposed to at least some aspects of 'human rights'.

'HUMAN RIGHTS', 'RELIGION' AND THE 'SECULAR'

Having given some preliminary consideration to the meaning of the basic realities signified by the terminology of 'religion' and 'human rights' and the relationships between them, this chapter now moves on to focus on its central argument concerning the relationships between 'religion' and 'human rights'.

In doing so, the central argument of this chapter is that, in a world existing on the other side of the impact of a historical condition known as modernity,[8] the relationships between 'religion' and 'human rights' can only be appropriately considered within the context of a critical understanding of, and engagement with, the impact of another basic reality that is signified by the terminology of the 'secular'. This, it is argued, represents the often 'silent' – present if unarticulated – dimension of the 'in between' when the relationships between 'religion' and 'human rights' are discussed.

It is often argued that it has been the rise of the 'secular' spirit and its increasing adoption by states and societies that has enabled some degree of religious co-existence to overcome the inheritance of religious absolutism. In the judgement of post-Enlightenment secular liberals, religions

8 The present historical period is described in this way in order to leave on one side the debates over the extent to which the conditions of what is identified as 'post-modernity' have either superseded or live alongside those of modernity. This is not to ignore the importance of that debate, aspects of which will be referred to in the conclusion of the paper in so far as they have a bearing on particular interpretations of the 'secular'. But for the purposes of this part of the paper's argument, the critical issue to note is the transformation that has occurred from previous predominantly pre-modern or agrarian visions of society – constituted on the basis of Weber's *Gemeinschaften* – to forms of social organisation that can be characterised by Weber's *Gesellschaften*.

have been responsible for an enormous amount of bloodshed and human suffering, and for this reason it is safer to keep them marginalised from public life. Notwithstanding the already noted nostalgia for a previous order and way of being still to be found among some 'religious' people, that there is considerable truth in this judgement should be, and often is, acknowledged by the 'religions'.

The emergence of the 'secular' as a basis for social and political life and organisation is clearly, at least in part, a historical reaction to the horror of the European inheritance of the Inquisition and the impact of the seventeenth century Wars of Religion. This reaction and these new developments issued into the nineteenth- and twentieth-century conflicts between liberalism, socialism and 'religion' that gave birth to the contemporary idea and reality of the 'secular', which this chapter argues needs to be considered alongside, and as part of, any reflection of the contemporary relationship between 'human rights' and 'religion'.

But 'secular', like 'religion' and 'human rights', is also not a straightforward theoretical concept. It too manifests itself in a wide variety of historical forms. However, it is commonly the case that, in debates on the relationship between 'human rights' and 'religion', when its presence is specifically articulated, the dimension of the 'secular' is frequently referred to in ways that appear to view its meaning as self-evident and unproblematic. This, in turn, contributes to the phenomenon noted earlier – namely, that discussions on the relationship between 'religion' and 'human rights' often end up being constructed in terms of the problems of 'human rights' that arise from 'religion'.

It is, however, the argument of this chapter that, while it remains important to acknowledge that such problems exist and to engage with them, it may also be the case that at least some of the problems and issues in the relationship between 'human rights' and 'religion' can be located in particular theoretical understandings and historical actualisations of the 'secular'. Furthermore, it is argued that this is especially likely to be the case where the meaning and import of the 'secular' is not explicitly considered but remains an unspoken, invisible and assumed – yet ever present – dimension of the debate.

This can be illustrated from a November 1998 Council of Europe seminar that took place under the title, 'Religion and the Integration of Immigrants'. The title of the seminar, of course, in itself already implicitly indicates where the locus of the problem was seen to lie –primarily with 'migrants' and 'religion' rather than with the 'host' societies and their 'secular' states. In an all-European context, issues relating to migration and immigration were, of course, historically the predominant concerns of western European capitalist states and societies, rather than of the countries in eastern and central Europe with communist governments. Thus, in the European setting at the end of the twentieth century, the challenges arising from religious diversity had often been framed on the basis of generally shared western European liberal capitalist assumptions about the nature of the 'secular'.[9]

However, the particular Council of Europe seminar under consideration took place at a time when the post-communist transitional states and societies of central and eastern Europe were also beginning to wrestle with the issues arising from the development of more pluralizing populations. Partly because of the different history of the 'secular' from which these states and societies had only recently emerged,[10] the seminar took an interestingly different turn when it recognised not only the need to examine the challenges posed by the integration of the various religions in a plural society, but also the need to think critically about what might differentially be meant by the 'secular' as an often assumed framework for such integration. Thus, one of the conclusions of the seminar was that 'It was underlined that the use of the term "secular", referring to the relationship between the State and religion, should be re-examined and clarified on a pan-European level, with a view to reaching a common understanding.'[11]

If such diversity of understanding about the 'secular' exists in Europe as a context for the relationship between 'religion' and 'human rights' then, when considered in global perspective, the possible meanings and significance of the 'secular' may be even more diverse. Thus, in an article on 'religion' and 'secularity' in Nigeria, Dopamu identifies eight alternative meanings of the 'secular state' and argues that

9 Notwithstanding the considerable differences that actually existed between, say, *laïcité* in France, the presence of Church of England bishops in the House of Lords in England, and the 'corporatist' system of the Federal Republic of Germany.

10 In other words one that was informed by Marxist–Leninist historical materialism and the monopolising claims of 'the Party' with regard to the public sphere.

11 Council of Europe Directorate of Social and Economic Affairs, *Religion and the Integration of Immigrants*, 173.

> a secular state is one where one or a combination of the following is prevalent: (*a*) A state where religion is suppressed. (*b*) A state where religion is not given official recognition. (*c*) A state where the government is neutral in matters of religion. (*d*) A state where there is freedom of worship. (*e*) A state where no religion is imposed on the people or where there is no state religion. (*f*) A state where advancing science and technology have limited the sphere of influence of religion. (*g*) A state where there is a waning of institutional religion or where fewer people regularly attend religious services. (*h*) A state where there is a separation of religious from political, legal, economic or other institutions.[12]

Each of these basic alternative understandings of the 'secular' can lead to significantly different constitutional, legal and practical consequences for the relationships between 'human rights' and 'religion'. And it is to exploring four broad constitutional, social, political and historical 'contextual patterns' for these relationships, each of which has historical and contemporary examples, that the present discussion now turns.

In relation to each of the identified 'contextual patterns', there are also a variety of subtle variants, the full range of which cannot be explored here due to limitations of space. But an exploration of four basic patterns will at least illustrate the historical, political and philosophical diversity that is associated with understandings of the 'secular' and which can therefore – as the third part of the dynamic – have a bearing upon the relationship between 'religion' and 'human rights'.

SEPARATION OF CHURCH AND STATE (WITH RELIGIOSITY)

One of the most famous 'contextual patterns' for how the 'secular' frames the relationship between 'religion' and 'human rights' is the historical, constitutional and legal inheritance of the United States of America, with its constitutional guarantees of religious freedom and separation between religion and the state. Franklin Littell has argued that the roots of this way of dealing with both cultural and religious plurality are to be found in the history of the emigration to the New World, in which, of

12 Dopamu, 'Religion in a Secular State'.

course, many people migrated at least partly in search of greater religious freedom.[13]

Nevertheless, both before and at the time of American independence there was actually a considerable variety of practice regarding both the free exercise and the establishment of religion. Lord Baltimore's Roman Catholic colony of Maryland had a high degree of freedom, as did the Pennsylvania of the Quaker William Penn. However, the Articles of Confederation required neither separation nor liberty. In the young Republic such questions were initially matters for the individual states to decide. Nevertheless, strong traditions of religious liberty and the separation of religion and State did emerge – some of them being themselves rooted in a religious vision of the world. For example, in 1636 Roger Williams (who became a Baptist in 1639, founded the first Baptist church in North America and was author of the famous *The Bloudy Tenent of Persecution for Cause of Conscience*) founded the State of Rhode Island that upheld freedom for all, including non-believers.

One of the traditional explanations for why the non-establishment of religion took hold in the USA is that the number and variety of Churches made establishment impractical. For some, such as Benjamin Franklin, this was indeed a key pragmatic argument. But it should be noted that Anglo-Saxon Protestants dominated the fifty-six signatories of the American Declaration of Independence. Regarding the Anglicans and Presbyterians among the founding figures of the USA, Scottish journalist Stewart Lamont commented that 'The remarkable factor was that these men broke with tradition and created for the first time a system which made religion free from state intervention.'[14]

James Madison advocated the non-establishment of religion on the basis of a conviction that the highest form of religion is based on the voluntary principle. In the 1786 Virginian Act for Establishing Religious Freedom, promoted by Thomas Jefferson and James Madison, it was stated:

> Be it enacted by the General Assembly, That no man shall be compelled to frequent or support any religious worship, place of ministry whatsoever, nor shall be enforced, restrained, molested,

13 Littell, *From State Church to Religious Pluralism.*

14 Lamont, *Church and State*, 58.

> or burthened in his body or goods, nor shall otherwise suffer on account of his religious opinions or belief; but that all men shall be free to profess, and by argument to maintain, their opinion in matters of religion; and that the same shall in no wise diminish, enlarge, or affect their civil capabilities.[15]

It was further declared that 'the rights hereby asserted are of the natural rights of mankind, and that if any act shall be hereafter passed to repeal the present, or to narrow its operation, such act will be an infringement of natural right.' This was not, therefore, the granting of a grudging toleration arising out of political expediency. Rather, it was the recognition of what was seen as a pre-existing and natural human right that led to the First Amendment to the United States Constitution, signed on 17 September 1789. This stated that 'Congress shall make no law respecting an establishment of religion, or prohibiting the exercise thereof". This amendment in due course became known as 'The Jeffersonian Wall' after Thomas Jefferson who, in 1802, referred to the amendment as 'a wall separating church from state.'

However, while the basic constitutional position has been maintained, the scope, application and effect of the First Amendment has long been debated in the American courts, and its meaning and significance has been contested among the American public.[16] Case law regarding establishment issues has not always been consistent, and considerable debate has taken place concerning the balance between the 'no establishment' and the 'free exercise' clauses of the constitution. The debate, whose basic shape has been explored by a number of writers, has been between those holding that the constitution implies a strict 'separationist' position and, on the other hand, those seen as 'accommodationists.'[17]

In practice, one clause of the First Amendment has often been seen as superior to, and a precondition of, the other. Following the Second World War, the Supreme Court took a more so-called 'Jeffersonian' view of the need for a 'wall' between religion and state. In the 1960s, secularists had morning prayer banned in schools, emphasising 'neutrality'

15 Quoted in Lamont, 58.

16 See Murphy, *Religious Freedom: Separation and Free Exercise.*

17 See Abraham, 'The Status of the First Amendment's Religion Clauses'; Baker, 'Belief and Action'; Pfeffer, *God, Caesar and the Constitution*; 'The Establishment Clause: the never-ending conflict', in White and Zimmerman, *An Unsettled Arena*, 69–71.

and the 'non-establishment' of religion as the underlying theme of the establishment clause. At other times, the 'free exercise' of religion has been emphasised.

In fact, issues relating to schooling have often been a focus for these constitutional debates. And, as a result of a reaction by religious people to a trend in the constitutional decisions that seemed to marginalise religion, the Supreme Court began to distinguish between what has been argued to be an allowable indirect support for the 'pupil welfare' of those attending religious schools and what came to be known as direct 'parochial' help. In a landmark of the debate over the First Amendment provisions, in the case of *Lemon* v. *Kurtzman* (1971), a so-called 'tripartite hermeneutic' was developed for interpreting and applying the Constitution. This case involved the states of Rhode Island and Pennsylvania giving financial support to secular materials and teachers in non-public schools – a practice eventually found to be unconstitutional. However, the hermeneutic principles established through this case were that religion should neither be inhibited nor advanced; that government should not become excessively entangled with religion; and that government should maintain its secular purpose.

The case of *Wisconsin* v. *Yoder* set forth three principles of 'free exercise' to balance the 'no establishment' principles of *Lemon*. These principles concern whether a belief is legitimately religious and an activity restricted by a state pervasively religious; whether the state action burdens or inhibits free exercise; and whether it is justified by a compelling state interest which requires these, rather than less restrictive, means. More recently, the Religious Freedom Restoration Act 1993 prohibited Federal and State governmental bodies from 'substantially [burdening] religious exercise without compelling justification' of a kind that 'is the least restrictive means of furthering that . . . interest.'[18]

One of the paradoxes of the position in the USA is, of course, that alongside the basic principle of the separation of Church and State, courtroom oaths and 'swearings-in' are also found. Then there are the national holidays of Thanksgiving and Memorial Day and the rituals associated with the American flag and the pledge of allegiance to a 'Nation under God'. There is the national motto of 'In God We Trust' and there are the

18 *Religious Freedom Restoration Act*, sections 2(a)(3) and 3(b)(2), respectively.

investitures of presidents who often appeal to 'God-language' in a way that is rare among European politicians. Thus, while there is a constitutional separation between particular religions and the state, this is not based on an ideology of secularism. Rather, the religiosity of civil society is an important part of the public and political culture.

Reflecting on this phenomenon, Mirsky has argued that civil religion is a necessary response of a disestablished society, arguing that 'Its abiding presence seems to speak to some curious need for religious symbols and rhetoric in a seemingly disestablished republic.'[19] Taking this further, Piérard and Linder have defined 'civil religion' in the American sense of the word as 'the widespread acceptance by a people of perceived religio-political traits regarding their nation's history and destiny. It relates their society to the realm of absolute meaning, enables them to look at their political community in a special sense, and provides the vision which ties the nation together as an integrated whole.'[20]

Others have critiqued this phenomenon on either theological or political grounds. Theologically, it can be seen as confused and inchoate. Politically, it has been argued that, as a binding myth, it can be internally exclusive of those groups of people that did not generate or share in the myths. Externally, it can manifest itself in a 'zealous nationalism'[21] that pits its forces of 'good' against those of 'evil' in an almost Manichean way, and which is then projected globally through the use of overwhelming economic and military power.

THE SECULARIST SECULAR TRADITION

A 'contextual pattern' for the 'secular' in the relationship between 'religion' and 'human rights' contrasting to that identified in the USA can be found in the French revolutionary republican tradition of the 'Rights of Man' and of 'secularism'. Like the 'no establishment' and 'free exercise' tradition of the USA, this tradition also emerged to some extent as a protest against the 'nationalised monopoly' forms of relationship

19 Mirsky, 'Civil Religion and the Establishment Clause', 1240.
20 Piérard and Lindar, *Civil Religion and the Presidency*, 22–23.
21 Jewett and Lawrence, *Captain America and the Crusade Against Evil.*

between religion(s), state and society that were previously characteristic of European history.[22]

But in contrast with the position in the USA where separation is combined with a high degree of religiosity in public life, in the revolutionary republic tradition separation is accompanied by an often 'secularist' ethos – in other words, one that is concerned with a philosophical and political challenge to the claims of religion, especially in relation to public life. The values that historically have been associated with this form of the 'secular' were strongly anti-clerical and rationalist in origin, and are rooted in an approach to individual 'human rights' that itself was based on a philosophical and political dethronement of God.

Positively, the 'secularist secular' tradition is linked with the promotion of the citizenship principles of Liberty, Equality and Fraternity. Taken together, these values give rise in France to the strong French tradition of *laïcité* (a word not fully translated into English by the oft-used approximation 'secular'). Arising from this, republican French society and politics has traditionally been organised on the basis of a strong conviction that religion is a matter for the private sphere alone and is therefore opposed to any possible 'contamination' of the public sphere by religion.

In recent times, following the Stasi Commission report on 'Laïcité et République',[23] this approach of *laïcité* has manifested itself in the state's action to prevent the wearing of religious symbols in public schools – including headscarves for Muslim girls, *kippahs* for Jewish boys, and crucifixes for young Christians.[24] Even in France, though, there have been some exceptions to the general approach of *laïcité*, for example, in the specific context of the *departement* of Alsace-Moselle, where the influence of the Franco-German historical inheritance has meant that a closer relationship subsists between religion(s) and public life than is the case in other parts of the Republic.

But it was the 'secularist' aspects of the revolutionary republican tradition that spread beyond France itself to influence many other emergent nationalist and socialist movements of the late nineteenth and twentieth

22 For the phrase 'nationalised monopoly' as it relates to religion see Buchanan, *Cut the Connection*, 11–19.

23 Stasi, *Laïcité et Republique*.

24 Terray, 'Headscarf Hysteria'.

centuries. One example of the influence of this tradition upon nationalist movements can be seen in the unique historical and contemporary setting of Turkey as a country with both Asian and European borders, a majority Muslim society, and a historical background as the centre of the Ottoman Islamic empires. As explained by Hakan Yavuz and John Esposito, 'In many developing countries, secularism has become a theology of progress and development' and 'normative fault lines of modernity are nowhere else as clear as in Turkey.'[25]

In the twentieth century, Turkey's story is dominated by the ideology of Mustafa Kemal Ataturk (1881–1938), the founder of the modern Turkish state who abolished the Muslim caliphate in 1924. Yavuz and Esposito point out that in Kemalist ideology, 'modernity and democracy require secularism.'[26] The version of secularism dominant in Turkey is what these authors call a 'radical Jacobin laicism', in which secularism is treated 'as above and outside politics' and in which, therefore, 'secularism draws the boundaries of public reasoning.'[27] Thus, until very recently, any attempts to use religious language in public debate could result in the banning of any political party that did so and, notwithstanding recent developments following the electoral victory of Recep Tayyip Erdogan, leader of the Justice and Development Party (*Adalet ve Kalkinma Partisi*, or AKP), ongoing conflicts related to the historical inheritance are, as yet, to be fully resolved.

However, the 'secularist secular' inheritance of the revolutionary and republican tradition also influenced the various socialist movements that emerged in the nineteenth century. These traditions, of course, reached their apotheosis in Marxist dialectical materialism in which, for much of the second half of the twentieth century, Communist parties in the former Eastern-bloc countries governed on the basis of a state-sponsored atheist ideology. Here, the previous national and state forms of religion were largely removed from public life either by force or by other coercive measures, and an effort was made to replace them with an ideology that restricted freedom of religious expression and organisation.

In ways more or less vigorously pursued according to specific national contexts, this tradition attempted – as a minimum – at least to keep

25 Yavuz and Esposito, 'Islam in Turkey: Retreat From the Secular Path?', xvii.
26 Ibid., xxiii.
27 Ibid., xvi.

religion restricted to the private sphere. But also among countries with Communist party governments there were significant variations.[28] At one extreme was the militant atheism of Enver Hoxha's Albania. Then there were the more ambiguous relationships between the Orthodox Church and Ceaucescu's Romania. In the former German Democratic Republic there was the official stance of 'critical solidarity' adopted by the Churches, while in the People's Republic of Poland religion continued as a social force of some considerable significance and power.[29]

This revolutionary republic tradition, then, has manifested itself in a variety of ways in connection to the meanings and implications of the 'secular' with regard to the relationship between 'religion' and 'human rights'. But while there is diversity among the range of 'secularist secular' approaches, as Yakuz and Esposito explain, there remains an overall contrast with the tradition of 'separation of Church and State (with religiosity)' that 'evolved from the Anglo-American experience'. In the latter, 'secularism shielded diverse religions from state manipulation' and has been concerned with seeking to 'protect religions from state intervention and encourage faith-based social networking to consolidate civil society'.[30]

By contrast, Yakuz and Esposito maintain that, in the secularism evolving out of the more general European experience, the 'philosophers and politicians tried to expand the power of the state and restrict religion to the private sphere' and that the 'secularism, or *laïcisme*, which evolved in France is antireligious and seeks to eliminate or control religion.'[31] It is this latter tradition that has broadly informed the 'secularist secular' tradition of many modernist nationalist and most Marxist movements.

'PILLARISATION'

An alternative European 'contextual pattern' relating to 'secularity' and the relationship between 'religion' and 'human rights' can be found in the distinctive history of the Netherlands where, historically, a policy

28 Beeson, *Discretion and Valour*.

29 See Gilarek, 'The Mainline Churches as Counterbalance to the State'.

30 H. Yavuz and J. Esposito, 'Islam in Turkey: Retreat From the Secular Path?', in H. Yavuz and J. Esposito (eds), *Turkish Islam and the Secular State: The Gulen Movement* (Syracuse, New York: Syracuse University Press, 2003), xv–xvi.

31 Yavuz and Esposito, xv–xvi.

was followed known as '*Verzuiling*'.[32] Often translated into English by means of the not very elegant term 'pillarisation', this approach was one of the key historic ways in which, following its modern establishment as an independent polity, the Netherlands had sought to accommodate religious and social difference. Explaining this approach, Ahmed Andrews described this 'pillarisation' in the following terms:

> At its most fully developed the structure of *verzuiling* enabled a person to live their whole life within their confessional or secular bloc. Once born into the system it has been possible to be educated in one particular bloc from school to University: join a confessional or non-confessional trade union or professional body and be employed within the same bloc. Marriage within the bloc was also the general rule. In addition, one could read a newspaper published within one's bloc and even receive television and radio broadcasts put out by the confessional or secular segment of society to which one belonged. Finally one's social and sporting activities were catered for within the bloc, owing to each having its own sports and social clubs.[33]

The beginnings of this policy lay in the origins of the country itself, which emerged out of a revolt inspired by Calvinist Christianity against Spanish Roman Catholic rule. This resulted in the foundation of a Calvinist state in which the Dutch Reformed Church was the only officially recognised Church. There were a number of Roman Catholic geographical enclaves and, although they were initially excluded from holding public office, the religious worshipping life of Protestant dissenters, Jews and Roman Catholics was tolerated.

In his book on Dutch society, Goudsblom argued that the commercial interests of the Dutch burghers and merchants modified the religious zealotry of the Calvinists, with the result that a Dutch society of 'varied religious composition' came into being.[34] Originally, the Dutch state was a republic but, in 1813, after the period of Napoleonic domination, it became a monarchy. Since 1848, its monarchy has played a similar con-

32 Dobbelaere, 'Secularisation, Pillarisation, Religious Involvement and Religious Change in the Low Countries'.

33 Andrews, 'The Inter-Faith Movement in the UK', 127.

34 Goudsblom, *Dutch Society*, 18.

stitutional role to the monarchy in Britain, and Goudsblom notes that 'religious diversity has remained a pervasive determinant of social and cultural distinctions, giving rise to the curious phenomenon of "bloc" formation known as *verzuiling*'.[35]

Historically, conflicts between the 'blocs', which have included not only the religious, but also the humanistic, liberal and socialist orientations, have generally been managed within the overall framework of this system. Like Christopher Bagley,[36] who undertook previous comparative work on race relations in the Netherlands and the UK, Andrews, when writing in the mid-1990s, argued that this model may still have something positive to offer other societies with different histories. While acknowledging that 'At first sight this segmentation of Dutch society might appear to lead to social instability', and noting that 'it is not as strong as it was in the 1960s', he nevertheless maintained that the approach of *verzuiling* is still a 'useful illustration of how a segmented society, a plural society, has met the needs of various conflicting groups and achieved a stability based, since the late 1800s, on equal treatment for all'.[37] And indeed, in its promotion of a combination of social and political openness and stability, the apparent social dynamics of the Netherlands as a multi-cultural society were often held up as an example for other European countries wrestling with the challenges and implications of growing cultural and religious plurality. According to Andrews' evaluation:

> Its success is, I believe, due to two factors. Firstly, the *verzuiling* structure arose in a society which was already clear about its national identity to which all groups had an attachment, unlike India or Pakistan, for example, where attachment to one's state or ethnic region often appears to be stronger than attachment to the nation. Secondly, all blocs have equal access to resources.[38]

However, questions have increasingly been raised about the extent to which this structural inheritance did, in fact, accommodate new Muslim

---

35 Ibid., 71–3.

36 Bagley, *Community Relations in the Netherlands*; id., *Race Relations and Social Structure in the Netherlands and Britain*; id., 'Immigrant minorities in the Netherlands'.

37 Andrews, 127.

38 Ibid.

migrants.[39] In addition, the idea of *verzuiling* itself became subject to considerable debate in the Netherlands, with some arguing that it should be seen as a relic of a previous age rather than having anything positive to offer the present or the future.[40] Most recently, the murder of the film maker Theo van Gogh[41] in November 2004 brought to the surface the severe strains that had already been apparent in Dutch society since the emergence of the populist and what might be called 'cultural nationalist' libertarian political movement known as the *List Pim Fortuyn*, or LPF, led by the Dutch politician Pim Fortuyn until his assassination (by a white collar environmentalist) in 2002.[42]

In the light of this and ensuing developments in the Netherlands, and with the advantage of hindsight, Vincent Cable's basically positive evaluation that 'Holland has been more successful than most other countries at assimilating non-whites (especially from Indonesia) and allowing strong and competing religious faiths to coexist with libertarian social legislation (for abortion, euthanasia and prostitution)'[43] seems to have been overly optimistic.

THE 'SECULAR' AGAINST THE COMMUNAL

Outside of the northern hemisphere, the notion of the 'secular' can be found in still other modes. This includes the strong foundational idea of the state as 'secular' that is present in the history and constitutional tradition of the Republic of India. However, this 'contextual pattern' contrasts in several important ways with both the more 'individualist' approach to the freedom and non-establishment of religion typified by the USA, and

39 See Bagley. *Race Relations and Social Structure*; Shadid and van Koningsveld, 'Dutch Political Views on the Multi-Cultural Society'; Feirabend and Rath, 'Making a Place for Islam in Politics'.

40 See Gowricharn and Mungra, 'The Politics of Integration in the Netherlands'.

41 Van Gogh had a history of controversial relations with Muslims, frequently referring to them as *geitenneukers* (or 'goat-fuckers'). However, the murder took place in reaction to a ten minute film called *Submission*, which was about violence against women in Muslim societies, and depicted four abused and naked women in see-through dresses with verses from the Qur'an painted on their bodies.

42 Fortuyn argued that Islam was backward and called for an end to any further Muslim immigration to the Netherlands.

43 Cable, *The World's New Fissures*, 71–2.

also with the tendency on the part of the broad European tradition that sees the 'secular' as anti-religious or, at the least, as non-religious.

Following independence, India was governed by the Congress Party, which had been influenced by the ideals of socialism. Rather than seeing what was called the 'secular' nature of the independent state as being fundamentally opposed to religion, it was understood and argued to be a defence against the threats posed to the nascent republic by religious communalism. The term 'communalism' was first used by British colonists to describe the situation in colonies such as India and Malaysia where religious and ethnic minorities existed alongside majority groups and where there is evidence that, in order to 'divide and rule', the colonists played the 'communal card' of highlighting religious differences.[44]

In 1947, amidst the horrific violence between communities, the Indian state was divided, on the basis of religious difference, into India and what then became the Muslim states of East and West Pakistan, with East Pakistan later becoming the independent state of Bangladesh. As the Indian Christian theologian and former director of the World Council of Churches' Sub-Unit on Dialogue with People of Living Faiths and Ideologies Stanley Samartha notes in a chapter on 'Religious Identities in a Secular State':

> With the tragic memories of partition still fresh in the minds of people, India opted for a socialist, democratic and secular state. There has been an enormous amount of discussion on the content and character of the 'secular' state in India. So many different interpretations are given that it is almost impossible to define it. What can, however, be said, is that the 'secular' state in India, sensitive to the lurking violence beneath the surface of a multi-religious society, was established in a way that sought to be impartial in its dealings with different religious communities, particularly its religious and ethnic minorities.[45]

And as Samartha observed, 'Probably no other single factor has so strongly militated against the role of religion in public life in independent India as the charge of communalism. The horrors of communal vio-

44 See Beckerlegge, ' 'Strong' cultures and distinctive religions'.
45 Samartha, *One Christ – Many Religions*, 48.

lence make a mockery of the principle of tolerance.[46] Thus in his 1987 book, *Communal Violence in India*, P. R. Rajagopal records that during the 1950s, 381 communal riots took place, resulting in 153 people being killed. In the 1960s there were 2,689 riots in which 3,247 people were killed. In the 1970s there were 2,608 riots with 1,108 people killed; and, for the first five years alone of the 1980s, there were 2,771 riots with 2,772 people killed. And this strand of Indian life has continued down to the present. At the close of the twentieth century and the beginning of the twenty-first century, a rise in Hindu nationalism – symbolised most dramatically by the destruction of the mosque at Ayodyha – and the impact of Islamic militancy in relation to Kashmir has led to further outbreaks of violent communalism.

In a 1986 article, 'Communalism: The Way Out', Bipin Chandra argued that communalism arises in three stages. First, he stated, common beliefs are identified with common economic, political and cultural interests; second, these interests are then seen as being different from those of other religions; finally, different interests are seen to be not only different, but also antagonistic.[47] At the same time, 'communalism' itself is capable of being understood in relation to a number of different types of 'communalisms'. Thus, in a piece entitled 'On the Varieties of Communalism in India', K. Ooommen differentiates between six different types of communalism, which he identifies in the following way:

1. 'Assimilationist communalism', which, in India, is expressed in terms of 'devices to identify non-Hindus as Hindus'.[48]
2. 'Welfarist communalism': in which communal actions are intended to bring benefit to one's community, as a 'resultant of co-terminality between caste and class'.[49]
3. 'Retreatist communalism': which entails withdrawal from political activity in which 'presumed non-action is action'.[50]
4. 'Retaliatory communalism': in which celebrations take place as 'provocations' that involve 'hurting the feelings or sentiments of others'.[51]

46 Ibid., 50.
47 Chandra, 'Communalism: The Way Out', 11 f.
48 Ooommen, 'On the Varieties of Communalism in India', 7.
49 Ibid., 8.
50 Ibid., 9.
51 Ibid.

5. 'Separatist communalism': which is a kind of 'cultural nationalism' within the state.[52]
6. 'Sucessionist communalism': which 'insists that a religious group is a political entity, and therefore it should have a separate political roof, an independent sovereign polity'.[53]

Oommen argues that 'the six varieties of communalism that I have talked about are qualitatively different'[54] and that 'If we really want to arrive at authentic solutions we must identify the different dimensions of the phenomenon under analysis. I believe the very existence of different varieties of communalism does indicate different causes. And the different causes will have to be dealt with separately rather than treated together. This is the first step in any meaningful analysis.'[55]

In his *New Left Review* article, 'Reflections on communalism and nationalism in India', Achin Vanaik acknowledges the problems involved in defining the principle of 'secularism' but points out that

> Notwithstanding the enduring problems of precise definition, the term 'secular' does possess an agreed core meaning: state neutrality with regard to religion. In a multireligious society like that of India this can mean either a fundamental separation of the state from religious activity and affiliation, or state impartiality on all issues relating to the religious interests of the different communities.[56]

Vanaik's view is that 'In practice, "Indian secularism" has been a mixture of the two: an unsatisfactory attempt to reconcile what some consider to be essentially incompatible approaches.'[57] He also draws attention to an attempt to create a 'third position', although in his view this has largely been part of academic, rather than activist or popular, debate. He characterises this 'third position' as encouraging 'the use of "authentic" resources of faith to create a socio-political culture with a more deeply-rooted and genuine tolerance of diversity and pluralism than "Western

52 Ibid., 10.
53 Ibid., 11.
54 Ibid., 12.
55 Ibid., 13.
56 Vanaik, 'Reflections on communalism and nationalism in India', 43.
57 Ibid., 43.

secularism" can ever generate. Religion itself is to be the key resource in the struggle against communalism.'[58]

Samartha might be taken as an exponent of the 'third position' criticised by Vanaik. Samartha argued that 'during the past four decades the secular state, fearful of all religions, has failed to provide creative space for religions to make any serious contribution to the moral life of the nation.'[59] Samartha's vision of the role of religions is one in which, 'In an age dominated by science and secularism one of the tasks of genuinely religious people is to draw attention to the Mystery of transcendence, a centre of values, a source of meaning, an object of loyalty beyond the smaller loyalties to one's particular caste, language or religion.'[60] In recognition of such an approach, Vanaik argues that the communalisation and politicisation of religion should clearly be differentiated from the political dimensions of religion, a distinction he believes a fearful 'secularism' has not properly understood:

> To say that politics and religion should be kept separate is understandable, especially at a time like ours. But what it really should mean is that politicians should not use religions for short-term political ends and religious leaders should not use politicians for narrowly communal gains. But surely every religion has a social and public dimension. To say that religions should be a private affair is to misunderstand both religion and politics.[61]

COMPARISONS AND CONTRASTS

As was acknowledged at the start of this exploration of the four basic 'contextual patterns' of the 'secular' (found in the US tradition of 'free exercise' and 'non-establishment' of religion, the Revolutionary Republican tradition of *laïcité* and 'secularism', the Dutch approach of 'pillarisation', and the 'secular state' against communalism of India), there are other 'contextual patterns' than those, which there is no space to explore here. In addition, there are also multiple variations within and among the basic patterns outlined here.

58 Ibid., 44.
59 Samartha, 48.
60 Ibid., 57.
61 Vanaik, 56.

But within a global historical and temporal perspective, it is worth remembering that it is the 'secular' that must be considered a new experiment in social organisation and integration. Furthermore, it is important to note that, associated with the 'secular' – as with 'religion' – have been horrors and serious conflicts with 'human rights', as well as the promotion of them. While there is no doubt that religions have been responsible for very considerable amounts of human suffering, so too have groups and movements espousing secular ideologies of various kinds.

Thus the formation of the modern nation-states and the operation of modern 'secular' ideologies can hardly be uncritically glorified in light of the nineteenth and twentieth centuries, which saw immense suffering experienced in the Two Thirds World: the experience of imperialism, colonialism and capitalism; the gas chambers of Nazism; the gulags of Stalinism; and the rape of the planet caused by the unsustainable and headlong technological exploitation of finite natural resources to feed a frenzy of material consumption artificially stimulated by the power of mass media advertising in order to meet the demands of profit.

Seen in such a light, it is little wonder that from the perspective of religious people and traditions some forms of the 'secular' can seem no less dangerous than some forms of 'religion'. Therefore, while questions need to continue to be posed to and within 'religions' about their relationships with 'human rights', the question needs to be asked whether there might not be too easy a moral superiority among secularist critics of religion who are blind to the problems of 'human rights' deriving from a 'secular' approach to living in community – problems encompassing both the wider community in general and those who live by religious convictions in a predominantly secular environment.

In considering the place of 'religions' in relation to the 'secular', Marc Luyckx, formerly of the European Commission's Forward Studies Unit, has suggested that, in Europe, it is possible to identify three 'social cosmologies' concerned with the relationship between 'religion' and the 'secular'. Luyckx calls these 'social cosmologies' the 'agrarian', the 'scientific-industrial' and the 'post-industrial'.[62] And while these categories were originally developed in relation to the future of Europe, it is arguable that they could also have wider relevance in the context of a globalising world

62 See Luyckx, 'The Vocation of Europe Today'.

in which all three 'social cosmologies' can be identified, albeit in different forms of constellation compared with the current situation in Europe.

The 'agrarian' cosmology is associated with traditional religious inheritances in societies and/or groups in which organic unities – Weber's *Gemeinschaften* – and pyramidical hierarchies operate. Then there is what Luyckx calls the 'scientific-industrial' 'social cosmology'. This is associated with the 'secularist' projects of modernity in which the previous organic unities are broken up, leading to the compartmentalisation, increased specialisation and fragmentation that is characteristic of a modernity, in which Weber's *Gemeinschaften* become transformed into *Gesellschaften*, and such an understanding has either initiated or reinforced movements for the separation of religion and politics and religion and the state.

But as distinct from these 'agrarian' and 'scientific-industrial' 'social cosmologies', Luyckx instead argues for what he calls a 'post-industrial' model, which he characterises by the image of a roundtable, and which he argues is the only theoretically adequate and socially sound approach for a pluralistic environment. While acknowledging that the project of the nation state was an attempt, on the basis of the 'scientific-industrial' approach, to address the question of how to achieve cohesion in the context of the breakdown of the previously existing organic unities, Luyckx argues that such a model is ultimately incompatible with the lifestyles of the 'agrarian', pre-modern communities that continue to exist in Europe, not least through migration of communities with Third World origins that were often rural in nature.

The complexity and diversity of contemporary societies means that nostalgia for pre-modern models, while pursued by some, can in the end not overcome the broad historical dynamics and developments foreseen by the historian Arnold Toynbee. Toynbee, as long ago as 1956, perceived that migration and pluralisation would be one of the determining features of the present century when he observed that

> The adherents of each religion . . . seem likely to come gradually to be distributed all over the 'oikoumene', but it may also be expected that, in the process, they will come to be intermingled everywhere with adherents of all other faiths, as the Jews are already intermingled with Muslims and Christians, and the Parsees with Muslims

> and Hindus. As a result, the appearance of the religious map of the 'oikoumene' may be expected to change from a pattern of a patchwork quilt to the texture of a piece of shot silk.[63]

Thus the increasingly global social reality of 'shot silk' rather than 'patchwork quilt' societies presents a serious difficulty for 'agrarian'/'pre-modern' and 'scientific-industrial'/'modern' 'social cosmologies' since it is increasingly clear that neither the 'pre-modern' approach based on organic unities nor the 'modernist' approach of trying to maintain the privatisation of religions is a realistic or effective option for the future.

In addition, in reflecting on the relationships between 'religion' and 'secularity' and the implications of these for the arena in which 'human rights' operates, the *reactive* origins of the 'secular' need to be understood as having originally been located in the European inheritance of the Inquisition; the historic existence of 'nationalised monopolies of religion'; the impact of the seventeenth century Wars of Religion, and the responses to these: economic liberalism, revolutionary republicanism and, finally, the emergence of socialism and Marxism.

These were, of course, all historical phases, forms and movements located in particular social, cultural and religious histories, although to some degree globalised due to the impact of European imperialism and colonialism on the world. But the currents of historical development are now moving away from many of these reactive origins, just as the inherited forms of organised and institutional religion in Europe are also changing, especially those concerned with former patterns of 'nationalised monopolies' of religion. An example of this is the Lutheran Church of Sweden which, despite its long historical tradition of being a state Church on the Scandinavian model, found this form of the relationship ended in 2002. From this, it is clear that basic 'contextual patterns' in the relationship between 'religion' and the 'secular' are not only diverse, but also changing – in this instance, completing for the moment a social and legal transition from a state and society with an established religion but a strongly 'secular' ethos, to a 'secular' state in the 'modern' tradition.

Of course, this change did not take place overnight. Nor, in this instance, was it something externally forced on the Church of Sweden. Rather, it was the product of a re-evaluation on the part of both Church

63 Toynbee, *An Historian's Approach to Religion*, 139.

and society occurring over a number of years and based on the achievement of a broad religious and secular consensus around this change. But the fact that it did ultimately happen is a reminder that it is indeed possible for such changes to take place on the basis of agreement.[64]

But just as much as 'religion' and its traditional forms need to be re-evaluated, so also the 'secular' needs contemporary hermeneutical review, particularly because it is the European roots of the 'secular' dimension that can make that dimension problematic for societies whose other experience of imports from Europe has been in terms of colonial and imperial imposition. It is thus very important that from within their own traditions people from diverse cultural and religious backgrounds work on the relationships between 'religion', the 'secular' and 'human rights' in order to try and see what might be possible to fully affirm in common while doing so from the integrity of diverse religious and cultural standpoints. An example of such an attempt is the work of the Global Ethics and Religion Forum which, in 2000, developed a draft of a Universal Declaration of Human Rights by the World's Religions[65]

Given the Muslim community's size as the largest non-Christian global religious tradition, and the existence of severe ruptures in the global community along fault-lines related to the interface between Muslim and other identities, it is particularly important that any contemporary consideration of the relationship between 'religion', 'human rights' and the meaning and role of the 'secular' gives careful consideration to the 'contextual patterns' that have, in the past, been familiar to Muslims, and which continue to exercise a strong influence upon the Muslim imagination today as historic alternatives to either modern secularist or Islamicist approaches.[66]

---

64 For an argument of how such a change might work in the case of the Church of England, see Weller, *Time for a Change*.

65 See Runzo, Martin and Sharma, 141–7.

66 There is considerable terminological variety and confusion involved in both journalistic and scholarly attempts to indicate the range of contemporary Muslim perspectives on what is viewed as being the ideal relationship between Islam, state and society. The term 'Islamist' is, perhaps, that which is most frequently used when external commentators seek to describe those who hold a form of Islamic vision that differs from the assumptions of liberal democratic forms of government.

However, 'Islamist' is now used almost as frequently and imprecisely as 'fundamentalist', and can sometimes misleadingly be applied to what are really much more 'traditionalist' forms of Muslim governance. Because of this, I have chosen here

Thus, in parts of the world where Islam has had particularly strong influence, such as in the Middle East, the image of a 'mosaic' has historically been invoked as one that can be an appropriate 'contextual pattern'. The classical expression of this kind of pattern was the 'millet system' of the Ottoman Empire that has often been held up by Muslims as an example of the Islamic accommodation of plurality of beliefs and is claimed to have been relatively successful within the boundaries of the predominantly Muslim societies in which it has operated.

As testimony to this from beyond Muslim *apologias*, it is interesting to note the example of Leonard Busher, an English Baptist Christian who was one of the earliest advocates of religious freedom writing in the English language. In his 1614 *Religion's Peace*,[67] as well as arguing for liberty of religion and conscience on theological grounds, Busher also challenged Christians by reference to historical descriptions of the Muslim treatment of both Christians and Jews in Constantinople. Thus he remarked,

> I read that a bishop of Rome would have constrained a Turkish emperor to the Christian faith, unto whom the emperor answered, 'I believe that Christ was an excellent prophet, but he did never, so far as I understand, command that men should, with the power of weapons, be constrained to believe his law: and verily I also do force no man to Mahomet's law.' And I read that Jews, Christians, and Turks are tolerated in Constantinople, and yet are peaceable, though so contrary the one to the other.[68]

In the 'contextual pattern' of the 'mosaic', each individual community forms a part of a wider whole, but its own distinctiveness remains clear and the boundaries that distinguish it from other communities generally

---

to use the word 'Islamicist'. By use of this word, I intend to an indicate a vision of the relationship between religion, state and society that is a radical polar opposite to what I have described as a 'secularist' secular vision.

In other words, in the sense that I am meaning it here, an 'Islamicist' approach is one that espouses a 'modern' vision in which Islam is seen to function as an ideology that rests on force (of either the revolutionary variety bringing about change, or the state variety imposing conformity) that should, in a given Muslim society or societies, ideally supplant all other forms and mechanisms of political governance.

67 Busher, 'Religion's Peace'.

68 Ibid., 21.

remain sharp. The system was based on the notion of 'treaties' between Islamic and other communities. In this approach, the Christian and Jewish communities were granted a limited degree of autonomy within which they were allowed to manage their own religious and educational affairs and personal status issues such as marriage.[69]

Of course, despite Busher's praise for what he had heard of Constantinople, there could often be a gap between ideal and reality. Christians and Jews were frequently treated by the state and the majority population as inferior members of the Islamic empires.[70] In the nineteenth century, Ottoman Empire reforms officially granted Christians and Jews equality within the political community, but those who insisted on their legal rights of emancipation were often bitterly opposed.

It is also the case that, within the Islamic Empires, Muslims other than the majority Sunnis, such as the Shi'as, Ismailis, 'Alawis and Druzes, have been even more strongly opposed, since they were viewed as being unorthodox or, at best, heterodox. They were therefore sometimes seen as even more of a threat to the unity of the *'ummah* than religious traditions and communities completely distinct from the household of Islam.

However, the contemporary position of the Middle Eastern Christian communities is one in which, as minorities, they have suffered considerable social and demographic pressure and consequent population attrition in their key areas of historic geographic presence in Syria, Turkey and other similar countries, where the ancient Christian Churches have been struggling to maintain a social foothold.[71]

Notwithstanding this, Muslims still generally appeal to a traditional mosaic model as a basis for accommodating a variety of religious beliefs and practices in public life. But while this traditional 'mosaic' model might be able to claim some historical success in relation to diverse populations of broadly settled geographies, its weakness is that it admits of little movement or change. It is therefore questionable how adequate it is in the context of globalised population movements and the highly mixed societies[72] that result from migration and globalisation and are reflected in Toynbee's image of 'shot silk' as compared with the more traditional

69 Braude and Lewis, *Christians and Jews in the Ottoman Empire.*

70 Ma'oz, 'Islamic-Arabism versus Pluralism'.

71 Wessels, *Arab and Christian? Christians in the Middle East.*

72 See Laszlo, *The Multi-Cultural Planet.*

'patchwork quilt' of the 'social mosaics' that have historically formed the backcloth for such traditional Muslim approaches.

Even so, also in contemporary Europe some adaptations of this classic 'treaty-based' approach exist that might to a certain extent resonate with what Muslims may well realistically hope for in a European context where they are in the minority rather than majority position.[73] An example of this can be found in the not widely known but significant *Acuerdo de Cooperacíon del Estado Español con las Comisíon islamica de España*.[74] This is an agreement between the Spanish state and its Islamic communities that is parallel to other treaties of a similar kind established with both Protestant Christian and Jewish communities. It guarantees a range of rights for Muslims such as civil recognition of religious marriages and the declaration of mosques as inviolable. As Peter Antes commented, 'The treaty is the most comprehensive recognition of Muslim rights signed in Europe so far'.[75]

There are no easy solutions here. But, while there do continue to be significant tensions and sometimes conflicts between advocacy of particular forms of 'religion' and 'human rights', it is the argument of this chapter that acknowledgement of the need to explicitly consider the 'secular' in the discussion, more often framed as taking place between 'religion' and 'human rights', is of great importance. Making this 'third dimension' of the discussion visible and explicit could, at the very least, result in formerly 'common sense' formulations of problems and issues being turned on their head, making it possible to see them from new and previously unrecognised perspectives. This, in turn, might make a significant contribution to the important task of finding a new, and yet more inclusive, consensus around a body of generally affirmed values and perspectives, which it might then be possible to reflect in the further development of instruments of national and international law that seek to uphold, promote and protect human dignity and opportunity in our diverse world.

---

73 See Abumalham, 'The Muslim Presence in Spain'.

74 (Co-Operation Agreement of the Spanish State with the Islamic Commission of Spain). For more background to, and information about this, see P. Antes, 'Islam in Europe', in S. Gill, G. D'Costa, and U. King (eds), *Religion in Europe: Contemporary Perspectives* (Kampen: Kok Pharos, 1994), 49–50.

75 Antes, 'Islam in Europe', 50.

BIBLIOGRAPHY

Religious Freedom Restoration Act, section 2(a)(3)
Religious Freedom Restoration Act, section 3(b)(2)

Abraham, H., 'The Status of the First Amendment's Religion Clauses: Some Reflections on Lines and Limits', *Journal of Church and State,* 22 (1980), 215–31.

Abumalham, M., 'The Muslim Presence in Spain', in W. Shadid and P. Van Koningsveld (eds), *Muslims in the Margin: Political Responses to the Presence of Islam in Western Europe* (Kampen: Kok Pharos, 1996), 80–92.

Andrews, A., 'The Inter-Faith Movement in the UK: Towards Religious Pluralism', *The Indo-British Review* 22 (1994), 123–30.

Antes, P., 'Islam in Europe', in S. Gill, G. D'Costa, and U. King (eds), *Religion in Europe: Contemporary Perspectives* (Kampen: Kok Pharos, 1994), 46–67.

Bagley, C., *Community Relations in the Netherlands: A Model for Britain?* (London: The Race Relations Committee of the Society of Friends, n.d.)

———, *Race Relations and Social Structure in the Netherlands and Britain* (London: Institute of Race Relations, 1971)

———, 'Immigrant Minorities in the Netherlands: Integration and Assimilation', *International Migration Review* 5 (1971), 18–35.

Baker, J., 'Belief and Action: Limitations on the Free Exercise of Religion', in J. Hensel (ed.), *Church, State and Politics* (Washington DC: The Roscoe Pound Foundation, 1981), 41–72.

Beckerlegge, G., ' 'Strong' Cultures and Distinctive Religions: The Influence of Imperialism upon British Communities of South Asian Origin', *New Community,* 17 (1991), 201–10.

Beeson, T., *Discretion and Valour* (Glasgow: Collins, 1974).

Berman, D., *A History of Atheism in Britain: From Hobbes to Russell* (London: Croon Helm, 1988).

Braude, B., and B. Lewis (eds), *Christians and Jews in the Ottoman Empire,* 2 vols (Holmes and Meier, 1982).

Buchanan, C., *Cut the Connection: Disestablishment and the Church of England* (London: Darton, Longman and Todd, 1994).

Busher, L., 'Religion's Peace: Or a Plea for Liberty of Conscience', in

E. Underhill (ed.), *Tracts on the Liberty of Conscience and Persecution, 1614–1667* (London: Hanserd Knollys Society, 1846), 1–81.

Cable, V., *The World's New Fissures: Identities in Crisis* (London: Demos, 1994).

Chandra, B., 'Communalism: The Way Out', in *Mainstream*, 24 (May 24, 1986).

Council of Europe Directorate of Social and Economic Affairs, *Religion and the Integration of Immigrants* (Strasbourg: Council of Europe Publishing, 1999).

Dobbelaere, K., 'Secularisation, Pillarisation, Religious Involvement and Religious Change in the Low Countries', in T. Gannon (ed.), *World Catholicism in Transition* (New York: Macmillan, 1988), 80–115.

Dopamu, P. Ade, 'Religion in a Secular State: Problems and Possibilities within the Nigerian Context', in *The Indo-British Review*, 20/1 (1994), 177–189.

Esposito, J. (ed.), *Islam in Asia: Religion, Politics and Society* (Oxford: OUP, 1987).

Feirabend, J., and J. Rath, 'Making a Place for Islam in Politics: Local Authorities Dealing with Islamic Associations', in W. Shadid and P. van Koningsveld (eds), *Muslims in the Margin: Political Responses to the Presence of Islam in Western Europe* (Kampen: Kok Pharos, 1996), 243–58.

Fitzgerald, T., *The Ideology of Religious Studies* (Oxford: OUP, 2000).

Gannon, T., (ed.), *World Catholicism in Transition* (New York: Macmillan, 1988), 80–115.

Gilarek, K., 'The Mainline Churches as Counterbalance to the State: The Church of England in the Thatcher Period and the Catholic Church in Poland under the Communist Regime', in T. Inglis, Z. Mach, R. Mazanek (eds), *Religion and Politics: East-West Contrast from Contemporary Europe* (Dublin: University College Press, 2000), 129–46.

Goudsblom, J., *Dutch Society* (New York: Random House, 1967).

Gowricharn, R., and B. Mungra, 'The Politics of Integration in the Netherlands', in W. Shadid and P. van Koningsveld (eds), *Muslims in the Margin: Political Responses to the Presence of Islam in Western Europe* (Kampen: Kok Pharos, 1996), 114–29.

Harmati, B., 'The Importance of Religiosity and Basic Values for Nation and State in Asia', in *Lutheran World Federation Documentation*, 20 (1986), 1–7.

Harmati, B., (ed.). *The Church and Civil Religion in the Nordic Countries of Europe* (Geneva: Lutheran World Federation, 1984).

Hensel, J. (ed.), *Church, State and Politics* (Washington DC: The Roscoe Pound Foundation, 1981).

Janis, W., and C. Evans (eds), *Religion and International Law* (Leiden: Martinus Nijhoff, 1999).

Jewett, R., and J. S. Lawrence, *Captain America and the Crusade Against Evil: The Dilemma of Zealous Nationalism* (Cambridge: William B. Eerdmans, 2003).

Jordan, W., *The Development of Religious Toleration in England*, 2 vols (London: George Allen & Unwin, 1932, 1936).

Kroef, K. van der, 'Patterns of Intergroup Accommodation in South-east Asia: Is Democrative Pluralism Possible?', in N. Rhoodie (ed.), *Intergroup Accommodation in Plural Societies* (Macmillan, 1978), 143–73.

Lamont, S., *Church and State: Uneasy Alliances* (London: Bodley Head, 1989).

Laszlo, E. (ed.), *The Multi-Cultural Planet: The Report of a UNESCO International Expert Group* (Oxford: One World, 1993).

Littell, F., *From State Church to Religious Pluralism: A Protestant Interpretation of Religion in American History* (Garden City: Doubleday and Company, 1962).

Luyckx, M., 'The Vocation of Europe Today', unpublished paper (European Commission, 25th May 1994), quoted in P. Weller, 'The Salman Rushdie Controversy, Religious Plurality and Established Religion in England' (unpublished doctoral dissertation, University of Leeds, 1996).

Ma'oz, M., 'Islamic-Arabism versus Pluralism: The Failure of Intergroup Accommodation in the Middle East', in N. Rhoodie (ed.), *Intergroup Accommodation in Plural Societies*, 115–42.

Mirsky, Y., 'Civil Religion and the Establishment Clause', *Yale Law Journal*, 95 (1986), 1237–57.

Murphy, P. (ed.), *Religious Freedom: Separation and Free Exercise*, 2 vols (Garland, 1990).

Ooommen, K., 'On the Varieties of Communalism in India', in S. Arokiasamy (ed.), *Responding to Communalism: The Task of Religions and Theology* (Anand: Gujarat Sahitya Prakash, 1991), 3–13.

Pfeffer, L., *God, Caesar and the Constitution: The Court as Referee of Church–State Relations* (Boston: Beacon, 1975).

——, 'The Establishment Clause: The Never-ending Conflict', in R. White, Jr and A. Zimmerman (eds), *An Unsettled Arena: Religion and the Bill of Rights* (Grand Rapdis: Eerdmans, 1986), 69–71.

Piérard, R., and R. Lindar, *Civil Religion and the Presidency* (Grand Rapids: Zondervan, 1988).

Rajagopal, P., *Communal Violence in India* (New Delhi: Uppal, 1987).
Runzo, J., N. Martin, and A. Sharma (eds), *Human Rights and Responsibilities in the World Religions* (Oxford: One World Publications, 2003).
Ruston. R., *Human Rights and the Image of God* (London: SCM, 2004).
Samartha, S., *One Christ – Many Religions: Towards a Revised Christology* (New York: Orbis, 1991).
Shadid, W., and S. van Koningsveld, 'Dutch Political Views on the Multi-Cultural Society', in W. Shadid and P. van Koningsveld (eds), *Muslims in the Margin: Political Responses to the Presence of Islam in Western Europe* (Kampen: Kok Pharos, 1996), 93–113.
Stasi, B., *Laïcité et Republique. Rapport de la Commision de Reflection sur l'Application du Principe de Laïcité dans la Republique* (Paris : La Documentation Francaise, 2004).
Stern, M., 'Freedom of Religion and the United States Constitution', in *Patterns of Prejudice*, 21 (1987), 15–30.
Terray, E., 'Headscarf Hysteria', in *New Left Review*, 2nd series, 26 (2004), 118–27.
Toynbee, A., *An Historian's Approach to Religion* (London: Oxford University Press, 1956).
Vanaik, A., 'Reflections on Communalism and Nationalism in India', in *New Left Review*, 196 (1992), 43–62.
Weller, P., 'The Dimensions and Dynamics of Religious Discrimination', in N. Ghanea (ed.), *The Challenge of Religious Discrimination at the Dawn of the New Millennium* (Leiden: Martinus Nijhoff, 2003), 57–81.
———, *Time for a Change: Reconfiguring, Religion State and Society* (London: T & T Clark, 2005).
Wessels, A., *Arab and Christian? Christians in the Middle East* (Kampen: Kok Pharos, 1995).
White, Jr, R., and A. Zimmerman (eds), *An Unsettled Arena: Religion and the Bill of Rights* (Grand Rapids, Eerdmans, 1986).
Williams, R., *The Bloudy Tenent of Persecution for Cause of Conscience: Discussed in a Conference Between Truth and Peace*, ed. R. Groves (Macon, Georgia: Mercer University Press, 2001).
Yavuz, H., and J. Esposito (eds), *Turkish Islam and the Secular State: The Gülen Movement* (Syracuse, New York: Syracuse University Press, 2003).
Yavuz, H., and J. Esposito, 'Islam in Turkey: Retreat From the Secular Path?', in H. Yavuz and J. Esposito (eds), ibid., xiii–xxxiii.

CHAPTER 10

Freedom of Religion and Belief in the Light of Recent Challenges: Needs, Clashes and Solutions

Dennis de Jong

INTRODUCTION

Does God believe in human rights? My immediate answer would be to the negative: by definition, God cannot believe in anything but God. God stands for the Supreme Being, and God's truth is therefore the ultimate, universal truth. You cannot make God's truth dependent on a greater truth, even if it relates to human rights or fundamental freedoms.

There is, however, more to be said about the relationship between religion or belief and international human rights law than this rather philosophical answer, though this premise does help in understanding the tensions between religion and human rights. In practice, it is not the question of whether God believes in human rights that really matters, but how the adherents of religions and beliefs perceive human rights. For though no one can bind God, the adherents of religions and beliefs are bound to human rights law, whether they 'believe' in them or not.

In this essay I shall first examine why religions and beliefs matter, and what makes the freedom of religion or belief special. Secondly, I shall look at a number of potential clashes between the precepts of religions or beliefs and human rights law. Finally, I shall try to draw some guidelines for governments to overcome these tensions and clashes.

1. WHY RELIGIONS AND BELIEFS MATTER

□ *Needs*

In the second half of the twentieth century, Western Europe and North America went through a so-called 'secularisation process'. This has often been looked upon as a process whereby many adherents of traditional faiths, especially Christians, left their denominations, or at least stopped being active members. This is certainly one aspect of the secularisation process, but it is only half the story. Turning their backs on traditional religious organisations did not make the people concerned non-believers. Many of them took an interest in new, partly individualised, forms of belief; in this regard, one can mention the New Age movement and the sudden increase of followers of Baghwan, Hare Krishna and other more 'exotic' groups. What happened was not that people suddenly believed there was nothing between heaven and earth, but that social pressures to stick to traditional religions decreased, giving people a chance to seek their own ways of fulfilling their spiritual needs.

It was often assumed that as a consequence of the secularisation process in Western Europe and North America the rest of the world would automatically follow. This conception was wrong in two respects. First, the Western world itself was not consistent in its attitude. On the one hand, organisations engaged in development cooperation and rooted in Christian beliefs went through a phase of reorientation that frequently led to a stronger emphasis on social objectives and less on proselytism. In this manner, mainstream development organisations 'secularised'. On the other hand, large-scale conversions to Catholicism and, more recently, to evangelical Protestant Churches continued through other organisations and movements.

Secondly, reference should be made to the effects of decolonisation. During the period of colonisation, evangelism and missionary activities were seen as a normal part of the objective 'to bring civilisation', but when decolonisation set in this official platform of course vanished. Insofar as Christianity was associated with colonial powers, its traditionally privileged position worked against it. Other, traditional religions and beliefs such as Islam, Hinduism, Buddhism and animistic beliefs were then in a much better position to act as unifying forces for nations in post-colonial days. Although in the context of this essay it is impossible to present an in-depth analysis of the various trends during the period of decolonisation, it seems justified to say that decolonisation worked in favour of traditional religions, at least in some parts of the world, and that secularisation remained a phenomenon largely reserved for Europe and North America. In the rest of the world, religion remained as important as it had been.

Mention should also be made of a different aspect of secularisation. It has already been mentioned that the secularisation process led to a wider variety of religions or beliefs in the Western world. This meant that it became increasingly difficult for governments to be seen as associated with one 'official' religion. Although not all European countries have done away with official or 'established' Churches, since the 1960s a definite trend towards separation of State and religion can be noted, even in countries where this principle was not part of the national heritage. Outside Western Europe and North America, however, no such trend towards separation of State and religion can be observed. On the contrary, the Islamic revolution in Iran and the emergence of the Hindutva movement in India are but two examples of a closer identification of the State with a particular religion. In order to understand what is going on in much of the world, one has therefore to think of religion or belief not only as an important instrument for personal development, but also for State identity.

It is remarkable that the importance of religion or belief has received little attention in such fields as international-relations theory until recently. Hans Morgenthau's theory of power, for example, denied the importance of cultural or religious factors.[1] The Islamic revolution in Iran therefore came as a shock to many analysts. This deliberate qualification of religion or belief as a 'nuisance factor' for the application of rational political theory may also help in explaining why originally the effects of globalisation, which became clearly visible towards the end of the twentieth century, were deemed to be only positive; after all, globalisation was supposed to lead to better worldwide economic prospects and, insofar as culture or religion was concerned, globalisation was believed to lead to more exchanges between cultures and religious beliefs, which was considered interesting and positive.

In reality, however, globalisation as it has been taking place since the 1980s is not value-free. The entire concept of globalisation is based on a firm belief in international trade through open markets. It presupposes a way of thinking that is often referred to as 'neo-liberal'. In cultural terms, it implies the existence of a human being who acts in an economically rational manner. Citizens become consumers, and everyone is offered ever more 'choice' in order to make the market do its work. Religion is either seen as a completely private affair with no implications for at

1 Hans J. Morgenthau, *Politics among Nations*, 5th edn (New York, 1973).

least the economic aspects of daily life, or as an incentive for economic behaviour insofar as its teachings are in harmony with such behaviour. In other words, the globalisation process to date has been a purely economically driven one with no particular place for spirituality, national cultural traditions or even social justice.

If the globalisation process had just created better economic opportunities without affecting national societies, it would not have mattered what its major drive was. However, the effects of globalisation go far beyond the economic realm. Bigger markets have led to a concentration of firms and to the growing influence of transnational corporations. Traditional, national products give way to products that can be distributed worldwide. National traditions and policies are often seen as obstacles to free trade or economic growth and are gradually giving way to more universal patterns. Valentine's Day, for example, is being exported to ever more countries, including even Iraq. Similarly, Santa Claus seems to be everywhere these days; in the Netherlands, for example, a constant battle must be fought to convince shop owners to heed the competing national tradition of *Sinterklaas*, which takes place on 5–6 December instead of at Christmas. Commercial interests are the driving force behind these developments.

Once again, this essay is not the place to enumerate all the cultural effects of globalisation, but in my opinion there is a definite tendency towards 'cultural harmonisation' as a consequence of the mainly economic agenda of globalisation. This holds for every part of the world, including Western Europe. Traditional religions or beliefs often become rare shelters where one can find traces of national identity. In a world full of insecurity, religions or beliefs can act as catalysts for spiritual, cultural and even social needs. Because globalisation emphasises individualisation and rational (i.e. economically inspired) behaviour, other values such as spirituality, brotherhood and charity are neglected. But these are just as essential for mankind as economic needs. Religions and beliefs fulfil those needs. They are also better equipped than other, political, movements to resist the pressures stemming from the globalisation process. Based on old scriptures and traditions, most religions and beliefs provide a coherent set of views as opposed to the pragmatic or even opportunistic views held by the protagonists of economic globalisation.

Globalisation also works in favour of religions or beliefs in another, more direct way. Most religions have always been internationally organised, but more recently they have fully exploited the new possibilities offered by the communication and physical infrastructure to strengthen the bonds between their adherents worldwide and to propagate their beliefs in the furthest corners of the world.[2] In this way, they have become more powerful players. On the one hand, they seem to gain importance because they can fulfil needs economic globalisation cannot; on the other hand, they themselves become more globalised and are therefore able to extend their influence beyond traditional geographical boundaries.

□ *Clashes*

Before discussing the clashes between religions and beliefs and international human rights law, it seems valid to question the values underlying human rights themselves. Can human rights be seen as a mainly Western invention, perhaps even as part of the process of 'cultural harmonisation' referred to above? In other words, are human rights instruments of economic globalisation?

Since international human rights law is based on international negotiations and claims to have universal value, it can be considered part of the general globalisation process. However, it is also heavily inspired by religious, and especially Christian, values and it protects religion or belief through the recognition of the freedom of thought, conscience and religion or belief.[3] Freedom of religion and belief as codified in, for example, the UN Covenant on Civil and Political Rights (ICCPR) has even been given a special position as one of the non-derogable rights, with a

2 See, for example, the contributions to the seminar 'Religion, Transnationalism, and Radicalism' organised by ISIM et al., 20–21 June 2003 in Amsterdam <http://www.iias.nl/iias/agenda/archief/20062003.html>.

3 Although from the very beginning representatives from, for example, Islamic and communist countries were actively participating in the negotiations on UN-standards in the field of human rights and fundamental freedoms, it cannot be denied that during the first two decades of the UN's existence, Western countries with a Christian background had an enormous influence on the negotiating process. For a differing view, see Gerrie ter Haar, *Rats, Cockroaches and People Like Us: Views of Humanity and Human Rights* (Inaugural Address, International Institute of Social Studies, 2000). In her opinion, 'the human rights concept as expressed in the Universal Declaration is at root a secular idea'. The author does continue though by pointing out the underlying 'value-based' ideas that the negotiators from countries with different dominating beliefs wished to bring out through the adoption of a world-wide Universal Declaration.

more restricted set of limitation grounds than other human rights, and it was one of the Four Freedoms identified by President Roosevelt which formed the basis for the entire human rights codification process in the context of the United Nations. In this sense, human rights recognises the importance of spirituality.[4] Considering the special attention paid to economic, social and cultural rights, international human rights law must be said to recognise the importance of brotherhood and charity. It would therefore be unfair to put international human rights law on the same footing as economic globalisation, even if it claims to represent universal truth.[5]

2. POTENTIAL CLASHES BETWEEN THE PRECEPTS OF RELIGIONS OR BELIEFS AND HUMAN RIGHTS LAW

The relationship between international human rights law and religions or beliefs is complicated. Sometimes, human rights serve as a means of liberation (they have, for example, improved the position of religious minorities worldwide, or the position of religion in communist states). Sometimes, human rights are seen as a form of globalisation emanating from 'the West' and therefore suspect, especially insofar as they restrict religious practices. I would like, therefore, to discuss at this point some of the clashes between international human rights law and manifestations of religions and beliefs.

4 Bas de Gaay Fortman and M. A. Mohamed Salih state that 'human rights and religion are mutually reinforcing insofar as human rights is related to spiritual roots and hence not conceived as "a secular religion" and provided that religion is seen within the full dynamic context of the life and times of its adherence' ('The Life and Times of Religion and Human Rights', paper presented at the Second International Conference on Human Rights, Mofid University, Qom, Iran, 17–18 May 2003, p. 2).

5 The World Conference on Human Rights, which was held in Vienna in 1993, confirmed the universal value of international human rights law. In para. 5 of the Vienna Declaration it is stated that 'all human rights are universal, indivisible and interdependent and interrelated' and that 'the international community must treat human rights globally in a fair and equal manner, on the same footing, and with the same emphasis'. According to the Declaration, 'while the significance of national and regional particularities and various historical, cultural and religious backgrounds must be borne in mind, it is the duty of States, regardless of their political, economic and cultural systems, to promote and protect all human rights and fundamental freedoms'.

□ *The Principle of non-discrimination*

Most religions love to be cherished by the State, i.e. they love to obtain some kind of official status. This strengthens them. Moreover, for the realisation of certain religious precepts (e.g. family law or penal law) religions or beliefs need the State. This is explained by the fact that, by definition, religions and beliefs offer a basis for defining one's outlook on life. They do not confine themselves to the private, spiritual domain, but tend to guide their adherents in all aspects of life. This is reflected in the recognition that everyone is free to manifest his or her religion in public or private, as, for example, in Article 18 of the ICCPR. However, in accordance with international human rights law, the State must remain neutral and not discriminate against any religions or beliefs.

This general principle holds irrespective of how many citizens adhere to a certain religion or belief. There are bound to be religious minorities, no matter how small. Moreover, freedom of religion is a dynamic right. It includes the right to change one's religion or belief. The State should therefore not provide incentives for people to remain members of the dominant religion or belief.

Globalisation implies that people and ideas move around the world: migration increases and so does people's knowledge of religions and beliefs other than their traditional ones. For some religions or beliefs, this development offers a window of opportunity. As I noted above, they can use new infrastructure and communication techniques for spreading the Word. Other religions, though, may feel threatened; for them it becomes all the more important for the State to endorse their 'official' nature. In Russia, the Russian Orthodox Church is the official one, and it exerts its influence into, *inter alia*, educational policies, thus ensuring its teachings are included in the school curriculum. It also encourages the implementation of restrictive policies requiring religious communities to register before fully enjoying the freedom to manifest their religion and belief.[6] Smaller movements, such as the evangelical Protestant churches, are either excluded from registration altogether or subjected to severe restrictions. This attitude can at least partly be explained by what the

6 Karel Blei in *Freedom of Religion and Belief: Europe's Story* (Assen: 2002), 160–1, briefly describes how the Orthodox Churches in Eastern Europe felt threatened after the fall of the Iron Curtain.

Orthodox Church sees as 'unfair competition' by non-traditional religions or beliefs. According to the Orthodox Church, evangelical movements especially arrive with financial and other incentives (such as free education in the United States), and are therefore attractive in a country with a high poverty rate, such as Russia.

A similar development can be noticed in the Islamic world. In the context of the debates in the United Nations, representatives from Muslim countries often complained about the aggressive activities of Christian missionaries in their countries. Although Christian minorities in most of these countries are nowadays small in number, the idea that Islam is threatened by Christian proselytism has probably never disappeared altogether. Moreover, within the Islamic movements it was felt that, as a consequence of the globalisation process, they were confronted with ever more facets of the Western lifestyle. The clash between cultural and social traditions and the 'modern', Western lifestyle is perhaps nowhere as clear as in the Islamic world. Pressure by Islamic movements on governments to be clear about the Islamic nature of the State and to base national legislation on the Shari'a has only increased as globalisation has set in.

□ *Freedom to change one's religion or belief*

International human rights law is neutral itself and requires free access to information about competing religions or beliefs, e.g. in education and as part of freedom of expression (or freedom to manifest one's religion or belief). Article 18 of the Universal Declaration of Human Rights explicitly recognises the freedom to change one's religion or belief. For religions or beliefs who take a traditionally privileged place in society, these 'freedoms' may seem threatening. For example, Islamic countries generally have not accepted this particular freedom as it contradicts the precepts of Islam. In the case of Saudi Arabia, this reference was the reason it did not vote in favour of the Universal Declaration of Human Rights.[7]

During more recent codification debates, it has proved impossible to obtain consensus on the wording directly derived from the Universal

7 For the codification history see Cornelis D. de Jong, *The Freedom of Thought, Conscience and Religion or Belief in the United Nations (1946-1992)* (Antwerp: 2000), 34–48.

Declaration. Instead, Article 18 of the ICCPR speaks of the freedom to have or to adopt a religion or belief of one's choice, and Article 1 of the Declaration on the Elimination of All Forms of Intolerance and of Discrimination Based on Religion or Belief recognises the freedom to have a religion or belief of one's choice. In its General Comment on the freedom of religion and belief, as enshrined in the ICCPR, the Human Rights Committee clearly states that this freedom includes the freedom to change one's religion or belief, no matter how it had to be worded in Article 18. This corresponds with the prevailing views among authors and with the right to be free from coercion recognised in Article 18(2) of the ICCPR. Coercion does not relate to proselytism only, but also to a case of someone wanting to abandon his or her previous religion or belief but being forced to remain with it.

It is understandable that religions or beliefs who feel threatened emphasise that such a principle goes against their precepts to convert to another religion or belief. However, they cannot expect the State to implement their policies even if conversion has social consequences. Former co-believers may reject the convert, but it runs counter to international human rights law for the State to exert pressure or impose sanctions on converts.[8] One may even assume a positive obligation for the State to protect converts against pressures amounting to 'coercion'.

□ *Violence*

All religions and beliefs aim at peace and harmony. However, hardly any religion or belief is pacifist. Especially when threatened, but also in

8 Mohamed Eltayeb in 'Religion and State in Islamic perspective', in J. M. M. Naber (ed.), *Freedom of Religion: A Precious Human Right* (Assen: 2000), 111, mentions Sudanese legislation as an example of legislation penalising 'apostasy'. He also quotes the former Special Rapporteur for the Sudan, Mr Caspar Biro, as calling this type of legislation a flagrant violation of Art. 18 of the ICCPR. Maurice Berger, 'On Legislation and Jurisprudence in Egypt', quoted in 'Apostasy and Public Policy in Contemporary Egypt: An Evaluation of Recent Cases from Egypt's Highest Courts', *Human Rights Quarterly*, 25 (2003), 720–40. Ann Elizabeth Mayer in 'Freedom of Religion in Islamic Human Rights Schemes', in *OSCE–ODIHR Bulletin*, 5/2 (1997), argues that 'it is ironic that the apostasy penalty of the pre-modern Shari'a has been revived after developments had suggested that many thoughtful Muslims were prepared to reform or discard the principles of pre-modern Islamic jurisprudence on this topic and accept the concept of religious freedom'. She points, *inter alia*, to the fact that there is no verse in the Koran that stipulates any earthly penalty for apostasy.

order to spread their message throughout the world, most religions or beliefs can be interpreted in a way permitting the acceptance of violence if necessary. Compare the Crusades and colonialism of Christianity,[9] the (external) *jihad* of Islam, and the Hindutva or radical Buddhism. Such religiously inspired violence is in direct conflict with international human rights and humanitarian law.

This type of violence should not be confused with the abuse of religion or belief for political purposes. It has often been argued that religions or beliefs, even if peaceful in themselves, can become powerful and dangerous weapons in the hands of those seeking a rallying force to obtain support for their political causes. As I noted initially, it is a mistake to think that religion or belief will disappear from public life just because the Western world is in a process of secularisation. The past decade has showed a re-emergence of religion in politics in all parts of the world, even in the Western world itself. Contrast, for example, references to evangelical Christian values by the Bush administration with references to the Koran by moderate and extremist Islamic movements and governments. Perhaps this is best reflected in words written on a wall near the demolished World Trade Centre: 'Our God is bigger than yours.'[10] Since religions pertain to the most fundamental elements of one's outlook on life, it is very attractive to capture a religion or belief for political purposes. Making a convincing argument that 'God is on our side' not only gains the backing of the believers concerned, it ensures their most heartfelt support.

The current war against terrorism, for example, has many religious overtones. Yet I maintain that in fact it is not a war of religions but a political war. A recent study carried out by the Jordan-based Center for Strategic Studies held that 'Arab public opinion does not perceive the tensions between the Arab world and the West in either religious or cultural terms.' Instead, the study concludes that 'the Arab public disagrees with the foreign policies of the US and UK, and that it is these policies which are at the root of anti-American and subsequently anti-Western sentiments.'[11] The study goes on to say that 'Arabs associate Western

9 See, for example, Karel Blei, *op. cit.*, 54–61.

10 See Thijs Broer, 'Het geloof is terug', *Vrij Nederland* (19 April 2003).

11 The study, called 'Revisiting the Arab Street – Research from Within' (2005) can be downloaded from <http://www.css-jordan.org/new/index.html>. The quotes have

societies with liberalism, individual liberty, democracy and technological progress, but also with increased levels of societal problems', and that 'they see their societies as maintaining stronger values of tradition and family, and as being less plagued with social problems'. This seems to imply a clash between the primacy of the economic imperative, as is increasingly prevalent in the Western world, and the more spiritual and social values prevalent in Arab societies. The study clearly states, however, that 'Arabs do not see Islam, or religious differences with the West, as a significant reason for hostility between East and West'.

Consistent with these findings, targets of terrorist attacks are seldom religious in nature, but normally symbols of Western political and economic power and of Western lifestyle. The WTC and the Pentagon were of course very clear symbols of economic and military power. Also the more recent attacks on Madrid's and London's public transportation cannot be regarded as attacks on religious targets. If the terrorists had been fighting a religious war, they would have chosen other targets, such as the Vatican or the seat of the Archbishop of Canterbury. Moreover, suicide is forbidden under Islam.[12] It was therefore only after religious precepts had been re-interpreted that they could be used to 'legitimise' these terrorist attacks. Similarly, the response by the USA and the UK in Iraq is not a religious response. The official reasons given for the intervention in Iraq are based on considerations relating to security and democratisation. The fact that both the US president and the prime minister of the UK are making no secrets of their – incidentally, differing – religious backgrounds, may appeal to some of their religious constituency; in a sense, doing so was essential for President Bush's re-election. But this does not make the intervention in Iraq a religious war. The Iraqis do not have to convert to Christianity. They do, however, have to adopt our Western economic and political system, and furthermore they will have to respect the international division of power: in other words, the objectives of the USA and the UK are similarly economic and political rather than religious.

---

been taken from the executive summary, pp. 3 and 6. Similarly, Abdullahi An-Naim, ''The Best of Times' and 'the Worst of Times': Human Agency and Human Rights in Islamic Societies', *Muslim World Journal of Human Rights*, 1/1 (2004).

12 This thesis has been developed by Ariel Merari, 'The Readiness to Kill and Die', in Walter Reich (ed.), *Origins of Terrorism* (Cambridge, 1990).

□ *The rights of women*

Certain clashes are caused by the precepts of religions or beliefs relating to gender and sexuality. It is by no means possible to speak of a single set of precepts of religions or beliefs, since there are always various interpretations of the sacred texts to be found in religious teachings, but it is interesting to notice a number of recurring precepts that may give rise to such clashes. Although it is impossible in this context to enumerate the many precepts or interpretations which discriminate against women, reference can be made to the common practice of many religions to reserve clerical posts for men. Such practices can be found in the Catholic Church, in Judaism, in Islam and in Buddhism. Moreover, in accordance with traditional interpretations of the Koran, women do not enjoy similar rights before the courts since their testimonies do not have equal value to men's testimonies. In Judaism and Islam, difference can also be found in respect of inheritance laws and marriage and divorce laws.

Article 1 of the UN Convention on the Elimination of All Forms of Discrimination against Women contains a wide-ranging definition of non-discrimination:

> For the purposes of the present Convention, the term 'discrimination against women' shall mean any distinction, exclusion or restriction made on the basis of sex which has the effect of impairing or nullifying the recognition, enjoyment or exercise by women, irrespective of their marital status, on a basis of equality of men and women, of human rights and fundamental freedoms in the political, economic, social, cultural, civil or any other field.

The external manifestations of practices like those mentioned above easily come under this definition. Article 14 of the ICCPR stipulates that all persons shall be equal before the courts and tribunals. This implies that giving unequal weight to women's testimonies compared to men's impairs the right of women to treatment in accordance with Article 14. Similarly, Article 23 of the ICCPR states that States Parties shall take appropriate steps to ensure equality of rights and responsibilities of spouses before and during marriage and its dissolution. Here too, an important human right would be impaired by unequal treatment of men and women concerning marriage rights.

It is more difficult when practices confined to the realm of religious organisations are at issue. The basic question arises as to whether one can speak of discrimination if the women concerned do not object to such practices. Normally, international human rights law allows for some discretion here. No one ought to be forced to join a specific religious organisation. Women who object to certain practices have the right to establish a new organisation based on the same religion but with differing practices. Their freedom of religion is therefore not necessarily violated. This would only stop being the case if coercion were exerted upon them to remain within the religious organisation.

□ *Sacrilege versus incitement to hatred*

Because of the spiritual nature of religions, certain statements and acts can be considered sacrilege by believers, thus becoming an emotional matter, with escalatory processes just around the corner. Although international human rights law does, to some extent, protect religions or beliefs in this respect, it also protects the freedom of expression. Clashes result.

In accordance with Article 20 of the ICCPR, any advocacy of national, racial or religious hatred that constitutes incitement to discrimination, hostility or violence shall be prohibited by law. Although at the time of its codification many Western countries objected to this article, considering it vague and therefore a potential threat to the freedom of expression, over time it does seem to have become a yardstick for measuring what is to be tolerated and what is not.

In accordance with Article 20, hurt feelings as such do not matter. In the Netherlands in the 1960s, the use of the 'Our Father' for exposing national addiction to television (comparing God with the power of television) stirred up emotions and led to a particular television series being taking off the air. This can be seen as self-censorship by the public broadcasting service, but it has nothing to do with human rights law. However, speeches aimed at mobilising parts of the population against adherents of a particular religion or belief do come under the realm of Article 20 and are therefore prohibited.

It is sometimes argued that religious manifestations are in this regard privileged in comparison with non-religious manifestations. In the Netherlands, a number of cases came before the court concerning Islamic and Christian sermons or literature condemning homosexuality. Those manifestations were generally held to be consistent with national and international law, provided they only concerned religious precepts for the followers of that particular religion. If, however, sermons or literature contain language exhorting followers to persecute homosexuals who do not belong to the same religion or belief, such manifestations are not protected by the freedom of religion and belief and are to be prohibited in accordance with Article 20.

Some countries have adopted legislation forbidding blasphemy against a specific religion – normally the 'official' one. This approach goes much beyond the scope of Article 20. It is contrary to the principle of non-discrimination to single out a particular religion or belief. Article 20 does not make any distinction between grounds for hatred, such as nationality, race or religion. There is, however, a tension between these provisions under international human rights law and the emotional impact of blasphemy on believers. It is very tempting for a State with an official religion to protect the rights of believers in this respect. This is therefore a good example of another dilemma that easily results in clashes between international human rights law and a particular religion or belief.

3. GUIDELINES FOR GOVERNMENTS TO OVERCOME CLASHES BETWEEN RELIGION AND HUMAN RIGHTS

(*a*) *Recognition of the importance of religion or belief for meeting the needs of people in matters relating to spirituality, brotherhood, and charity*

As I argued in the first part of this discussion, religions and beliefs meet certain basic human needs. It is therefore not a coincidence that freedom of religion or belief is one of the fundamental human rights. I also defended the thesis that the real clash is not so much between religions or between religions and international human rights law, but between values such as spirituality, brotherhood and charity on the one hand and the introduction of a rational, economic lifestyle throughout the world on the other. Against the 'neo-liberal' theory of rational economic behaviour, religions and beliefs together with human rights movements can develop an alternative based on respect of the rights of everyone, irrespective of his/her economic position.

In the context of development policies, human rights come to the fore as part of good governance practices. Good governance is often seen as yet another instrument that forces governments of developing countries to open up their markets and promote a good investment climate. Against this background, it is important to emphasise that there is not a one-to-one relationship between human rights law and good – economic – governance. Human rights protect everyone, irrespective of his or her economic or social position. Moreover, there are tendencies within the UN organs devoted to the protection of human rights to pay attention to the responsibilities of transnational corporations. Such efforts are concerned with the social, economic and cultural rights that aim to promote a fair society, and this does not necessarily coincide with the effects of an unrestricted market economy.

International human rights law focuses on the effects of policies vis-à-vis people; it does not prescribe a particular economic system, nor does it identify solely with Western societies. Instead, it reflects basic values and norms common to practically all religions or beliefs. Even if there are clashes between certain religious manifestations and human rights norms, this does not mean there cannot be widespread consensus with regard to the basic underlying values. International human rights lawyers may have a public-relations problem with religions as suppressors of human rights, but if presented in the right manner I am certain that most religions and beliefs will rather be allies than enemies of international human rights standards.

(*b*) *Adoption of a non-discriminatory and open approach by States vis-à-vis religions and beliefs*

In accordance with international human rights law, States may not discriminate against any religion or belief. Instead, they should treat all religions and beliefs similarly. Although in my opinion it is hardly possible to combine non-discriminatory policies with the existence of an 'official' religion,[13] international human rights law does not prohibit this, even

13 The mere fact that there is an 'official' religion is in my opinion already a setback for adherents of other religions or beliefs. Not belonging to the 'official' religion places

if the Human Rights Committee tends to examine these situations very carefully. What matters is that religions or beliefs other than the official religion obtain similar rights.

An open approach towards religions and beliefs implies that instead of restricting the freedom of religion or belief, States ought to concentrate on making manifestations of all religions or beliefs possible. I am well aware of the fact that this goes against the present tendency in many parts of the world. In the context of the war against terrorism many human rights are being restricted, and freedom of religion or belief is no exception. In this context, Ferrari mentions the effects on missionary activities of stringent provisions regarding the granting of visas, the transferring of funds across borders and the registration of foreign organisations.[14] One could easily add the recent legislative and administrative measures aimed at barring religious symbols from public institutions and, as Ferrari also mentions, the increasing political interference with the internal affairs of religious organisations, which goes as far as national security services examining sermons by imams in Europe and North America. It is striking, as Ferrari points out, that the UK Terrorism Act of 2000 defines terrorism as 'the use or threat of action . . . designed to influence the government or to intimidate the public . . . and made for the purpose of advancing a political, religious or ideological cause'. This definition almost makes the war against terrorism a religious war,[15] whereas in reality its political and ideological character is paramount, as argued above. The effect of many of these measures may well be that believers turn inwards, seek shelter with their co-believers and possibly become more aware of their religious identity than before.[16] This can

them outside the mainstream, and the State is unlikely to offer any kind of compensation for this effect. See Cornelis D. de Jong, *op. cit.*, 286.

14 'Religion and Security in Europe after September 11: A Gloomy Perspective?', in *Proceedings of the Tenth Annual International Law and Religion Symposium: Religious Pluralism, Difference and Social Stability*, organised at Brigham Young University, Provo, Utah, USA (5–8 October 2003) <http://www.iclrs.org>.

15 Ferrari, *op. cit.*, points out that neither the UN Declaration on Measures to Eliminate International Terrorism nor the preceding UK Prevention of Terrorism Act 1989 mentioned religion, other than as a factor that could be abused for political, terrorist purposes.

16 Referring to recent French legislation prohibiting the wearing of religious symbols at French public schools, Dr. William F. Vendley questions the neutrality of the French secular state: 'But, is the public square truly neutral when the government

easily bring about an escalatory process: the more religious movements feel threatened, the more prone they may be to extremist views, leading to more interference, etc.

Instead, States should return to what the international human rights instruments teach them to do, i.e. enable people to adhere to the religion or belief of their choice and manifest it in public and in private, alone or in community with others. I shall take the example of recent French legislation barring headscarves from public schools. Although this measure did not give rise to as much tension at schools as might have been expected, and though the European Court of Human Rights has already held that this type of measure is not in violation of article 9 of the European Convention on Human Rights,[17] there is a serious concern that many Muslim girls may now prefer (or be forced) to join Islamic schools rather than public ones. In that case, the net result of these measures is that the target group does not integrate into the secular system but instead turns further away from it.

If governments were to give ample room to manifestations of religions and beliefs, it would create room for inter- and intra-religious debates. This would make it possible to expose extremist views, but it would also diminish the risk of religious groups isolating themselves, with all the dangers that brings for further radicalisation of the beliefs concerned.

Governments do not have to refrain from expressing their opinions of certain manifestations. I shall develop this argument further with respect to possible violations of other human rights and fundamental freedoms in the name of certain religions or beliefs. The State has a clear role to play here. But also within the realm of freedom of religion or belief itself

---

restricts religious expression in this way? Does French secularism have some of the features of a *de facto* civil religion with some fundamentalistic characteristics? It seems an honest question to raise along with the question of religious fundamentalism' ('Secular Fundamentalism', remarks made during the Symposium on Inter-religious Dialogue in the Face of Fundamentalism, Paris, France (21 March 2004)).

17 Case of *Lela Sahin* v. *Turkey* Application 44774/98, (2004) and the case of *Dahlab* v. *Switzerland* Application 42393/98, (2001). Channa Samkalden ('De Staat van de Godsdienstvrijheid – De Staat vrij van Godsdienst?', in NJCM–*Bulletin*, 29/4B (2004), 582–3) shows that in Germany the *Bundesverfassungsgericht* came to a different conclusion, which immediately prompted a number of *Länder* to adopt legislation explicitly prohibiting the wearing of religious symbols in public schools. Similar questions came up in Italy and even in the United States (concerning the 'pledge of alliance to the flag' at schools).

there is the need for an active State. If certain religions or beliefs condemn conversion to other religions or beliefs, the State ought to make sure that the persons concerned are protected. In a formal sense, this means that there ought not to be State legislation which enforces any such negative effects. I am referring in this respect to aspects of family and inheritance law in some Islamic countries. Even if Islam prescribes that the marriages of apostates must be dissolved and that apostates lose their right of inheritance, States should remain far from such clear violations of human rights. I only have to refer in this respect to Article 18(3) of the UN Covenant on Civil and Political Rights that prescribes freedom from coercion.

States also bear responsibilities in the field of education: not only are they responsible for public educational systems, they also set the framework for educational standards in private educational institutions. This offers a unique opportunity for States to ensure that children are not indoctrinated with a single religion or belief but are taught about all the main ones. Some will argue that this contradicts what I stated above regarding the barring of headscarves from public schools. However, I don't see any contradiction. In a way, it is even more powerful if a teacher wearing a headscarf teaches children, some of whom also wear headscarves, about the main tenets of Christianity, Judaism, Buddhism, Hinduism, humanism and even atheism. Others might argue that prescribing such a form of education violates the right of parents to have their religious and philosophical convictions respected where the education of their children is concerned.[18] However, in accordance with the jurisprudence of the European Court of Human Rights, 'the state is obligated to ensure the communication of information and knowledge in an objective and pluralistic manner'.[19] This is precisely what such a prescription aims at. Furthermore, Article 13 of the UN Covenant on Economic, Social and Cultural Rights stipulates that 'education shall enable all persons to participate effectively in a free society, promote understanding, tolerance and friendship among all nations and all racial, ethnic or religious groups, and further the activities of the United Nations for the maintenance of peace'. The proposed measure would serve this very objective.

---

18 European Convention on Human Rights, Article 2 of Protocol 1.

19 *Kjeldsen, Busk Madsen and Pederson* Series A No 23, (1976) ECHR).

(c) *Maintaining a right balance between the rights of adherents of clashing beliefs*

Once the State is seen to be open and non-discriminatory in respect of religions and beliefs, it finds itself in a much better position to prevent and resolve tensions in a society based on clashing beliefs. This may take the form of promoting dialogue and tolerance, but at this point I would like to address cases where repressive action of the State is at issue.

A particular dilemma governments may have to face is how to deal with clashes involving expressions considered blasphemy by adherents of a specific religion or belief as opposed to manifestations of the freedom of religion and belief that may be held offensive to people who do not adhere to the religion or belief concerned.

First of all, it should be recognised that, by definition, freedom of religion protects what is most important in one's outlook on life.[20] Therefore, religion or belief is more than a mere opinion, and people can feel seriously hurt when someone attacks what they have defined as their identity. At the same time, there is also freedom of expression. Recently, there has been a lot of turmoil in the Netherlands about a movie called 'Submission', which contains images offensive to many Muslims. The murder of Theo van Gogh, the film maker, by a Muslim extremist was not only justified by him as part of the *jihad*, but was also directly related to this man's sacrilege. It caused an animated debate in the media on the need to protect freedom of expression against these manifestations of religious extremism. Many in and outside politics claimed that governments ought to curtail freedom of religion or belief in order to protect freedom of expression. It was argued that though freedom of religion did not, of course, protect violence (such as murder), it did provide the basis for the idea that a religion had to be protected against blasphemy. Moreover, reference was made to radical statements against homosexuality that were permitted when made on the basis of a particular religion, while criticisms of religion were often found to be illegal.

20 In this respect, reference can be made to the preamble of the 1981 UN Declaration on the Elimination of All Forms of Intolerance and of Discrimination based on Religion or Belief, which states that religion or belief, for anyone who professes either, is one of the fundamental elements in his conception of life and that freedom of religion or belief should be fully respected and guaranteed.

As I argued earlier, protection against incitement to discrimination, hostility or violence is not confined to religions. The fact that manifestations of freedom of religion and belief are more difficult to restrict than manifestations of freedom of expression is a direct consequence of the way in which international human rights law has been set up, since the limitation grounds are more restrictive in the case of freedom of religion or belief than in the case of freedom of expression. In the Otto-Preminger case, the European Court of Human Rights stated:

> Those who choose to exercise the freedom to manifest their religion, irrespective of whether they do so as members of a religious majority or a minority, cannot reasonably expect to be exempt from all criticism. They must tolerate and accept the denial by others of their religious beliefs and even the propagation by others of doctrines hostile to their faith. However, the manner in which religious beliefs and doctrines are opposed or denied is a matter which may engage the responsibility of the State, notably its responsibility to ensure the peaceful enjoyment of the right guaranteed under Article 9 to the holders of those beliefs and doctrines. Indeed, in extreme cases the effect of particular methods of opposing or denying religious beliefs can be such as to inhibit those who hold such beliefs from exercising their freedom to hold and express them.[21]

I do not see why the recent events in the Netherlands or elsewhere should change this line of reasoning. Freedom to express one's opinion is important, but an opinion may change overnight, whereas adherence to a religion or belief tends to be much more deeply rooted. It seems therefore justified to limit freedom of expression if not doing so would result in people not feeling free to manifest their religion or belief. Theo van Gogh's movie, one could argue, was made specifically to attack certain Islamic precepts. It was made in a way guaranteed to shock Muslims as much as possible. Although careful weighing up of all relevant points is necessary, I cannot rule out that prohibiting this movie from being screened might have been justified.[22]

---

21 No 295 ECHR.

22 Willi Fuhrmann ('Perspectives on Religious Freedom from the Vantage Point of the European Court of Human Rights', *Brigham Young University Law Review*,

Clashes are of course not confined to blasphemy: they can take any form ranging from hostility and discrimination to violence. In each case, the State has to act. Discriminatory and violent acts cannot be tolerated, no matter who is the victim. When, after the murder of van Gogh, mosques, churches and religious schools were vandalised, the Netherlands prime minister made a very clear statement condemning these acts, irrespective of whose religion was at issue. The perpetrators were prosecuted and are awaiting trial. That is the only right course of action in such cases.

(*d*) *Promotion of dialogue among adherents of different and opposing beliefs*

Whereas repressive measures may sometimes be necessary, it is of course much better to avoid clashes between religions and beliefs, or at least to prevent these from leading to violence. At times when tensions related to religion or belief seem to be increasing, States ought to put more energy into engaging and promoting dialogue with and among all concerned. According to the judgement of the European Court of Human Rights quoted above, there is even a State obligation for active involvement. This dialogue does not have to be restrained by 'sensitivities' on the part of the believers. In general, humour and even satire can help in creating a more open atmosphere and should certainly not be prohibited. But the overall tone should be constructive, not humiliating, and respectful of each other's position.[23]

(2000), 837) emphasises the need for such a weighing of circumstances, when he concludes that 'there must be a balance of proportionality between the manner in which the antireligious sentiment is expressed and the state's repressive measures and penalties'. Paul Cliteur (in 'Godslastering en zelfcensuur na de moord op Theo van Gogh', *Nederlands Juristen Blad*, 45/46 (Dec. 2004), 2328–35) calls for respect of the freedom of expression and is afraid of the self-censorship that a more restrictive approach might bring about in this respect.

23 True dialogue presupposes mutual respect. As Javaid Rehman points out: 'Religions and beliefs also have the tendency to become rigid, and their followers intolerant towards other competing religious values and philosophies. . . . This intolerance can lead a follower to the view that "I am in the right and you are wrong. When you are stronger, you ought to tolerate me; for it is your duty to tolerate truth. But when I am stronger, I shall persecute you; since it is my duty to persecute you"' ('Accommodating Religious Identities in an Islamic State: International Law, Freedom of Religion and the Rights of Religious Minorities', *International Journal on Minority and Group Rights*, 7/2 (Feb. 2000), 139–65). Real tolerance is based on respect, which in

Generally, religious organisations are ready to engage in such dialogue. Reference can be made to a number of initiatives in this regard. The World Conference of Religions for Peace, for example, devotes much of its time and energy to establishing and maintaining inter-religious councils. At local, sub-regional and regional levels, these councils can be instrumental in promoting inter- and intra-religious dialogue. The International Association for Religious Freedom (IARF) has drawn up a 'Declaration of Religious Freedom and Responsibility' which, when adopted by an increasing number of religions and beliefs, should contribute to harmony and tolerance. Moreover, the IARF is currently engaged in a project preparing teaching materials to be used at grass-roots level. The materials promote dialogue among adherents of different religions and beliefs. In the Netherlands, religious movements work together at national and local levels and constitute platforms for discussions on themes that may otherwise lead to tensions in society.

In 2001, President Khatami of the Islamic Republic of Iran called for a dialogue among civilisations. This initiative was welcomed by the UN, which adopted the Agenda for Dialogue among Civilisations that same year. As Hans Küng and others put it, 'it is better to have a dialogue among civilisations than a clash among civilisations' (alluding to Huntington's famous concept).[24] Although dialogue among civilisations is broader than inter-religious dialogue, the latter can certainly contribute to the broader process. This is clearly evident when looking at Unesco's work in this respect. Through its series of conferences and declarations, Unesco aims at promoting dialogue, thereby trying to diminish the tensions caused, *inter alia*, by international terrorism. Part of these activities is directly related to inter-religious dialogue.[25]

Governments can take a number of initiatives to promote dialogue. They can encourage non-governmental organisations based on religion or belief to set up platforms for dialogue, *inter alia* by funding such

turn is based on the acceptance that what may be 'truth' for oneself may not represent 'truth' for the other.

24 *Crossing the Divide: Dialogue among Civilizations* (South Orange, New Jersey, 2001). Based on an initiative by the Islamic Republic of Iran (speech by President Khatami before the General Assembly in 1998, and res. A/53/22 of 16 November 1998). The year 2001 became the UN Year of the Dialogue among Civilizations.

25 Information on Unesco's programme can be found on <http://www.unesco.org/dialogue2001>.

projects. At national and local levels, governments can also create such platforms themselves. People often have a false idea of each other, fed by incidents that catch the media's attention. When adherents of opposing beliefs meet each other, many of the stereotypes suddenly do not fit anymore. Creating meeting places, both of a formal and of an informal nature, may therefore be very helpful in diminishing tensions.

As observed above, another important instrument governments have at their disposal is education. In a recent study, 'Religion and Schooling in an Open Society: A Framework for Informed Dialogue',[26] the Open Society Institute recognises the importance of education for the promotion of tolerance. However, while it is stated that teaching about religions as a nonconfessional model of religious education may be an appropriate policy for an open society, it is also questioned whether teaching about religions, in itself, is sufficient, and whether this will actually develop tolerance and social cohesion. Unesco has already done a lot of work in this field, but the development of teaching tools and methodologies ought to be encouraged in order to take into account the present-day situation, where competing religions and beliefs are struggling in a world facing growing tensions, *inter alia* as a consequence of the abuse of religion by international terrorists and, as far as Europe is concerned, by the arrival of large communities of immigrants with different beliefs than those that were the norm in most European countries. In this respect, the conclusions of the seminar organised by the Commissioner of Human Rights of the Council of Europe on religion and education are interesting, especially the recommendation 'that a working group be established to examine how an international Institute for cooperation in the field of the education of religions in schools might best be established and what its mandate might be'.[27] It will be interesting to see what follow-up the Council of Europe gives to this initiative.

(e) *Promotion of debates on interpretation of religious precepts*

So far I have called for a rather positive approach towards religions or beliefs. It cannot be denied, however, that some religious precepts are at odds with international human rights standards. The previous part of

26 Open Society Institute, December 2004, Ljubljana, Slovenia.

27 CommDH(2004)9, which can be downloaded from <http://www.coe.int/commissioner>.

this essay, dealing with actual and potential clashes, already mentioned a number of such tensions. The State cannot remain indifferent to this phenomenon. In the case of clear violations of human rights, States will have to take repressive measures. Moreover, as I already stated, the State itself should never be associated with practices running counter to human rights or fundamental freedoms.

There are, however, other ways of influencing religions and beliefs without interfering directly with their internal affairs. In all world religions there has always been and will continue to be discussion regarding the correct interpretation of sacred texts. These texts normally stem from a of time completely different to our modern world. Many of the ongoing discussions of world religions relate to the question of whether the texts can be re-interpreted to take account of the present situation. Governments can stimulate such debates: taking an interest in such discussions does not amount to interference with internal religious affairs, since, after all, many in our societies are affected by them.

This is true particularly for countries where there is no separation of State and religion. Engaging in discussions on the interpretation of religious texts is, for the governments of these countries, sometimes essential, in order to be able to bring their legislation, insofar as it is based upon or inspired by certain religions or beliefs, into line with international human rights law. In this respect, reference can be made to the careful steps taken by the Moroccan government to improve the rights of women, e.g. in the field of family law. Simply changing the laws might have been interpreted as a concession to Western influence. However, the changes in law were directly based on interpretations of the Koran, showing that there need not be a conflict between religious teachings and international human rights law.

CONCLUSIONS

The search for spirituality is not a thing of the past, and probably never will be. It is an essential need for every human being, though each of us may have a different way of fulfilling it. The freedom of religion and belief is a reflection of this need. Those who favour a world based on economic values will have to come to terms with the reality that people do not live 'by bread alone'. The need for spirituality together with the need for brotherhood are not met by an economic paradigm based on the assumption that people solely make economically rational decisions based on their economic self-interest. If there is a clash of civilisations, perhaps this is the overriding one – the clash between economic theories that take the shape of a new world religion and existing religions and beliefs.

Instead of unduly restricting the freedom of religion or belief, governments ought to recognise its significance and act upon it. The present legal framework leaves plenty of scope for governments to limit manifestations of this freedom. The limitation grounds have been carefully worded because of the precious (and vulnerable) nature of this particular fundamental freedom. However, if the fundamental rights and freedoms of others are at issue, it must remain possible to restrict the freedom to manifest one's religion or belief.

At the same time, it cannot be denied that most governments face challenges arising out of religion or belief. Abuse of religion or belief for political purposes, as well as the existence of precepts running counter to international human rights law, are challenges that must be addressed. Sometimes, a government will have to act against repressive means being used in the name of religion. Most often, however, it is of overriding importance that the government takes an open approach towards all religions or beliefs, is neutral in that respect, and never becomes hostile to any particular religion or belief. It will then be in the best possible position to engage in dialogue with religions and beliefs, and to encourage inter- and intra-religious dialogue whenever relevant. Through dialogue and education, it will be possible to further a harmonious society based on values and beliefs that go beyond economic imperatives.

CHAPTER 11

Triumphalism and Respect for Diversity

Conor Gearty

IN THIS BRIEF ESSAY I would like to consider the question of the conflict between human rights and religion.

The first proposition is that religion and human rights have plenty of similarities. I think Professor Javaid Rehman in his essay is right to challenge the inevitability of the clash. I think Professor Avrom Sherr, in his, is right to echo him. In this essay I shall first describe some of those similarities, then draw attention to some of the tensions between the two, and finally address, in the context of those tensions, some of the points that have been raised.

Firstly, human rights and religion both make universal claims. Melanie Phillips, in her contribution, starts by discussing dignity and the Bible. She then slightly pulls back from that and suggests that human rights may be vacuous. I do not think that the idea is. I think the generality of the claims human rights makes is pretty big, and that the subject shares with religion this – rather ambitious – universality.

Secondly, human rights does put culture in its place. I think that when human rights is being 'polite', it suggests that it is deferential to the culture of the place in which the idea is to be found. But among friends, human rights is rather more bombastic than that; I think there is in human rights, as there is in religion, a slightly universalist triumphalism. The point is that there are indeed, at certain levels of generality, elements of cultural imperialism here. Melanie Phillips is right that the European Court of Human Rights' decisions in the case regarding the gays in Ireland and in Cyprus[1] were not well received in their places of origin on the whole. There indeed was a way here in which human rights was not deferring to the local community. In this respect, the subject shares with religion a kind of deference to the local without being slave to it. Hence you find anthropologists who are quite critical of human rights, as they often are of religions that claim universality.

1 *Norris* v. *Ireland* (1988) 13 EHRR 186; *Modinos* v. *Cyprus* (1993) 16 EHRR 485.

Thirdly, I think that at their core, human rights and religion share a commitment to the dignity of the person in a way which manifests itself in a commitment to the dignity of others. This is one of the things that really links them. Human rights are certainly concerned with the self, but they are also concerned with other persons – and not just one's immediate family, or village, or community, or region or state. Human rights actually require people to imagine the situation of an individual outside their own zone. This is a significant and, I think, quite a religious concept. A remarkable paper, delivered as the Aquinas Lecture in Oxford by Oliver Davis, talks about compassion as the idea that underpins an approach to human rights, and this is consistent with certain strands of Christian thinking. This is a very interesting approach indeed.

Elsewhere in the current volume, Nazila Ghanea mentions the notion of 'the invisible'. I have thought often that human rights is a kind of visibility project. It is about drawing people to other people's attention. These are the ways in which human rights and religion share many similarities.

Whence the tension?

Both human rights and religion have got real problems with postmodernism – which is the prevailing *zeitgeist*, in the West anyway. Human rights have, perhaps, coped with it better than religion, in ways I shall discuss below. What are those problems? Well, Melanie Phillips is right that in what is rudely called the pre-Enlightenment-period, duty was prior to rights. Religion was in its pomp. It was the only show in town. Only in the Enlightenment period did liberals develop a strong belief in an alternative truth outside the Church available for discovery – a truth requiring more than just turning to the priest for directions. This is not the current approach of our society, however, which is much rooted in a *rejection* not just of Church authority but also of this kind of rationalist foundationalism.

The challenge for both human rights and religion is how to deal with the problem of difference. In my own faith there is kind of real tension between a universalistic demand to regard everybody as a *potential* Catholic, and a recognition that the Holy Spirit on an 'off' day might have manifested the commitment to truth via some other religion; and various very bright people – Jesuits usually – try and say this without being excommunicated. In every religion you find people trying to work within the culture to say, 'Look, you know, they're not *all* going to burn in—' (fill the gap).

Human rights has solved this matter in a slightly different way. Human rights is a subject which has thrived in the anti-foundationalist, post-modern era, and that is odd and unexpected. The reason for its success, I think, lies in not taking its claim to foundationalism seriously. What instead?

It has developed a different approach – the one Melanie Phillips, in a most useful way, attacks. It is an approach which focuses precisely not on personal gratification. Melanie Phillips allied personal happiness with personal gratification, as though they were the same; but actually there is a very important difference between personal gratification and personal happiness. Human rights in the post-modern era tries to say: 'Let's focus on personal flourishing, on personal growth, on personal development in the private sphere.' That *may* involve sexual orientation being fully reflected in practices. It may involve degrees of departure from the prevailing norm. It does not have to do so, there is no compulsion about it, but the human rights agenda does require respect for difference.

Human rights has also got a public dimension, because democracy suits human rights beautifully. Democracy is a perfect post-modern notion. 'Truth' is whatever passing majorities say it should be, and that suits the contemporary human rights message perfectly. So there is the commitment to personal growth, but also the commitment to a public good which is defined by reference to the people themselves – not by reference to God, or a professor, or a philosopher, but by reference to the people. This is what human rights today is about. It is not about equality as identicality. It is about constructing a society which, within limits, gives everybody a chance to lead the life they want to lead and aim for the best chance they have for personal flourishing. This is how human rights in a way has got ahead of religion. I think religion is seeking to accommodate this notion of respect for diversity within it in many of its different forms, and one of the interesting things in the next few years will be to see how it manages to do that. Human rights when at its highpoint tended to regard religion as irrational and irrelevant. A human rights chastened by recent events is more inclined to see that there is more to the person than the mind: 'post-modern human rights' is more open than the intellectually superior form that preceded it.

I shall end with the following thought. Watch the debate in the UK about incitement to religious hatred. That will be a good test of where people stand on human rights. Do they emphasise the prohibition on religious criticism, or do they emphasise the notion of an incitement to hatred? At this moment in our culture we have no space in our discourse for any kind of hatred: whether it is religiously inspired or racially motivated should remain a secondary consideration. As someone committed to human rights and to the dignity of the individual, I have no anxieties about a properly regulated approach to the problem of persons who set about inciting hatred in our society. Others less committed to equality and dignity of the person than to free speech as the basic building block of our society would take a different approach. It is an interesting debate in which to work out where one stands.

CHAPTER 12

'Phobias' and 'Isms': Recognition of Difference or the Slippery Slope of Particularisms?

Nazila Ghanea

In recent years, new terminology has been emerging at the international level, especially at UN forums, suggesting a typology of language for the racial and religious discrimination suffered by various groups. To the existing language on 'anti-Semitism' has been added 'Islamophobia' and 'Christianophobia.'

This chapter asks where this accumulation of new terms is going to end, and, more importantly, what purpose it really serves in international human rights law. 'Special rights' and differences of treatment have been recognised in human rights as serving a particular role in addressing previously neglected arenas where violations were being suffered but not sufficiently recognised, as, for example, in relation to the rights of children or migrants, who had previously been bundled under the term 'everyone.' However, the question is whether highlighting Islamophobia or Christianophobia serves a similar end. Do these terms highlight a new and significantly different nexus of human rights violations that remain untouched by the overarching terms of racial or religious discrimination?

Taking a victim-centred approach, the main question is whether the identification of such separate hatreds and discrimination enhances legal and other approaches to combating them. This will be the criteria used to assess the utility of expanding particularisms during the course of this chapter.

New Language at the International Level: The Durban Legacy?

The 2001 World Conference Against Racism can be seen as a pivotal moment, when the international community clashed bitterly over comparisons of suffering and the attempt at identifying hierarchies of racisms. The distasteful competition of injustices and the divisions of

Durban were to be entrenched yet further by the legacy of September 11, 2001, just three days after the World Conference Against Racism ended.[1] While the identification of different kinds of race and religious discriminations at the international level cannot solely be traced to Durban or 9/11, these were clearly monumental events in this practice. Since then, it has increasingly become standard to list a series of such hatreds and discriminations, often with little attention as to why in fact this is actually so.

Examples of this practice will be taken in this initial part of the chapter from the UN Commission of Human Rights (henceforth 'Commission'), because Commission resolutions engage the majority of states, whether members of that 53-state body during that session or not. The wording of its resolutions are, therefore, a significant indicator of international opinion on a matter at any particular time. Attention will be given below to both the context within which this matter arose in Commission resolutions and the language of those resolutions.

April 2004 was the first time the Commission resolution on 'the incompatibility between democracy and racism' listed anti-Semitism, Islamophobia, and Christianophobia.[2] This was in the context of expressing deep concern about the increase in these phenomena. Even that list was not seen to be sufficient, and deep concern was also expressed with regard to 'the emergence of racial and violent movements based on racism and discriminatory ideas against Arab, Christian, Jewish and Muslim communities, as well as communities of people of African descent and communities of people of Asian descent, and other communities'.[3] In 2003 the same resolution merely referred to 'racism, racial discrimination, xenophobia and related intolerance' throughout the document.[4] The same language of phobias and communities was repeated in the

1 World Conference Against Racism 2001, Durban Declaration and Programme of Action, linked from <http://www.ohchr.org/english/law/index.htm> accessed 13 June 2005.

2 UN Doc. E/CN.4/2004/38, 'The Incompatibility between Democracy and Racism', Commission on Human Rights resolution, adopted at the 55th meeting, 19 April 2004, para. 5.

3 UN Doc. E/CN.4/2004/38, para. 5.

4 UN Doc. E/CN.4/2003/41, 'The Incompatibility between Democracy and Racism', Commission on Human Rights resolution, adopted at the 58th meeting, 23 April 2003.

World Conference against Racism resolution as well, again in noting deep concern with the increase in these phenomena.[5] More worryingly, the annual Commission resolution on religious intolerance in 2004 also adopted the same listing for the first time but in a different order: 'Islamophobia, anti-Semitism and Christianophobia'.[6] This was repeated in the 2005 resolution on religious intolerance.[7] In both instances, these mentions were in the context of recognising deep concern with the rise in instances of such intolerance and the violence motivated by these phenomena. But the question is why these three hatreds were singled out from the general category of religious intolerance.

The separation of Islamophobia from the broader scourge of religious discrimination was asserted in a further 2005 Commission resolution as well. The resolution, 'Combating Defamation of Religions', had been tabled since 1999. Religious defamation is contextualised in the broader framework of respect for all, harmony in all societies, religious and cultural diversity, tolerance and freedom of religion and belief, concern about the negative stereotyping of religions, attacks on religious sites and symbols, the prohibition of racist and xenophobic ideas and the defamation of religions. However, it is not clear why every single one of the eight examples given of such defamation and discrimination in this broader context highlight only Muslims. The references are to the negative impact of events against 'Muslim minorities and communities in some non-Muslim countries and the negative projection of Islam in the media'; laws that 'discriminate against and target Muslims'; the attack especially in human rights forums on 'Islam and Muslims'; the ethnic and

5 UN Doc. E/CN.4/2004/88, World Conference against Racism, Racial Discrimination, Xenophobia and Related Intolerance, and the comprehensive implementation of and follow-up to the Durban Declaration and Programme of Action, Commission on Human Rights resolution, adopted at the 59th meeting, 22 April 2004, preambular para. 6.

6 UN Doc. E/CN.4/2004/36, 'Elimination of all Forms of Religious Intolerance', Commission on Human Rights Resolution, adopted at the 55th meeting, 19 April 2004, preambular para. 14.

7 Paragraph 6 '*Recognizes with deep concern* the overall rise in instances of intolerance and violence directed against members of many religious communities in various parts of the world, including cases motivated by Islamophobia, anti-Semitism and Christianophobia' (UN Doc E/CN.4/2005/40, 'Elimination of all Forms of Intolerance and of Discrimination Based on Religion or Belief', Commission on Human Rights resolution, adopted at the 49th meeting, 14 April 2005).

religious profiling of 'Muslim minorities', the wrongful association with human rights violations and terrorism of 'Islam'; the use of the media to incite violence and intolerance towards 'Islam or any other religion'; the need to effectively combat defamation of 'all religions, Islam and Muslims in particular, especially in human rights forums'; and, finally, a request to the Special Rapporteur on contemporary forms of racism, racial discrimination, xenophobia and related intolerance 'to continue to examine the situation of Muslims and Arab peoples in various parts of the world' and the discrimination faced by them.[8]

Examination of these examples of references at international forums suggests that the use of these terms is such as to be to the detriment of attention to the broader and more general challenges of religious and racial discrimination. Before revisiting the impact of this, let us turn to the question of whether the phenomena of anti-Semitism, Islamophobia and Christianophobia are in themselves so distinct as to require separate mention?

WHAT IS ANTI-SEMITISM, ISLAMOPHOBIA AND CHRISTIANOPHOBIA, AND HOW DO THEY DIFFER?

The separate identification of anti-Semitism has a long history. Indeed the dreadful scourge of anti-Semitism played a historical role in lending impetus to the very creation of the United Nations. At a recent United Nations special session specifically on anti-Semitism held at UN headquarters in June 2004,[9] UN Secretary-General Kofi Annan emphasised that 'The United Nations must never forget that it was created as a response to the evil of Nazism, or that the horror of the Holocaust helped to shape its mission. That response is enshrined in our Charter, and in

8 UN Doc. E/CN.4/2005/3, 'Combating Defamation of Religions', Commission on Human Rights resolution, adopted at the 44th meeting, 12 April 2005, preliminary paras. 12 and 15 and operative paras. 3, 4, 6, 8 and 16.

9 The anti-Semitism seminar was the first in a series held by the UN Department of Public Information under the theme of 'Unlearning Intolerance'; see <http://www.un.org/apps/sg/sgstats.asp?nid=988> accessed 20 February 2005. Since then, another seminar has been held on 'Confronting Islamophobia' on 7 December 2004. For the text of the UN Secretary-General's address at that seminar see <http://www.un.org/apps/sg/sgstats.asp?nid=1217> accessed 20 Feb. 2005.

the Universal Declaration of Human Rights.'[10] The UN further marked the sixtieth anniversary of the liberation of Auschwitz with a General Assembly special session on 24 January 2005. Nevertheless, the UN has been severely criticised for an anti-Semitic record in more recent times. In a speech at the UN conference 'Confronting Anti-Semitism: Education for Tolerance and Understanding,' Anne Bayefsky asserted that

> [t]he UN took root in the ashes of the Jewish people, and according to its charter was to flower on the strength of a commitment to tolerance and equality for all men and women and of nations large and small. Today, however, the UN provides a platform for those who cast the victims of the Nazis as the Nazi counterparts of the twenty-first century. The UN has become the leading global purveyor of anti-Semitism – intolerance and inequality against the Jewish people and its state.[11]

She argues this point on the basis of, amongst other things, the fact that

> [t]here has never been a UN resolution specifically on anti-Semitism or a single report to a UN body dedicated to discrimination against Jews, in contrast to annual resolutions and reports focusing on the defamation of Islam and discrimination against Muslims and Arabs.[12]

Anti-Semitism, however, does specifically find mention within numerous more general UN documents, both within charter body and treaty body discussions of discrimination.

Is the apparent need to follow each mention of anti-Semitism in such documents with Islamophobia and Christianophobia just because parity is being sought by populous religions? In which case, where is this practice ultimately going to lead the international community – to

---

10 Secretary-General's statement to the Special Session of the General Assembly (New York, 24 Jan. 2005) <http://www.un.org/apps/sg/sgstats.asp?nid=1273> accessed 17 Feb. 2005.

11 Anne Bayefsky, 'One Small Step: Is the UN Finally Ready to get Serious about Anti-Semitism?', in *The Wall Street Journal*'s opinion journal, *On the Record* (21 June 2004), available online at <http://www.un.org/apps/sg/sgstats.asp?nid=988> accessed 13 June 2005.

12 Ibid.

the creation of endless new 'isms' and 'phobias' such as Hinduophobia, Buddhistophobia, Bahá'íophobia, Sikhophobia, Zoroastrianophobia and so on? Or is there a unique nexus of multiple discrimination and fundamentally different and cumulative manifestations of hatred that are being uncovered by the coining and utility of each of these terms?

□ *Anti-semitism*

Anti-Semitism's separate recognition has long been argued on the basis of both its unfortunate combining of racial and religious hatred and its unenviable historical legacy due to the Nazi genocide. The labelling imposed upon the victim of Semitic hatred is inescapable and entrenched. Semitic hatred has evolved a whole series of identifiable symbols and practices; its continuum of increasingly hateful practices can be deliberated, and are recognised across borders and cultures. It is an international phenomenon. Whilst the fact that the survivors of the Holocaust are still living is also sometimes given as a reason for continuing to highlight it, this may perhaps be recognised as a more emotive than legal stance. The key reasons for its *separate* recognition in international human rights can be summarised as including the following: entrenched and awful history; the combining of multiple hatreds – racial and religious; and the identifiable pattern of violations against the victims regardless of borders. How do these criteria compare in the cases of Christianophobia and Islamophobia?

□ *Christianophobia*

Whilst persecution against Christians on a global level continues in many countries, and is carefully followed by a number of organisations,[13] the Thirty Years War (1618–48) can be recognised as the period of the greatest bloodshed of Christians. In this complex series of wars, partly taking the shape of a religious war between Catholics, Lutherans and Calvinists, some estimates suggest that up to one third of the population of Europe was eradicated. Inter-Christian rivalries therefore seem to have characterised the heyday of the bloodshed of Christians. Another factor, both characterising that period as well as present-day persecution of Christians, is that this persecution can be escaped through conversion

---

13 e.g. The Center for Religious Freedom of Freedom House; see <http://www.freedomhouse.org/religion/> accessed 17 Feb. 2005.

– distinguishing it from the persecution of Jews as a racial group during the Holocaust. A glance at the persecution of Christians in various parts of the world today suggests that it is the practice of evangelism and the attracting of new converts by some Christian groups that gives rise to most persecution.[14] Examples of this stem, for example, from India, the Islamic Republic of Iran and China – though persecution against Christians in Egypt, Vietnam, Saudi Arabia and Nigeria incorporates further elements. The historical experience of Christianophobia therefore seems to distinguish itself from anti-Semitism in a number of ways, though this of course does not make it any more excusable. Nevertheless, it must be admitted that the whole phenomenon of Christianophobia is very difficult to analyse, as it is not a term that has attracted academic or policy attention to date. It is, in fact, a term created in the international arena in order to reflect parity of concern with the other phobias and 'isms'!

□ *Islamophobia*

Islamophobia as a recognised phenomenon has a recent history – just over two decades. Even today, and unlike anti-Semitism but like Christianophobia, there is a dearth of academic literature actually addressing the phenomenon in any depth. Most definitions draw upon the same sources, particularly the 1997 Runnymede Trust report, many are British and European in origin, and many originate from web sources and from organisations that also record incidents of Islamophobia.

The aforementioned and often-quoted 1997 study of Islamophobia in the UK provided the following elements in defining the term: 'dread or hatred of Islam . . . to fear or dislike . . . [of] all or most Muslims';[15] 'unfounded hostility towards Islam';[16] with the practical consequences of such hostility being 'unfair discrimination against Muslim individuals and communities' and their exclusion 'from mainstream political and social affairs.'[17] Overall the report asserts that this new term, which

---

14 One may make a distinction between Christian groups that are active in proselytising or evangelising and those that are more settled or traditional. There is a sharp distinction in some countries between the tolerance to the latter and repression of the former, Iran being a case in point.

15 The Runnymede Trust, *Commission on British Muslims and Islamophobia: Islamophobia, A Challenge For Us All*, (London: Runnymede Trust, Oct. 1997), 1.

16 Ibid., 4.

17 Ibid.

was first used in print in 1991,[18] described a new threat needing to be countered:

> The word 'Islamophobia' has been coined because there is a new reality which needs naming: anti-Muslim prejudice has grown so considerably and so rapidly in recent years that a new item in the vocabulary is needed so that it can be identified and acted against. . . . the mere use of the new word 'Islamophobia' will not in itself prevent tragic conflict and waste. But . . . it can play a valuable part in the long endeavour of correcting perceptions and improving relationships.[19]

A number of authors have emphasised that Islamophobia contains both racist and religious elements in its hatred of Muslims. In the context of the UK, for example, Modood argues that 'Just as hostility against Jews, in various times and places, has been a varying blend of anti-Judaism (hostility to a religion) and anti-Semitism (hostility to a racial group), so it is difficult to gauge to what extent contemporary British Islamophobia is "religious" and to what extent "racial".'[20]

The report also, very importantly, explains what Islamophobia is not:

> It is not intrinsically phobic or prejudiced, of course, to disagree with or to disapprove of Muslim beliefs, laws or practices. . . . It can be legitimate to criticise policies and practices of Muslim states and regimes, for example, especially when their governments do not subscribe to internationally recognised human rights, freedoms and democratic procedures, or to criticise and condemn terrorist movements which claim to be motivated by Islamic values.[21]

Modood reiterates this very succinctly in calling for the need for there to be 'analytical space for forthright criticism of aspects of Muslim doctrines, ideologies and practice without it being dismissed as Islamophobia

18 Ibid., 1 n. 4.

19 Ibid., 4.

20 Tariq Modood, 'The Place of Muslims in British Secular Multiculturalism', in N. Ghanea (ed.), *The Challenge of Religious Discrimination at the Dawn of the New Millennium* (Leiden: Martinus Nijhoff, 2003), 242.

21 The Runnymede Trust, *Commission on British Muslims and Islamophobia*, 4.

– this being exactly the parallel problem of distinguishing anti-Zionism and anti-Semitism.'[22] The clarity with which this distinction is stated is very welcome, but it is a far cry from the record at the international level of, for example, a whole range of UN Commission on Human Rights resolutions. It would indeed be appropriate to explore what the parallels to this are for Christianophobia and Islamophobia.

Since 1999, the UN has adopted annual resolutions variously entitled 'Combating Defamation of Religions', 'Defamation of Religions' or 'Combating Defamation of Religions as a Means to Promote Human Rights, Social Harmony, and Religious and Cultural Diversity'.[23] All of these resolutions have been notable in their attempt primarily to protect the religion of Islam and no other – despite their title suggesting a broader mandate – rather than the rights of Muslims per se. The 1999 resolution for example addresses the stereotyping of religions,[24] expresses concern at the association of Islam with human rights violations and terrorism,[25] and even talks of incitement of violence and discrimination against Islam rather than Muslims.[26] What is not clear is how a religion per se can be discriminated against (and how this tallies with freedom of speech for example) and, further, how this would be a human rights concern. The 2000[27] and 2001[28] resolutions are very similar, and the 2002 resolution adds the element of strongly deploring 'physical attacks and assaults on businesses, cultural centres and places of worship of all religions, in particular of Muslims in many parts of the world'.[29] The 2003 resolution's

22 Modood, 'Muslims in British Secular Multiculturalism', 234.

23 See UN Doc. E/CN.4/1999/82 adopted 30 April 1999, UN Doc. E/CN.4/2000/84 adopted 26 April 2000, UN Doc. E/CN.4/2001/4 adopted 18 April 2001, UN Doc. E/CN.4/2002/9 adopted 15 April 2002, UN Doc. E/CN.4/2003/4 adopted 14 April 2003, UN Doc. E/CN.4/2004/6 adopted 13 April 2004 and E/CN.4/2005/3 adopted 12 April 2005.

24 UN Doc. E/CN.4/1999/82, 'Defamation of Religions', Commission on Human Rights resolution, adopted at the 62nd meeting, 30 April 1999, para. 1.

25 Ibid., para. 2.

26 Ibid., para. 3.

27 UN Doc. E/CN.4/2000/84, 'Defamation of Religions', Commission on Human Rights resolution, adopted at the 67th meeting, 26 April 2000.

28 UN Doc. E/CN.4/2001/4, 'Combating Defamation of Religions as a Means to Promote Human Rights, Social Harmony and Religious and Cultural Diversity', Commission on Human Rights resolution, adopted at the 61st meeting, 18 April 2001.

29 UN Doc E/CN.4/2002/9, 'Combating Defamation of Religion', Commission

concern with combating 'hatred, discrimination, intolerance and acts of violence, intimidation and coercion motivated by religious intolerance, including attacks on religious places',[30] was at least more clear in intention and general to all religions. The 2004 resolution combines, in the same sentence, concern with a campaign of defamation of religions and the 'ethnic and religious profiling of Muslim minorities' since 9/11.[31] Its reference to incitement of 'acts of violence, xenophobia or related intolerance and discrimination' is confusingly not to particular believers but 'towards Islam or any other religion'.[32] The same protectionism towards religion and particularly Islam per se, rather than Muslims, continues in 2005. That year's resolution specifically stresses the need to 'effectively combat defamation of all religions, Islam and Muslims in particular, especially in human rights forums',[33] and urges states to take all possible measures to (in the same sentence) protect 'against acts of hatred, discrimination, intimidation and coercion resulting from defamation of religions', 'promote tolerance and respect for all religions and their value systems' and 'combat religious hatred and intolerance'.[34] This protectionism against Islam and Muslims in human rights forums is of particular concern. Clearly, no people and no practices – in whatever name they are carried out – should be exempt from legitimate scrutiny at international human rights bodies.

It is clear from these references that, whilst framed in human rights terms and adopted in a human rights body, the concern is almost exclusively with the corporate identity of the religion and attacks on it rather than on individuals. Whilst the latter could certainly be the subject of legislative and other measures, these are more suitably covered under domestic criminal law or other policies and not under international human rights law.

Another important dimension of the 1997 Runnymede report on

---

on Human Rights resolution, adopted at the 39th meeting, 15 April 2002, para. 7.

30 UN Doc E/CN.4/2003/4, 'Combating Defamation of Religions', Commission on Human Rights resolution, adopted at the 47th meeting, 14 April 2003, para. 7.

31 UN Doc E/CN.4/2004/6, 'Combating Defamation of Religions', Commission on Human Rights resolution, adopted at the 45th meeting, 13 April 2004, para. 6.

32 Ibid., para. 7.

33 UN Doc E/CN.4/2005/3, 'Combating Defamation of Religions', Commission on Human Rights resolution, adopted at the 44th meeting, 12 April 2005, para. 8.

34 Ibid., para. 10.

Islamophobia is its suggestion that the concept is in some ways Western-centric. Two of the eight components of the definition refer to the West. One component refers to the perceived inferiority of Islam in relation to the West and the second to the rejection of Islamic criticisms of the West.[35] Definitions from other sources also take on this Western-centric approach. Imam Dr Abduljalil Sajid, chairman of the UK Muslim Council for Religious and Racial Harmony, in his article 'Islamophobia: A New Name for an Old Fear', refers to the existence of the phenomenon of Islamophobia since the eighth century, but only in Europe and the West.[36] The same holds true in the 2004 report from the Commission on British Muslims and Islamophobia, which holds that 'Hostility towards Islam and Muslims has been a feature of European societies since the eighth century of the common era.'[37] Al-Maktabi's definition further supports the term's Western focus in arguing that 'the term "Islamophobia" does not adequately express the full range and depth of antipathy towards Islam and Muslims in the West today.'[38] He further argues that

> Attitudes and policies towards Muslims in Britain and Europe have a mixture of dread (phobia) and outright racism. Thus attitudes towards Muslims combine fear and active hostility. Islamophobia does not capture this marriage of fear and hostility, of dread and discrimination, of horror and harassment. A more accurate expression would be 'anti-Islamic racism' for it combines the elements of dislike of a religion and active discrimination against the people belonging to that religion. This discrimination is racist because it is based on the belief that no matter what such a person does s/he will never be acceptable to or in the West.[39]

The organisation Islamophobia Watch only lists twelve Western

35 See the Runnymede Trust, 'Islamophobia: A Challenge For Us All'.

36 Imam Dr Abduljalil Sajid, 'Islamophobia: A New Name for an Old Fear', *The American Muslim Journal*, (January–March 2005) <http://theamericanmuslim.org/2005jan_comments.php?id=558_0_31_0_C> accessed 7 June 2005.

37 Commission on British Muslims and Islamophobia, *Islamophobia: Issues, Challenges and Action*, (Stoke-on-Trent: Trentham Books, 2004), 7, found on-line on <http://www.insted.co.uk/islambook.pdf> accessed 7 June 2005.

38 Al-Maktabi, definition of 'Islamophobia', written for *Salaam* <http://www.salaam.co.uk/maktabi/islamophobia.html> accessed 7 June 2005.

39 Ibid.

countries on the 'categories of concern' part of its website; not, for example, China, Uzbekistan or Thailand.[40] The organisation describes itself as a non-profit-making project that aims to document 'fear of the Muslim peoples *of the world* and Islam as a religion' (my italics). It claims to have been founded

> with a determination not to allow the racist and imperialist ideology of Western Imperialism to gain common currency in its demonisation of Islam. Islamophobia, as a racist tool of Western Imperialism, is strongly advocated by the political right but has also found an echo in the left, particularly sections of the left in France and the countries that make up the United Kingdom.[41]

Anti-Muslim hatred certainly exists elsewhere, for example as shown in the massive anti-Muslim violence in Gujarat in 2002 and again in 2004. However, it is unclear why that is not referred to as an example of Islamophobia. It seems that the *worldwide* pattern of discrimination and hatred against Muslims, in both religious and racial terms, cannot be fully covered under the term 'Islamophobia.' It is not a term, therefore, that refers to the same phenomenon throughout the world – from China to Europe, or India to the USA and Central Asia, for example.

Another distinction that in some instances can be drawn between Islamophobia, Christianophobia and anti-Semitism is whether the possibility of opting in or out is admitted. Certainly anti-Semitic hatred often attaches to an individual due to his or her racial background and regardless of whether or not that person converts to another religion or does not consider themselves Jewish. Definitions and perceptions regarding who is considered a Christian or Muslim are usually less rigid.

Whilst it is difficult, and somewhat distasteful, to enter into a comparison of suffering, the intentionality and extent of the mass killings during the Holocaust certainly highlight unique elements of that unfortunate historical episode. However, if one looks more generally at anti-Semitism's equating of all Jews with stereotypical and negative

40 These countries listed are Spain, Australia, Belgium, France, Scotland, Austria, Germany, Italy, Canada, Netherlands, UK and USA. See the website of Islamophobia Watch: Documenting the War against Islam <http://www.islamophobia-watch.com/islamophobia-watch/> accessed 16/6/05.

41 Islamophobia Watch: Documenting the war against Islam <http://www.islamophobia-watch.com/islamophobia-watch/> accessed 16/6/05.

characterisations of personality, or its linkage of identity with political affiliation and behaviour on a whole range of matters, then Islamophobia and Christianophobia become more comparable to the phenomenon of anti-Semitism. Many victims, for example, would define Islamophobia as the stereotyping of all Muslims across time and space as one amorphous whole, equating them with violence, intolerance and terrorism.

However, the question is not merely whether these hatreds and stereotypes exist and how they compare, but why they cannot be identified together, rather than separately, in a human rights context as instances of racial and/or religious hatred?

COMBATING HATRED AND DISCRIMINATION: DO PARTICULARISMS HELP?

Are there unique elements to each of these hatreds that necessitates them being identified separately from the phenomenon of racial and religious hatred at the international level? Each of them has its own particular symbols, stereotypes, history and targeted insults. However, in the context of human rights this does not in itself justify separate identification. The reason why women, minorities and children, for example, spawned their own instruments and procedures is that the existing normative and legal language was considered not to have covered them adequately – they remained invisible within them. The experience of indivisibility within the alleged universality of human rights led to the realisation of the need for 'special rights' or 'differences of treatment' in relation to particular targets of human rights violations and discrimination. This realisation can, for example, be noted quite clearly in relation to the UN's handling of minority rights, where a conscious shift away from special provisions to non-discrimination was later followed by a return to the definite realisation of the necessity of special rights for minorities.

As the UN Fact Sheet on Minorities explains,

> In 1947, the system for the protection of minorities, as groups, established under the League of Nations and considered by the United Nations to have outlived its political expediency, was replaced by the Charter of the United Nations and the Universal Declaration of Human Rights. These instruments were based on

> the protection of individual human rights and freedoms and the principles of non-discrimination and equality. The view was that if the non-discrimination provisions were effectively implemented, special provisions for the rights of minorities would not be necessary. It was very soon evident, however, that further measures were needed in order to better protect persons belonging to minorities from discrimination and to promote their identity. To this end, special rights for minorities were elaborated and measures adopted to supplement the non-discrimination provisions in international human rights instruments.[42]

The UN now refers to 'special rights', 'differences of treatment' or 'affirmative action' for minorities, which, it explains, are not privileges but

> make it possible for minorities to preserve their identity, characteristics and traditions. Special rights are just as important in achieving equality of treatment as non-discrimination. Only when minorities are able to use their own languages, benefit from services they have themselves organised, as well as take part in the political and economic life of States can they begin to achieve the status which majorities take for granted. . . . This form of affirmative action may have to be sustained over a prolonged period in order to enable minority groups to benefit from society on an equal footing with the majority.[43]

So what the UN has concluded over its nearly sixty-years' experience with minority rights is that what is needed is actually both the 'effective implementation of the non-discrimination provisions' and 'special rights'.[44]

It is more dubious whether the detailed elaboration, within existing instruments, of racial and religious hatred, allied with hate speech, incitement and non-discrimination, do not adequately account for the

---

42 'Minority Rights', Fact Sheet No. 18 (Rev. 1), (Geneva: Office of the High Commissioner for Human Rights), <http://www.ohchr.org/english/about/publications/docs/fs18.htm> accessed 9/6/05.

43 Ibid.

44 Ibid.

hatreds of Islamophobia, Christianophobia and anti-Semitism.[45] The International Convention on the Elimination of All Forms of Racial Discrimination (henceforth 'Race Discrimination Convention') defines racial discrimination as 'any distinction, exclusion, restriction or preference based on race, colour, descent, or national or ethnic origin which has the purpose or effect of nullifying or impairing the recognition, enjoyment or exercise, on an equal footing, of human rights and fundamental freedoms in the political, economic, social, cultural or any other field of public life.'[46] The UN Declaration on the Elimination of All Forms of Intolerance and of Discrimination Based on Religion or Belief (henceforth 'Religious Discrimination Declaration') further defines intolerance and discrimination based on religion or belief as 'any distinction, exclusion, restriction or preference based on religion or belief and having as its purpose or as its effect nullification or impairment of the recognition, enjoyment or exercise of human rights and fundamental freedoms on an equal basis.'[47] The two definitions are almost identical in language, though the former is more specific about the fields in which the distinctions may be applied. The Race Discrimination Convention also specifically covers hate crimes, condemning this practice and obliging States Parties to 'adopt immediate and positive measures designed to eradicate all incitement to, or acts of such discrimination.'[48] Specifically, States Parties are to ban the dissemination of race supremacy and hatred and make it punishable by law. The Religious Discrimination Declaration does not cover hate crimes. Whereas the emergence of measures against race and religious discrimination at the UN shared a common early his-

---

45 If anything, it is smaller religions that are denied 'religious status' through restrictive government registration procedures that are much more likely to face problems in relation to the practice of their religion in particular domestic contexts. Such more recent or smaller religions or beliefs may face persecution. Examples include members of the Bahá'í Faith in Iran and the Ahmadiyyah in Pakistan. Certainly Christians, Jews and Muslims also face hatred and persecution in some jurisdictions, but this is very seldom as a result of the denial of their status as a religious and/or racial group.

46 International Convention on the Elimination of All Forms of Racial Discrimination, Art. 1(1), adopted in 1965.

47 'UN Declaration on All Forms of Intolerance and of Discrimination Based on Religion or Belief', Art. 2(2), adopted in 1981.

48 International Convention on the Elimination of All Forms of Racial Discrimination, Art. 4, adopted in 1965.

tory, their paths diverged after the first decade.[49] The stronger opposition to race hatred than to religious hatred in UN instruments is reflected also at the domestic level in certain instances. This seems attributable to the belief held by many that race hatred or crime is somehow more integral an assault on a person's identity than religious hatred. Furthermore, religious hatred may seem to be more problematic since religious communities are often organised in some form or another, whereas even where communities based around race are organised there is a multiplicity of organisations and they are more fluid.

In the UK, for example, proposed legislation on religious hatred already lags more than three decades behind similar legislation on race crimes.[50] But there is much public opposition to such proposed legislation. Concerns seem to surround the fact that such legislation will go beyond protecting members of a religion or belief and attempt to protect the belief itself, thereby compromising freedom of speech. Furthermore, those opposing such legislation point out that religious or other beliefs differ from race in that religion is a matter of personal choice – thus making it more appropriate a subject of debate. Whilst this position is self-evident, the question should not be that of debate but of a much higher threshold and burden of proof of *extreme hatred*. Many hold that the Bill owes more to domestic politics than concerns for justice, which could be met through means other than new legislation.

The point here is that religious hatred, both internationally and domestically, is considered by many as the lesser cause compared to incitement to racial hatred. Human rights instruments too frame religion or belief as fundamental to a person's 'conception of life'[51] and interlinked with 'thought' and 'conscience'.[52] The question of whether or not Islamophobia and Christianophobia include racial as well as religious

49 Nazila Ghanea, 'The 1981 UN Declaration on the Elimination of All Forms of Intolerance and of Discrimination Based on Religion or Belief: Some Observations', in Nazila Ghanea (ed.), *Religious Discrimination at the Dawn of the New Millennium* (Leiden: Martinus Nijhoff, 2003), 11.

50 The Race Relations Act 1976, amended in 2000. The legislation on religious hatred has been twice abandoned previously, the first attempt being made in 2002 and the second earlier in 2005. The Racial and Religious Hatred Bill was introduced in the House of Commons on 9 June 2005.

51 'UN Declaration on All Forms of Intolerance and of Discrimination Based on Religion or Belief', preambular para. 3.

52 The European Convention for the Protection of Human Rights and Fundamental

traces to the same extent as anti-Semitism, therefore, would be a significant consideration to many. Since this question is linked to that of comparing how integral religion or race is to a person's identity, an allied consideration is that of conversion out of the religion. Is this feasible realistically and practically? Or are the social, civil and political consequences so acute as to render it highly unlikely or force it underground?

Further to these pragmatic considerations are some more subjective considerations authors such as Modood and Weller raise. The first point is that the public–private divide and expectations of societal secularisation render religion a category policy makers are more reluctant to deal with than that of race. This is echoed in the social sciences themselves, where 'the dominant tradition has understood religion to be a dependent variable of ethnicity and/or culture' rather than recognising religion itself 'as a "social determinate"'.[53] Using the example of the UK, Weller explains how 'the politics of identity and diversity had become primarily concerned with issues related to race and ethnicity' in the 1970s and early 1980s; but 'in more recent times religion has begun to re-emerge as a marker of individual and community identity for a significant number of people'.[54]

Nevertheless, 'In actual populations, religion, ethnicity and culture are often closely linked as a consequence of the history of when and where religious traditions developed. However, the patterns of overlap between religion and ethnicity are not always straightforward, and most religious communities are ethnically diverse.'[55] Whilst this may be so, for a notable number of peoples reducing religion to racial categories has been reductionist and exclusionary. Modood even voices the sense some have that attempting to misplace Muslims in the UK into race relations categories has 'at worst' been seen 'as a conspiracy to prevent the emergence of a specifically Muslim socio-political formation'.[56] The fairest way forward in this minefield of religion, race, ethnicity and culture, therefore, would seem to be one where 'the development of policy and practice in relation

Freedoms, adopted 1950, protects religion in Article 9 under the overall scheme of 'Freedom of Thought, Conscience and Religion'.

53 Paul Weller, 'The Dimensions and Dynamics of Religious Discrimination: Findings and Analysis from the UK', in Ghanea, *Religious Discrimination*, 66.

54 Ibid., 61.

55 Ibid., 65.

56 Modood, 'Muslims in British Secular Multiculturalism', 225.

to self-definition . . . represents the . . . way forward.'[57] After all, and as Modood argues, 'a minority will respond to some forms of exclusion or inferiorisation and not to others. The ones it will respond to are those which relate in some way to its own sense of being.'[58] Therefore, 'which identity will emerge as important to a group at a particular time lies in the nature of the minority group in question.'[59] Modood adds a cautionary note here, that not all those that may identify with religious rather than racial categories are necessarily themselves religious. He suggests that this should not be subject to external censorship. After all, 'People may still feel passionate about the public recognition and resourcing of aspects of their community identity, even though as individuals they may not wish that resource for themselves.'[60] Self-descriptions are our best guide at the domestic level where legal policy and procedures must ensure that a loophole doesn't exist that either excludes religion as a category for race crimes or indirectly deals with religion as an ethnic category, thereby excluding a significant number. However, it should also be noted that the experience of hatred will never be an exact science, and a subjective understanding or element will always remain. For example, the distinction between prejudice and hatred itself is hard to draw. Weller distinguishes the two as follows:

> Attitudes of religious prejudice may result in no specific discriminatory outcomes. At the same time, when both [are] intensified and developed in a settled attitude of mind, emotion and will, 'religious prejudice' can spill over into, and fan, manifestations of 'religious hatred'. When such 'religious hatred' becomes intense, in certain circumstances it can result in intimidatory and/or violent behaviour towards the religiously 'other'. 'Religious hatred' can also be stimulated and nurtured by organised cadres such as those of extreme racist and fascist groups.[61]

Religious hatred, in turn, can be distinguished from religious persecution, which Eltayeb has defined as

57 Weller, 'Dynamics of Religious Discrimination', 66.
58 Modood, 'Muslims in British Secular Multiculturalism', 234.
59 Ibid.
60 Ibid., 235.
61 Weller, 'Dynamics of Religious Discrimination', 69.

> including a situation of gross violation of the right to freedom of thought, conscience, and religion or belief emanating from systematic and active state policy and action to harass, intimidate and punish individuals and religious groups in a manner that continuously infringes or threatens the right to life, personal integrity or personal security.[62]

Eltayeb has further categorised religious persecution into the following forms: 'inter-religious persecution; intra-religious persecution; secular v. religious; and religious v. secular.'[63] In this context, he strongly argues for a wider recognition of the phenomenon of intra-religious persecution, which 'entails a violation of the right to dissent within a religious tradition.'[64] The right to pluralism or dissent within one's religion or belief is the means by which intra-religious persecution can be avoided. His point is a very significant one, and one that is often neglected at the international level, especially in the context of freedom of religion or belief. It is a point that one needs to be very cognisant of when the attempt is made to protect a religious or belief system per se in the context of a human rights document or instrument. Human rights concerns should centre around the freedom of religion or belief of the individual, of the public manifestation of that religion or belief by an individual or individuals in community with others, and of the exercise of freedoms by a minority group – but none of these should infringe on what Eltayeb has labelled 'freedom to dissent.' One may infer that this freedom to dissent includes a package of associated rights including: freedom from coercion in matters of religion or belief and freedom of expression regarding matters of religion or belief (one may refer to this as freedom of 'interpretation' in the context of religion or belief). As in other areas, this is not to suggest that the tension between group rights, minority rights associated to religious minorities and the freedom to dissent will prove an easy one to draw; it will be subject to the dynamic considerations of balancing competing claims from which no area of human rights is immune.

On another front, however, consideration must be given to how the

62 Mohamed S. M. Eltayeb, 'A Human Rights Framework for Defining and Understanding Intra-Religious Persecution in Muslim Countries', in Ghanea, *Religious Discrimination*, 93.

63 Ibid., 84.

64 Ibid., 88.

broader cause of racial and religious discrimination in international human rights law is going to be harmed by the dissection of the larger fight against all forms of hatred and discrimination. Separating some of the more populous potential victims creates a hierarchy of suffering (currently a trinity of victims: Muslims, Christians and Jews) depending not on the extent of suffering inflicted on the victims but on how it feeds into the balance sheet of that particular hatred. This weakens the larger fight against the phenomenon of religious and racial discrimination at the international level. It seems, in fact, to hijack legal human rights principles in favour of the politics of separation.

The price to be paid for this politics of separation is that it downgrades the common scourge of racial and religious hatred to a sectarian concern and potentially dismembers a unified mobilisation of the international community against it. In relation to anti-Semitism in Britain, for example, the chief rabbi of the United Hebrew Congregations of the Commonwealth, Sir Jonathan Sacks, is reported to have acknowledged this same need in a domestic context. This context was of a sharp recorded increase in anti-Semitic attacks in the UK in recent years, a particularly deplorable and recurrent aspect being that of the desecration of Jewish cemeteries. The Jerusalem Post reported the Chief Rabbi as saying that 'The single most important thing is for our community to enlist others to join in the protest against the [anti-Semitic] attacks,' and, 'Jews must not be left to fight anti-Semitism alone.'[65] It would seem that the separate identification of Islamophobia, Christianophobia and anti-Semitism at international forums is doing precisely the opposite – separating support for combating racial and religious discrimination and hatred into sectarian lines. It is separating the support of various governments and NGOs into factional parity for the various causes. This is reflected, for example, in the different voting patters for each of the relevant resolutions at the 60th and 61st sessions of the UN Commission on Human Rights in 2004 and 2005: the resolution on 'The Incompatibility between Democracy and Racism,'[66] adopted without a vote, had Brazil as its main sponsor; the resolution on the 'World Conference against Racism, Racial

65 Daniella Peled, 'A darkness Falls on England', *Jerusalem Post* (15 Feb. 2005).

66 UN Doc. E/CN.4/2005/36, 'The Incompatibility between Democracy and Racism', Commission on Human Rights resolution, adopted at the 44th meeting, 12 April 2005.

Discrimination, Xenophobia and Related Intolerance'[67] had the African Group as its main sponsor and was adopted by a vote of 38 for, 1 against and 14 abstentions;[68] 'Elimination of All Forms of Religious Intolerance',[69] which was adopted without a vote, had the EU as its main sponsor; and the Organisation of Islamic Conference was the main sponsor of the resolution 'Combating Defamation of Religions'.[70] This was adopted with a vote of 31 for, 16 against and 5 abstentions.[71]

HIERARCHIES AND DIVERSITY OF SUFFERING: POLITICAL OR LEGAL PHENOMENON?

Whilst particularly egregious instances of Islamophobia, Christianophobia and anti-Semitism need to be acknowledged and combated effectively at the local, national and regional levels, this chapter has questioned the utility of doing so in general *international* human rights documents which already rest on the understanding of the wider scourge of discrimination, incitement and hatred.[72] Human rights, by definition, is not biased in favour of the majority – it cannot recognise particular instances

67 UN Doc. E/CN.4/2005/64, World Conference against Racism, Racial Discrimination, Xenophobia and Related Intolerance and the comprehensive implementation of and follow-up to the Durban Declaration and Programme of Action, Commission on Human Rights resolution, adopted at the 59th meeting, 22 April 2005.

68 The voting was as follows: 38–1–14, with the USA voting against and the following countries abstaining: Australia, Canada, Finland, France, Germany, Hungary, Ireland, Italy, Japan, Netherlands, Republic of Korea, Romania, Ukraine and UK.

69 UN Doc. E/CN.4/2005/40, 'Elimination of All Forms of Intolerance and of Discrimination Based on Religion or Belief', Commission on Human Rights resolution, adopted at the 57th meeting, 14 April 2005.

70 UN Doc. E/CN.4/2005/3, 'Combating Defamation of Religions', Commission on Human Rights resolution, adopted at the 44th meeting, 12 April 2005.

71 The adoption was by a vote of 31–16–5. Those who voted against were Australia, Canada, Dominican Republic, Finland, France, Germany, Guatemala, Hungary, Ireland, Italy, Japan, Netherlands, Romania, Ukraine, UK and USA. The five abstentions were Armenia, Honduras, India, Peru and the Republic of Korea.

72 At the European level, for example, the Council of Europe's European Commission against Racism and Intolerance (ECRI) has separate general policy recommendations on anti-Semitism (general policy recommendation no. 9 on the fight against anti-Semitism, adopted 25 June 2004) and discrimination against Muslims (general policy recommendation no. 5: Combating Intolerance and Discrimination against Muslims, adopted 27 April 2000). It does not use the term 'Islamophobia'. The general mandate and language of ECRI is that of 'racism, xenophobia, anti-Semitism and intolerance'.

of the self-same phenomenon purely on the grounds of the victims being part of a more populous group. Its concern is the individual victims, regardless of the commonality or otherwise of discrimination against them. It is only when egregious violations against particular victims have been neglected that human rights instruments have and should spawn new language in order to better protect. If the spawning of new language is neither uncovering new victims nor advancing protection, such language is spurious.

There is a concern that separating or distinguishing these hatreds is essentially political and separatist – rather than legal and victim-centred – in motive and impact. If the victims are not benefiting from these new developments, then who is lobbying for them and why? Is it particular states asserting authority, is it a particular breed of leaders whipping up popularity, is it perhaps just another subtle manifestation of cultural relativity? Whilst we may speculate about the causes and impacts, what this chapter makes clear is that it is not ultimately the cause of human rights that is being advanced through this process. The case has yet to be made for the assertion that the universalisation of these new political identities, the creation of these new 'global victims,' is of benefit to the alleviation of their plight in various domestic contexts where there already exists the legal accountability for racial and religious discrimination and hatred.

CONCLUSION

I am of the view that the evolution of new language merely detracts from the essential and shared experience of racial and/or religious discrimination, which, though well-established, remains an area highly neglected by recalcitrant governments. Particular terms, such as those mentioned above, may be useful in understanding features of specific historical instances of discrimination in specific contexts, even of current scourges of prejudice in specific *domestic* contexts, that need educational, legal and other measures to overcome them. However, their seeping into human rights documents at the international level should be avoided; they should only be used very sparingly when serving to *exemplify* such discrimination. They should not be used where doing so may detract from the commonality of the scourge itself. The way they are being selectively utilised at present falls far short of that need.

CHAPTER 13

Inciting Religious Hatred: Balancing Free Speech and Religious Sensibilities in a Multi-Faith Society

Peter Cumper

INTRODUCTION

One of the few things that people of every faith (or none) tend to agree on is the importance of free expression. It is, for example, rare for a religion not to encourage its followers to use their skills of communication to celebrate the divine and to foster closer ties with fellow believers. As a consequence, one can find, in most religious traditions, evidence of public prayer, group praise and communal worship.[1] But what are the limits of this freedom to express oneself? This 'gift' of free speech, which can be used so positively to bring communities together, can also be abused to drive them apart. Different faith groups and theologians will inevitably disagree on the extent to which God is willing to tolerate those who seek to provoke social disharmony by using words to sow the seeds of hatred. But while God's views on the limits of free speech are unclear, one thing is certainly beyond dispute – in every society there are few things that are more capable of causing offence than verbal attacks on, or the perceived criticism of, another's faith.[2]

History is replete with instances of deliberate or ill-chosen attacks on religious figures and beliefs that provoked outrage, social unrest and even violence. Of late, there have been a number of high profile incidents involving writers and performers incurring the wrath of religious organisations. These range from the murder of Dutch film maker Theo van Gogh and the reaffirmation of the fatwa against Salman Rushdie,

1 Indeed, in some religious traditions other forms of expression (e.g. music, poetry and dance) are used to celebrate one's faith. For example, in the Bible, we are told that King David danced before God (2 Samuel 6:14), and that he composed songs of praise, which he played on the harp (Amos 6:5).

2 For example, according to the Advertising Standards Authority, adverts that offended the religious sensibilities of Christians and were seen as being sacrilegious led to the most complaints in 2004 <http://www.asa.org.uk/asa/news/news/2005/ASA+more+effective+as+regulatory+role+expands+Annual+Report+2004.htm>.

to recent protests following a Birmingham theatre's decision to show a controversial play about a rape in a Sikh temple, and the BBC's decision to broadcast the musical *Jerry Springer the Opera*.[3] Such events clearly illustrate the challenge of balancing the rights of artists to shock or offend and the rights of faith groups to be protected from what they regard as hateful and iniquitous attacks on their beliefs.

In seeking to balance this 'conflict of rights', international human rights norms appear to offer little guidance. The problem is that international human rights law recognises both the principle of freedom of expression – which is invoked by artists who portray religion in less than flattering terms – and freedom of religion, which is invoked by religious groups who argue that the state has a duty to protect their faith from being vilified.[4] This challenge, of reconciling these apparently contradictory principles, recently came to the fore in Britain as a result of the Blair government's pledge to create an offence of incitement to hatred on religious grounds. Two previous efforts to introduce a religious incitement law failed in Autumn 2001 and in Spring 2005 because of opposition from peers in the House of Lords. However, at the time of writing, the government has, under the auspices of the Racial and Religious Hatred Bill, once again proposed a law banning the incitement of religious hatred.[5] The Bill introduces an amendment to Part III of the Public Order Act 1986, whereby it will be an offence to stir up hatred against people on both *racial* and *religious* grounds.[6] With the number of Labour peers in the House of Lords now matching those of the Conservative party,[7]

3 See 'Gunman Kills Dutch Film Director' <http://news.bbc.co.uk/1/hi/world/europe/3974179.stm>; 'Ayatollah Revives the Death Fatwa on Salman Rushdie', *The Times* (January 20, 2005) <http://www.timesonline.co.uk/article/0,,2-1448279,00.html>; 'Theatre Stormed in Sikh Protest' <http://news.bbc.co.uk/1/hi/england/west_midlands/4107437.stm>; 'Protests as BBC Screens Springer' <http://news.bbc.co.uk/1/hi/entertainment/tv_and_radio/4154071.stm>.

4 For example, freedom of expression is guaranteed by Article 10 of the European Convention on Human Rights (1950) and Article 19 of the International Covenant on Civil and Political Rights (1966); Freedom of Religion is guaranteed by Article 9 of the European Convention on Human Rights (1950) and Article 18 of the International Covenant on Civil and Political Rights (1966).

5 See <http://www.parliament.uk/commons/lib/research/rp2005/rp05-048.pdf>.

6 The law that prohibits incitement to *racial* hatred is found in Part III of the Public Order Act (§§ 17–29).

7 See 'Labour Peers Now Match Tories in the Lords', *The Guardian* (22 June

and ministers pledging to bypass the Lords by using the 'Parliament Act procedure' if peers defeat their proposals,[8] the enactment of the Racial and Religious Hatred Act 2005 seems inevitable.

But what is the justification for such legal reform? In this chapter I begin by considering the case for establishing an offence of incitement to hatred on religious grounds. I then discuss some of the challenges that will face the courts in interpreting the Racial and Religious Hatred legislation, before proceeding to examine a number of the assumptions that underpin this reform. My central thesis is that while, on the face of it, a plausible case can be made for the enactment of this legislation, there is a real risk that the government's plans for a religious incitement law could have a number of unforeseen consequences that might ultimately lead to an erosion of freedom of expression.

INCITEMENT TO RELIGIOUS HATRED – THE CASE FOR REFORM

Although freedom of expression 'constitutes one of the essential foundations of a [democratic] society',[9] there is general agreement that it is not an absolute right. Irrespective of one's response to the Racial and Religious Hatred Bill, a number of credible arguments can undeniably be put forward for the creation of an offence of incitement to hatred on religious grounds. Perhaps the most persuasive of these is the need to address the anomaly that only some religions come within the parameters of the law currently prohibiting incitement to *racial* hatred.[10] Thus, whilst members of the Jewish[11] and Sikh[12] communities are classified under British law as having both racial and religions identities, other groups, such as Muslims[13] and Rastafarians,[14] are not protected by the incitement to racial hatred legislation because they are deemed to be *religions* rather than *races*.

2005), 14.

8 See 'Labour Prepared to Use Parliamentary Act on Religious Hatred', *Muslim News* (15 April, 2005).

9 See *Handyside* v. *UK* (1976) 1 EHRR 737, para. 49.

10 See Charles Clarke, Hansard, HC, col. 678 (21 June 2005).

11 *Seide* v. *Gillette Industries Ltd* (1980) IRLR 427.

12 *Mandla* v. *Dowell Lee* (1983) 1 All ER 1062.

13 *J. H. Walker* v. *Hussain* (1996) IRLR 11, EAT.

14 *CRE* v. *Dutton* (1989) QB 783.

The Racial and Religious Hatred Bill rectifies this anomaly and offers protection to the members of all faiths from words or conduct that is likely or is intended to provoke hatred against them.[15] The enactment of the Bill would also mean that Far Right extremists, who often make inflammatory comments about Muslims with apparent impunity, could be fined or imprisoned for such actions.[16] A number of prominent Muslims[17] and senior Police Officers[18] have already identified a link between hateful statements by members of Far Right groups and violence against the Muslim community. The need to tackle this problem, which some insist has directly led to civil unrest and violence,[19] has long been one of the main reasons for the government's determination to enact an offence of incitement to religious hatred.[20] Indeed, one minister (Paul Goggins) has even suggested that had the Racial and Religious Hatred Bill been in force the race riots that took place in the north of England in 2001 could have been prevented.[21] Irrespective of the accuracy of such claims, a number of other arguments can be advanced for the introduction of an offence of incitement to hatred on religious grounds.[22]

15 See Home Office press release <http://www.homeoffice.gov.uk/pageprint.asp?item_id=1314>.

16 For example, in the absence of an offence of religious incitement, the law on incitement to racial hatred was 'stretched' when it was used as the legal basis for the arrest of the BNP's leader Nick Griffin, for allegedly calling Islam a 'wicked, vicious faith': *The Times* (15 Dec. 2004), 25. The deficiencies of this approach, however, are illustrated by the fact that Griffin was able to claim that his arrest had been politically motivated (ibid.), while the Islamic Human Rights Commission complained that, notwithstanding the arrest, Griffin was unlikely to face any 'sanction for his numerous deeply anti-Muslim and Islamophobic comments' <http://www.ihrc.org.uk/show.php?id=1323>.

17 For example, see Sadiq Khan, Hansard, HC, 21 col. 735 (June 2005), and Shahid Malik, Hansard, HC, col. 703 (21 June 2005).

18 For example, see the views expressed by Peter Fahy, deputy chief constable, Surry, and Martin Baines, inspector with the West Yorkshire police, *Select Committee on Religious Offences in England and Wales*, ii: *Oral Evidence* (House of Lords, Session 2002–2003), 32–41.

19 See 'Sideline the Extremists', Home Office Press Release 222/2004, (Home Secretary, 7 July 2004) <http://www.homeoffice.gov.uk/n_story.asp?item_id=993>.

20 See the comments of Caroline Flint, Hansard, HC, col. 1136 (7 Dec. 2004), and Baroness Scotland, Hansard, HL, col. 1646 (20 Dec. 2004).

21 See T. Branigan, 'New Hate Laws "could have stopped Riots"', *The Guardian* (10 June 2005), 8.

22 It must be noted, however, that the Racial and Religious Hatred Bill will have little effect on the Internet, one of the areas where material that incites religious hatred

For a start, the Racial and Religious Hatred Bill has the advantage of offering protection to *all* faiths.[23] In addition, it is argued that the narrow remit of the term 'hatred' means that the Bill's effect on free speech will be minimal.[24] Furthermore, it is possible that Britain's obligations under international human rights law may impose a positive obligation on the government to enact legislation prohibiting incitement to religious hatred.[25] Moreover, the enactment of an offence of incitement to hatred on religious grounds covering all religious faiths makes if easier for the government to justify repealing Britain's archaic blasphemy laws, which currently protect only the Christian faith.[26] And finally, the Racial and Religious Hatred Bill has the advantage of bringing the law in England and Wales into line with some other regions in the United Kingdom where a religious incitement law is being planned or is already on the statute book.[27]

The government and its supporters may have been convinced by these arguments of the need for an offence of incitement to religious hatred, but many others remain sceptical. Indeed, opposition to the government's proposals for reform has led to the creation of one of the most

---

is most likely to be found. On this generally see E. Kallen, 'Hate on the Net: A Question of Rights/A Question of Power', *Electronic Journal of Sociology* (1998) <http://www.sociology.org/>.

23 See Explanatory Notes to the Racial and Religious Hatred Bill <http://www.publications.parliament.uk/pa/cm200506/cmbills/011/en/06011x--.htm, para. 9>.

24 See Charles Clarke, Hansard, HC, col. 671 (21 June 2005).

25 For example, Article 20(2) of the International Covenant on the Civil and Political Rights (1966) provides that 'Any advocacy of national, racial or religious hatred that constitutes incitement to discrimination, hostility or violence shall be prohibited by law'. However, because this international treaty has not been incorporated into British law, its provisions are not legally binding within the United Kingdom. Therefore, Art 20(2) is ultimately of significance merely in terms of its moral or political value.

26 See *R* v. *Chief Metropolitan Stipendiary Magistrate, ex parte Choudhury* (1991) 1 All ER 306. There has been speculation in the press that the government is seriously considering the repeal of Britain's blasphemy laws. See A. Travis, 'Blasphemy law to be scrapped', *The Guardian* (18 October 2004). However, despite calls for the repeal of the blasphemy laws, ministers have so far refused to make any such specific commitment: see Charles Clarke, Hansard, HC, col. 681 (21 June 2005).

27 The Racial and Religious Hatred Bill only applies to England and Wales: Explanatory Notes, *op. cit.*, note 28, para. 8. On the Scottish Executive's proposals for an offence of incitement to religious hatred see <http://www.scotland.gov.uk/library5/society/trhr-05.asp>. A religious incitement law currently exists in Northern Ireland: see The Public Order (Northern Ireland) Order 1987, Part II, §§ 8–17.

unusual political alliances to be seen in Britain for many years. A coalition of strange political bed-fellows, including Christians,[28] secularists,[29] journalists,[30] authors,[31] artists,[32] comedians[33] and lawyers,[34] have secured cross-party support in order to resist the government's plans to create an offence of incitement to hatred on religious grounds.[35] Inevitably, each of these parties is motivated by different considerations, but what unites them is a shared belief that legal reform in this area risks placing unnecessary restrictions on freedom of expression.

Despite official protestations that such fears are ill-founded,[36] ministers have been forced to concede that they can only speculate on how the Racial and Religious Hatred Bill will be interpreted once it is on the statute book.[37] With this in mind, I proceed now to consider three of the main problems that will face those who are charged with interpreting the relevant legislation: (a) the challenge of defining 'religious' hatred; (b) the formidable task of distinguishing between attacks on faith communities and religious doctrines; and (c) the complexities of differentiating

28 See The Lawyers' Christian Fellowship, *Strength in Diversity* (September 2004), <http://www.lawcf.org/lawreformdetail.php?ID=97>.

29 See K. Porteous Wood, 'Incitement to Religious Hatred' <http://www.secularism.org.uk/index.php?option=content&task=view&id=141&Itemid=30>.

30 See P. Toynbee, 'I may be in bad company, but this law will not work', *The Guardian* (15 Dec. 2004), 22.

31 For example, Salman Rushdie has been a harsh critic of the government's religious incitement proposals. See: <http://www.indexonline.org/en/indexindex/articles/2005/1/britain-salman-rushdie-speaks-out-against-re.shtml>.

32 For example, the director of the National Theatre, Nicholas Hytner, has warned that legislation on incitement to religious hatred would 'strike fear' into institutions working in the field of the arts: *The Guardian* (2 Feb. 2005).

33 For example, Rowan Atkinson is a prominent opponent of the government's plans. See <http://www.eclipse.co.uk/thoughts/rowanatkinson.htm>.

34 See D. Pannick, 'A curb on free speech that should offend us all, whatever our religion', *The Times* (11 Jan. 2005), 4.

35 For example, an unusual alliance was forged in parliament between Conservative, Liberal Democrat and some Labour MPs in opposition to the proposals for an offence of incitement to religious hatred. See, respectively, the speeches of Andrew Selous, Hansard, HC, col. 1126 (7 December), Gordon Prentice, *ibid*, col. 1095 and Evan Harris, *ibid*, col. 1075.

36 See Baroness Scotland, Hansard, HL, col. 1647 (20 Dec. 2004), Charles Clarke, Hansard, HC, col. 671 (21 June 2005) and Paul Goggins, Hansard, HC, col. 758 (21 June 2005).

37 See Charles Clarke, Hansard, HC, col. 675 (21 June 2005).

between incitement to hatred on religious grounds and legitimate free speech.

THE RACIAL AND RELIGIOUS HATRED ACT 2005: PROBLEMS OF INTERPRETATION

(a) *The challenge of defining 'religious hatred'*

Once the Racial and Religious Hatred Act 2005 is in force, one of the most controversial issues will be its scope, especially in relation to the definition of 'religious hatred'.[38] The spectre of Satanists and members of controversial new religious movements receiving protection from the religious incitement legislation has provoked outrage in sections of the press,[39] and perhaps explains why government ministers have tended to make the case for legal reform primarily on the basis of the need to protect faiths such as Islam and Christianity.[40] However, the Explanatory Notes accompanying the Racial and Religious Hatred Bill make it clear that the interpretation to be given to 'religious hatred' in the Bill is a 'broad one' (para. 12). Accordingly, 'religious hatred' covers hatred against groups 'defined by their religious belief or lack of religious beliefs', (ibid.) and the Notes also suggest that the Bill will extend not merely to religions that are widely recognised in Britain (eg. 'Christianity, Islam, Hinduism, Judaism, Buddhism, Sikhism, Rastafarianism, Bahá'ísm, Zoroastrianism and Jainism'), but will also cover Atheism, Humanism and 'branches or sects within a religion' (ibid.).

Whilst the Explanatory Notes may be of some interpretative value, it will ultimately be for the courts to decide which of the nation's many diverse religious organisations should enjoy the protection of the proposed Racial and Religious Hatred law.[41] At present one can only specu-

38 For example, on this issue concern has been expressed by David Davis, Hansard, HC, col. 1067 (7 Dec. 2004); Baroness Perry, Hansard, HL, col. 1629 (20 Dec. 2004); and Lord Chan, Hansard, HL, col. 1639 (20 Dec. 2004).

39 For example see, 'Now You Face Jail for being Nasty to Satanists', *Daily Telegraph* (10 June 2001), 1 and R. Liddle, 'A Witch's Brew of Idiocy', *Sunday Times* (12 June 2005), 15.

40 See Fiona Mactaggart, Hansard, HC, col. 1101 (7 Dec. 2004). More recently, however, a Home Office minister, Paul Goggins, has been reported as suggesting that the Racial and Religious Hatred Bill will protect groups such as Satanists and Pagans: *The Guardian* (10 June 2005), 5.

41 According to the last census, 170 different faiths and belief systems can be found

late on the criteria judges will employ for this purpose.[42] There is not much guidance from the jurisprudence of the European Court of Human Rights on such matters,[43] and in the past there has been little consensus between judges in the common-law world as to what constitutes a 'religious belief'.[44] However, what is clear is that any decision to distinguish between the world's most well-established faiths and new religious movements would risk being in contravention of Britain's international human rights obligations, given that the UN's Human Rights Committee has stated that it 'views with concern any tendency to discriminate against any religion or belief for any reason, including the fact that they are newly established'.[45]

Nevertheless, it is almost inconceivable that absolutely every group claiming to be defined by its 'religious belief' (or lack of) will be so recognised. Accordingly, controversy is likely to surround the question of whether groups as diverse as Satanists, Moonies or even the 390,000 people who described themselves as 'Jedi Knights' in the last census will come within the remit of the Racial and Religious Hatred Act 2005.[46] Fears have already been expressed that religious incitement legislation will offer legal protection to 'any sect or cult',[47] including ones that 'express dangerous views'[48] and preach physical harm or death to non-believers.[49] Whilst the frequent misrepresentation of many new religious move-

in the United Kingdom: National Statistics Online: <http://www.statistics.gov.uk/>.

42 The Home Secretary has suggested that 'any religion must have a clear structure and belief system [and] any belief system will need to attain a certain level of cogency, cohesion and importance': Charles Clarke, Hansard, HC, col. 679 (21 June 2005).

43 On this generally see P. Cumper, 'The Legal Regulation of New Religious Movements', in P. Cumper and S. Wheatley (eds), *Minority Rights in the New Europe* (Kluwer Press, 1999), 173.

44 For example, in defining the term 'religion', the approach of British judges in *Re South Place Ethical Society; Barralet* v. AG (1980) 3 All ER 918 can be contrasted with that of the Australian judiciary in *Church of the New Faith* v. *Pay Roll Tax Commissioners* (1983) 57 *AJLR* 785.

45 See ICCPR General Comment no. 22: The right to freedom of thought, conscience and religion (Art. 18) 30 July 1993. The Human Rights Committee is the body responsible for interpreting the International Covenant on Civil and Political Rights (1966).

46 See <http://www.statistics.gov.uk/census2001/profiles/rank/jedi.asp>.

47 David Davis, Hansard, HC, col. 1067 (7 Dec. 2004).

48 Mark Hoban, Hansard, HC, col. 1119 (7 Dec. 2004).

49 See Earl of Mar and Kellie, Hansard, HL, col. 1638 (20 Dec. 2004).

ments in the press may explain such hysterical reactions,[50] the possibility of, say, a Far Right organisation wishing to use the cloak of 'religion' as a guise to retain the right to propagate racial hatred appears to pose an equally potent threat. There are, after all, white supremacist churches in the United States that claim to be manifesting their *religious* beliefs when they make vitriolic attacks on certain races.[51] And in the light of claims that some members of the British National Party worship a white supremacist god,[52] the possibility that right-wing extremists could try and take advantage of the Racial and Religious Hatred legislation cannot be discounted.[53] In having to distinguish between 'bona fide' and 'bogus' *religious* beliefs, the courts may find themselves mired in complex theological disputes as a result of the cases that are brought before them.

(*b*) *Distinguishing between attacks on faith communities and religious doctrines*

An equally taxing problem will be that of having to distinguish between the believer – who is protected under the Racial and Religious Hatred Bill – and his or her beliefs, which fall beyond the remit of the proposed legislation. Although government ministers,[54] as well as the Attorney General,[55] have emphasised that the offence of incitement to hatred on religious grounds is about 'protecting people from hatred, not faiths from criticism',[56] this distinction is likely to prove difficult to maintain in practice. As the comedian Rowan Atkinson succinctly puts it, 'Beliefs are only

---

50 On this generally see J. Beckford, 'Cults, Conflicts and Journalists', in R. Towler (ed.), *New Religions and the New Europe* (1995), 100.

51 For example see V. Larson, 'A Christian Religion for White Racists', *Christian Research Journal*, (Fall 1992) <http://go2cornerstone.com>.

52 See Dominic Grieve, Hansard, HC, col. 74 (21 June 2005).

53 Irrespective of whether Far Right parties will try to portray their racist philosophies as 'religious beliefs', there is a real risk that groups such as the BNP will seek to gain maximum support and publicity from any prosecutions for incitement to hatred on religious grounds. See *Racial and Religious Hatred Bill*, Liberty's Briefing for 2nd reading in the House of Commons, paras 4, 5 <www.liberty-human-rights.org.uk/resources/policy-papers/2004/organised-crime-2nd-reading-commons.PDF>.

54 See Caroline Flint, Hansard, HC, col. 1136 (7 Dec. 2004).

55 'Sideline the Extremists', Home Office Press Release 222/2004, (Home Secretary, 7 July 2004) <http://www.homeoffice.gov.uk/n_story.asp?item_id=993>.

56 Ibid.

invested with life and meaning by believers [and] you wouldn't need to criticise beliefs if no one believed them.'[57]

For many people of faith, any perceived slight or criticism of their most sacred religious figures is certainly an attack not just on their beliefs but also on them as members of a group. Therefore the portrayal of Jesus Christ as an inadequate fool wearing only a nappy in a televised broadcast of *Jerry Springer the Opera*[58] caused considerable offence to many within the Christian community.[59] In view of the fact that the term 'Christian' is derived from 'Christ', any vilification of the latter is also seen by some as constituting an attack on the former. In the same way, when the former editor of the *Daily Telegraph*, Charles Moore, provocatively posed the question of whether the Prophet Mohammed had been a paedophile for marrying a very young girl, many Muslims were outraged and felt personally aggrieved by his comments.[60] Indeed, there have even been suggestions that Moore's words may risk inciting hatred against Muslims. When a Home Office minister, Paul Goggins, was asked whether a question such as 'was the Prophet Mohammed a paedophile?' could contravene the Racial and Religious Hatred Bill, he answered in the affirmative.[61] Goggins' comment, that there would be an offence if the person who asked this question intended to incite religious hatred,[62] has attracted criticism for ignoring the fact that one does not solely have to *intend* to incite religious hatred to fall foul of the government's proposals.[63] Nevertheless, the most worrying aspect of his remark is the suggestion that an offensive statement about an important religious figure might constitute incitement to hatred on religious grounds.[64] By way of

57 As cited by Evan Harris, Hansard, HC, col. 739 (21 June 2005).

58 'Protests as BBC Screens Springer' <http://news.bbc.co.uk/1/hi/entertainment/tv_and_radio/4154071.stm>.

59 See <http://www.christianvoice.org.uk/springer12.html>.

60 C. Moore, 'Is it only Mr Bean who Resists this New Religious Intolerance?', *Daily Telegraph* (11 Dec. 2004), 24; I. Sacranie (secretary general of the Muslim Council of Britain), 'We Need Protection from the Peddlers of Religious Hatred', *Daily Telegraph* (14 Dec. 2004).

61 *Sunday*, BBC Radio 4 (8 AM, 12 June 2005).

62 Ibid.

63 See Gary Streeter, Hansard, HC, col. 721 (21 June 2005). The Explanatory Notes accompanying the Bill provide that 'for material to be likely to stir up racial or religious hatred it will need only be shown that it was likely to be seen by a person in whom it is likely to stir up racial or religious hatred'.

64 Clearly there are situations where the expression of views that the Prophet

implication, this suggests that scurrilous portrayals of, say, Jesus as the leader of a group of homosexuals,[65] the Virgin Mary as a sexually promiscuous woman[66] or L. Ron Hubbard (the founder of Scientology) as a money-grabbing crook[67] will also come within the remit of the Racial and Religious Hatred Bill. Such an interpretation risks blurring the distinction between granting protection to 'beliefs' rather than 'believers', and one MP has even implied that Salman Rushdie could be prosecuted for inciting religious hatred as a result of his book *The Satanic Verses*.[68]

These considerations have led to commentators such as the director of Liberty, Shami Chakrabarti, raising the possibility that the Racial and Religious Hatred Bill may ultimately become 'a dangerous new blasphemy law'.[69] Despite calls in the past for extension of the law of blasphemy to faiths other than Christianity,[70] any attempt to do so would have a significant impact on free speech, putting artists and comedians at risk of finding themselves prosecuted for ridiculing religious figures and beliefs.[71] Ministers have strongly rejected fears that the Racial and Religious Hatred Bill could be used to facilitate any extension of the blas-

---

Mohammed was a paedophile must be unlawful. For example, if someone makes these claims in a mosque, intending or aware that their conduct is likely to provoke unrest, he or she could be lawfully arrested under existing public order laws. However, it is argued that this scenario is significantly different from that of Charles Moore, who posed this question in a national newspaper in an effort to provoke discussion about one of the government's legislative proposals.

65 For example, Jesus is portrayed in such terms in the play *Corpus Christi*, the showing of which was investigated by the police in Scotland, in December 2004. See 'No action on "Gay Jesus" – Police' <http://news.bbc.co.uk/2/hi/uk_news/scotland/4085023.stm>.

66 For example, in *Otto-Preminger–Institut* v. *Austria* (1994) 19 EHRR 34, the European Court of Human Rights upheld a ban on a film that portrayed Mary in these terms.

67 Such claims were made by John Gummer, Hansard, HC, col. 705 (21 June).

68 See Khalid Mahmood, Hansard, HC, col. 1217 (7 Feb. 2005). Moreover, some opponents of the government's proposals have pointed out that government ministers have pointedly refused either to confirm or deny whether the *Satanic Verses* could be affected by the Racial and Religious Hatred Bill. See Evan Harris, Hansard, HC, col. 740 (21 June 2005).

69 *The Independent* (10 June 2005), 21.

70 For example, see the comments of King-Hamilton J in *R* v. *Lemon* (1979) AC 617.

71 For example, see the concerns of the comedian Rowan Atkinson <http://www.indexonline.org/news/20041207_britain.shtm1>.

phemy law.[72] On the contrary, guarantees have been offered that the Bill 'does not stop anybody telling jokes about religion',[73] and, on balance, it seems unlikely that artists will fall foul of the incitement to religious hatred provisions because a raft of safeguards (including those of the Crown Prosecution Service, the Director of Public Prosecutions, and the Attorney General) have been put in place to ensure that individuals are not subject to arbitrary prosecutions.[74] Furthermore, the existing incitement-to-racial-hatred laws have been rarely used, with only sixty-five prosecutions and forty-four convictions since the Public Order Act 1986 came into force on 1st April 1987.[75] And finally, there is no evidence that the existence of the offence of incitement to racial hatred has ever led to the prosecution of artists and comedians.[76] Whilst it is possible that some performers will, in future, engage in self-censorship, the likelihood that comedians or artists could be prosecuted for inciting religious hatred seems remote.

A matter of much greater concern, however, is the possibility that some members of the public will fail to distinguish between the rights of *believers* and their deeply held *beliefs*. There is even evidence to suggest that some religious leaders are confused about the scope of the religious incitement legislation. For example, it has been reported that the secretary general of the Muslim Council of Britain, Sir Iqbal Sacranie, speaking on BBC Radio 4's *Moral Maze* (14 July 2004), stated that 'any defamation in the character of the Prophet Muhammad (peace be upon him)' would be 'a direct insult and abuse on the Muslim community' and should be made illegal under a law on incitement to religious hatred.[77] Such a

72 See Charles Clarke, Hansard, HC, col. 673 (21 June 2005).

73 Ibid., col. 668.

74 Ibid, col. 671.

75 Lord Goldsmith, the Attorney General, Hansard, HL, col. WA 5 (31 Jan. 2005).

76 For example, the existing provisions governing incitement to racial hatred legislation were not used to ban *Behzti*, the controversial play depicting sex abuse and murder in a Sikh temple, the showing of which led to serious public disorder in Birmingham in December 2004. Presumably the reason for this was that the play's author Gurpreet Kaur Bhatti wished to highlight the hypocrisy of institutionalised religion rather than seek to incite hatred against Sikhs. In the absence of a 'public interest' defence under the Public Order Act 1986, such considerations are a matter for the discretion of the Attorney General.

77 See <http://www.barnabasfund.org/News/ITRHC/ITRHC.pdf>.

claim is clearly incompatible with the government's long held view that religious incitement legislation should be enacted to protect 'communities' rather than 'beliefs' from attack.[78] However, more recently, Sir Iqbal moved away from his earlier position when he stated that an offence of incitement to hatred on religious grounds would 'protect believers from incitement and not protect their faiths from criticism'.[79] This later clarification is clearly extremely important. Nevertheless, it is still hard to avoid the conclusion that, if one of the nation's most prominent religious leaders has been less than clear about the distinction between the protection of believers and their beliefs, many ordinary members of the public will struggle to comprehend such differences.

(c) *Differentiating between incitement to hatred and legitimate free-speech*

A third problem associated with the interpretation of the Racial and Religious Hatred Bill will be the need to distinguish between legitimate forms of freedom of expression and conduct that constitutes incitement to hatred on religious grounds. This task would have been less daunting had ministers not rejected a Liberal Democrat amendment designed to prevent the Far Right from using religion as a pretext for inciting racial hatred.[80] Endorsed by groups as diverse as Liberty,[81] the Muslim Parliament[82] and the Conservative Party,[83] it was nevertheless rejected by ministers on the basis that its remit was too narrow,[84] and that rather than merely extending to racist groups, the Racial and Religious Hatred Bill had the advantage of curbing the activities of 'extremists' in general.[85] Regrettably ministers failed to specify how they would define 'extremists', but it is almost certain that this term covers members of religious organisations that incite religious hatred.

---

78 For example, see David Blunkett, Hansard, HC, col. 1056 (7 Dec. 2004).

79 See <http://www.mcb.org.uk/presstext.php?ann_id=128>.

80 See Hansard, HC, cols 696, 697 (21 June 2005).

81 Home Office press release <http://www.homeoffice.gov.uk/pageprint.asp?item_id=1314>, para. 11.

82 This claim was made by Alistair Carmichael, Hansard, HC, col. 695 (21 June 2005).

83 See David Davis, Hansard, HC, col. 690 (21 June 2005).

84 On this generally see Paul Goggins, Hansard, HC, col. 648 (11 July 2005).

85 Ibid., col. 649.

The possibility that faith groups could fall foul of the Racial and Religious Hatred Bill has clearly alarmed a number of mainly Christian organisations.[86] They have warned that the creation of an offence of incitement to hatred on religious grounds could lead to bona fide religious bodies engaging in self-censorship out of fear that any criticism of other faiths could expose them to charges of inciting religious hatred.[87] And, with reports that the apparently lawful activities of some street preachers have recently been curtailed by overzealous police officers,[88] concern has been expressed that the Racial and Religious Hatred Bill will 'effectively lead to harassment of people who are legitimately proselytising their faith.'[89]

Government ministers have given short shrift to such fears, insisting that religious organisations will remain free to 'criticise the beliefs, teachings or practices' of other faiths.[90] Given that the Human Rights Act 1998 guarantees the principles of freedom of religion, expression and assembly, and that the courts have long recognised the rights of evangelists under British law, the vast majority of street preachers are unlikely to be affected by the Racial and Religious Hatred Bill.[91] But what of the minority of evangelists who, for example, attack members of other faiths by quoting directly from religious texts? One of the most difficult issues that will have to be resolved should the Bill become law is whether controversial passages from holy books, such as the Bible and the Koran, are ever capable of inciting religious hatred.

This is an extremely emotive issue, as is evidenced by the fact that, in a petition signed by more than one thousand churches, concern was expressed that if the Racial and Religious Hatred Bill is enacted, 'the

---

86 For example, see The Christian Institute, 'Blunkett Speech Causes Fear of Clamp Down on Christian Belief', *News Release* (7 July 2004) <http://www.christian.org.uk//pressreleases/2 with 004/july>.

87 For example, see the concerns of the Lawyers' Christian Fellowship, 'Strength in Diversity' (September 2004) <http://www.lawcf.org/lawreformdetail.php?ID=97>, and the Barnabas Fund <http://www.barnabasfund.org/News/Archive/United%20Kingdom/UK-20041206.htm>.

88 See Dominic Grieve, Hansard, HC, col. 706 (21 June 2005).

89 David Heath, Hansard, HC, col. 682 (21 June 2005).

90 See Paul Goggins, Hansard, HC, col. 758 (21 June 2005).

91 For example see *Redmond-Bate* v. DPP (1999) All ER (D) 864, where it was held that a police officer who had arrested three woman for disobeying his instructions to stop preaching on the steps of a cathedral, had acted unlawfully.

mere quoting of texts from both the Koran and the Bible could be ... criminalised.'[92] In an attempt to assuage fears, the Home Secretary has categorically rejected the suggestion that statements in the Bible, Koran and 'other faith books' could ever be regarded as constituting 'incitement to hatred.'[93] In a sense his reaction was predictable, because there would almost certainly have been outrage from the faith communities had a senior government minister suggested that sections of their most holy books were capable of inciting hatred. Nevertheless, considerations of political expediency aside, the Home Secretary's position is undoubtedly open to serious challenge.

There is, for example, plenty of evidence to suggest that, taken literally, a number of passages from both the Bible[94] and the Koran[95] are capable of inciting hatred on the grounds of religion. Indeed, one proponent of this view has even suggested that the enactment of the Racial and Religious Hatred Bill would mean that 'WH Smith will commit a crime every time a Bible or Koran is sold in its shops.'[96] While such claims appear to lack foundation, the Home Secretary's assertion that 'the private and public recitation of bits of the Koran is not incitement to hatred' is certainly open to question.[97] After all, in 2002 a Muslim was found guilty of inciting racial hatred for having distributed leaflets with quotations from the 'Hadith' that called on Muslims to fight and kill Jews.[98] McMullen J rejected the defendant's submission that he had only been quoting from a religious text, and concluded that 'words created 1400 years ago are equally capable of containing race hate as words created today.'[99] The court's ruling implicitly accepts that the Koran, like other holy books, should be read in context, and, if taken out of context, can be

92 See 'Hatred Bill Goes Ahead Despite Church Protests', *Daily Telegraph* (12 July 2005).

93 Charles Clarke, Hansard, HC, col. 671 (21 June 2005).

94 A number of examples are given by Edward Leigh, Hansard, HC, col. 729 (21 June 2005).

95 A number of examples are given by Boris Johnson, Hansard, HC, cols 733–4 (21 June 2005).

96 See A. Myrers, 'A crime to Tell the Truth', *New Law Journal* (24 June 2005), 957.

97 Charles Clarke, Hansard, HC, col. 682 (21 June 2005).

98 See 'Muslim guilty of inciting racial hatred' <http://news.bbc.co.uk/1/hi/england/1966839.stm>.

99 Ibid.

used to incite hatred. Thus, it is argued that there ought to be no reason why those who attack a faith community by deliberately misrepresenting its sacred texts should not fall foul of a law that seeks to prohibit incitement to hatred on religious grounds.[100]

Of course, it is not only the Koran that has generated controversy in this area. It has also been alleged that verses in the Bible are capable of inciting hatred. For example, in 2005 an evangelical Christian Swedish pastor was sentenced to thirty days in prison for having made offensive comments about homosexuals, before an appeal court quashed his conviction on the basis that his remarks merely reflected his personal interpretation of the Bible.[101] Furthermore, in Canada, attempts to criminalise inflammatory statements about homosexuals have led to a heated national debate as to whether particular verses of the Bible can constitute hate speech.[102] And finally, there have been claims that some of the comments attributed to Jesus in the New Testament could potentially incite religious hatred under the Racial and Religious Hatred Bill.[103]

In light of the examples above, there seems little doubt that sections of most religious holy books are capable, at least in principle, of inciting religious hatred. Yet, in some respects, this should perhaps not be a surprise. Many faiths exhort their followers to hate 'sin' and those who perpetrate evil. In the Bible, for example, David wrote 'O Lord, How I hate those who hate you! . . . I hate them with a total hatred' (Psalm 139.21). The fact that many faiths permit (or even encourage) their followers to 'hate' in certain circumstances is in marked contrast to the Racial and Religious Hatred Bill, which is based on the premise that, because hatred is inevitably linked to violence, any conduct that incites hatred is wrong. Yet such a blanket repudiation of 'hatred' is open to question.[104] The accident of birth means that *racial* hatred is inevitably irrational, and

100 For example, the spectre of Far Right extremists combing through the Koran in an attempt to find material that could be used to incite religious hatred may be unpalatable, but it cannot be totally discounted.

101 See 'Swedish Hate-Speech Verdict Reversed' <http://www.washingtonpost.com/wp-dyn/world/europe/westerneurope/sweden/>.

102 See 'Bible as "Hate Speech" Signed into Law' <http://www.worldnetdaily.com/news/article.asp?ARTICLE_ID=38268.>.

103 Edward Leigh, Hansard, HC, col. 729 (21 June 2005).

104 For example, as Liberty point out, 'It is not a crime to hate some thing' (*Racial and Religious Hatred Bill*, Liberty's Briefing for 2nd reading in the House of Commons, para. 3).

accordingly should never be condoned. However, there may be occasions where the toleration of *religious* hatred is permissible. For example, David Pannick has argued that hatred of the beliefs of sects that permit young children to be severely beaten to have evil spirits exorcised from their bodies is an 'appropriate reaction.'[105] In the same way, the case can be made that it is not unreasonable to hate 'religious' groups that engage in child sacrifice or teach that murder is a sacred duty.[106]

These are obviously extreme cases, but they cast doubt on the assumption underpinning the Racial and Religious Hatred Bill that incitement to hatred is *always* wrong. The extent to which groups that engage in such morally reprehensible acts are protected by these legislative proposals remains to be seen. But what is clear is that, in striking a fair balance between incitement to religious hatred and free speech, the question of whether sacred texts are capable of inciting religious hatred is almost certainly bound to provoke controversy.

INCITEMENT TO RELIGIOUS HATRED: FALSE PREMISES AND QUESTIONABLE ASSUMPTIONS

As was just noted in the context of 'hatred,' the Racial and Religious Hatred Bill is predicated on a number of assumptions, many of which are eminently rational. They include, for example, the premise that freedom of expression is not an absolute right; inciting religious hatred is immoral; that hate speech can lead to violence; and that the law can be used as an effective tool to protect the nation's faith communities. There are, however, three *false* premises that underpin the Bill. These are that incitement-to-religious-hatred legislation will enhance good community relations; that religion is analogous to race in relation to legislation that prohibits incitement to hatred; and that the ECHR is a valuable safeguard for religious speech.

105 See D. Pannick, 'The Devil Isn't in the Detail at this Time,' *The Times* (25 June 2005).

106 An example of a religious sect that one could justifiably hate is Thuggee, whose members practised robbing and murdering of travellers between the thirteenth and nineteenth centuries in India. On this generally see G. Bruce, *The Stranglers: The Cult of Thuggee and its Overthrow in British India* (New York: Harcourt, Brace and World, 1968).

□ *The questionable assumption that incitement-to-religious-hatred legislation will enhance good community relations*

Government ministers have long been insistent that the enactment of an offence of incitement to hatred on religious grounds is likely to improve community relations in Britain.[107] Regrettably, however, there are a number of reasons why this optimism may be misplaced.

First, there is a risk that the Racial and Religious Hatred legislation will have an adverse impact on interfaith relations. In view of the fact that the overwhelming majority of Muslims appear to be supportive of an incitement to religious hatred law[108] and a significant number of Christian groups oppose this reform,[109] the fault lines are possibly in place for conflicts between elements of these two faiths.[110] Secondly, *intra*-faith rivalries could lead to accusations of religious incitement, because under the proposed legislation 'branches of sects within a religion can be considered as religions or beliefs in their own right'.[111] Thirdly, notwithstanding the sanction of a fine or imprisonment, members of some groups may deliberately seek to be arrested and prosecuted for inciting religious hatred so as to attract publicity for their cause.[112] Already there have been reports that groups such as Christian Voice are planning to preach aggressively against other faiths so as to test the boundaries of the Racial

107 For example, see Baroness Scotland, Hansard, HL, col. 1645 (20 December 2004).

108 According to one recent survey, 81 per cent of British Muslims are in favour of a new law to make incitement to religious hatred a criminal offence, with only 15 per cent against the establishment of such a law (*The Guardian* (30 November 2004), 20).

109 For example, see The Christian Institute, 'Why a Religious Hatred Law Would Harm Religious Liberty and Freedom of Speech' <http://www.christian.org.uk//incitement2005/danielscot/index.html>.

110 However, it must also be noted that a minority of Muslims oppose the Racial and Religious Hatred Bill, just as some Christian denominations, such as the Methodists, welcome its enactment. See, retrospectively, Muslim Parliament Press Release (13 June 2005), as cited by Liberty, and <http://www.methodist.org.uk/index.cfm?fuseaction=news.content&cmid=963>.

111 Explanatory Notes, para. 12. For example, a potential area of conflict could be between mainstream Christian groups and breakaway 'Christian cults', or between some Muslims and groups such as Ahmadiyyas and Ismailis.

112 Anyone convicted of the offence of incitement to hatred on religious grounds could face a fine of up to £5,000 on conviction in a magistrates' court, or up to seven years in jail following conviction in a Crown court.

and Religious Hated legislation by portraying themselves as martyrs for their faith.[113] And finally, the absence of a law prohibiting incitement to hatred on the basis of one's sexuality will be difficult to justify once the Racial and Religious Hatred Bill is on the statute book.[114] Already calls have been made for the enactment of such legislation,[115] and should the government accede to these demands[116] it could be the catalyst for other groups, such as the disabled, to launch campaigns for equivalent legal protection.

While all of these factors could militate against the effectiveness of the Racial and Religious Hatred legislation, perhaps the most serious concern is the fact that a religious incitement law may create expectations that have no realistic chance of ever being fulfilled. As has been noted above, there is a risk that many people will fail to realise that the offence of incitement to hatred on religious grounds is narrowly defined and is intended to protect believers, rather than religious beliefs, from hateful attacks. In view of the fact that such distinctions are difficult to make, the Attorney General's decisions on whether to prosecute for religious incitement are likely to be controversial. In these circumstances, there is a risk that the Attorney General will be accused of displaying bias towards certain faiths. This would not merely pose a threat to the good administration of justice, but could lead to tension between those groups that have secured the Attorney General's consent for prosecutions and those that have been unsuccessful in this regard.[117]

The spectre of recriminations from bitter and aggrieved complainants, who are keen to gather evidence in order to corroborate their alle-

113 *Sunday*, BBC Radio 4 (8.00 AM, 12 June 2005).

114 In November 2003, the press carried reports that the police were investigating complaints that an Anglican Bishop had made illegal comments about homosexuals: 'Bishop's Anti-Gay Comments Spark Legal Investigation', *The Independent* (10 November 2003). Had there been a law prohibiting incitement to hatred on the basis of one's sexuality at the time when the Bishop made his remarks, it is possible that an offence would have been committed.

115 See Lynne Jones, Hansard, HC, col. 669 (21 June 2005).

116 During the second reading of the Racial and Religious Hatred Bill, the Home Secretary, Charles Clarke, did not entirely rule out this possibility: Hansard, HC, col. 669 (21 June 2005).

117 There have also been claims that the Attorney General may sanction prosecutions for incitement to hatred on religious grounds for political reasons. See Gary Streeter, Hansard, HC, col. 723 (21 June 2005).

gations, cannot be entirely discounted. Thus, a perception (however erroneous) that those of one faith have been attending the meetings of other religious organisations to gather evidence that could be used as the basis for a prosecution would further pose a serious threat to good community relations. Consequently, if the organisers of such meetings were to refuse to grant entry to those they suspected of being of a different faith, their actions would almost certainly jeopardise inter-faith dialogue and might culminate in allegations of religious discrimination. In spite of the fact that the vast majority of Britain's faith communities have excellent relations with one another, it cannot be denied that there have been periods in recent years when otherwise cordial relations between Britain's religious leaders have been strained.[118] These differences could be seized upon by a small minority of what has been called 'zealots and self-appointed religious vigilantes',[119] who might seek to use the Racial and Religious Hatred legislation as a way of attacking those who challenge their religious beliefs. It would therefore be tragic if a law that is intended to 'sideline the extremists'[120] could, paradoxically, polarise religious communities and act as a catalyst for inter-faith strife.

□ *The false premise that religion is analogous to race in relation to legislation that prohibits incitement to hatred*

The Racial and Religious Hatred Bill is based on the premise that activities which stir up hatred on religious grounds should be subject to the same prohibitions as those that currently govern racial hatred.[121] Whilst some deny that there is a necessary correlation between one's race and

---

118 For example, many Muslims expressed outrage at a speech of the former archbishop of Canterbury, George Carey, when he cast doubt on the value of Islamic culture and criticised some Muslim leaders for failing properly to condemn terrorism. See 'Muslim Dismay at Carey Speech', *The Guardian* (27 March 2004).

119 See Graham Allen, Hansard, HC, col. 719 (21 June 2005).

120 See Home Secretary, 'Sideline the Extremists' (Home Office Press Release 222/2004, 7 July 2004) <http://www.homeoffice.gov.uk/n_story.asp?item_id=993>.

121 See Charles Clarke, Hansard, HC, col. 675 (21 June 2005). Moreover, advocates of reform argue that just as the fears of those who thought that the offence of incitement to racial hatred would constitute a serious erosion of freedom of speech were mistaken, similar concerns about incitement to hatred on religious grounds will, in time, be shown to be unjustified. See David Winnick, Hansard, HC, col. 672 (21 June 2005).

religion,[122] government ministers are adamant that such a link exists, and they strongly emphasise 'the importance of faith to self-identity'.[123]

At first sight this argument appears to be persuasive. For many Britons, especially those of ethnic minority origin, there is a clear link between their faith and identity as citizens,[124] and on this basis the Commission for Racial Equality supports the creation of an offence of incitement to religious hatred.[125] Yet on closer inspection the latent assumption in this argument, that the law prohibiting incitement to *racial* hatred should be extended to *religion* because religion is inevitably analogous to race, can be attacked on a number of grounds.[126]

First, an important difference between race and religion is that the former is an inherited characteristic, while the latter involves a personal choice in the form of the voluntary acceptance of a system of ideas. Thus, a 'white' person of Christian parents can change his or her faith and become a Hindu, but he or she cannot change their race and become an Indian. Secondly, even though community, family and social pressures can militate against someone changing their faith, individuals still have a legal right to do so if they wish.[127] Thirdly, whilst the vast majority of people in Britain practise the religion of their parents, this does not obviate the reality of their choice of faith. For example, many people share the political affiliations of their parents, but the suggestion is never made that parental influence somehow diminishes one's freedom to support the political party of one's choice. A fourth difference between religion and race is that every religion has a code of beliefs or a set of rules (unlike

---

122 For example, see David Davis, Hansard, HC, col. 1067 (7 December 2004) and Boris Johnson, Hansard, HC, col. 732 (21 June 2005).

123 Baroness Scotland, Hansard, HL, col. 1648 (20 December 2004).

124 See T. Modood, 'Culture and Identity', in T. Modood et al., *Ethnic Minorities in Britain: Diversity and Disadvantage* (London: PSI, 1997), 297.

125 See submission of the CRE to the Select Committee on Religious Offences in England and Wales <http://www.parliament.thestationeryoffice.co.uk/pa/ld200203/ldselect/ldrelof/95/95w22.htm>.

126 It is conceded that there is a general perception within our society that there are closer ties between one's race and religion in relation to some groups than to others. For example, a Jew who chooses to become a Christian is usually regarded as remaining a Jew, while a Christian or a Muslim who decides to convert to Judaism is seen as no longer continuing to be a member of their original faith.

127 For example, Article 9(1) of the European Convention on Human Rights provides that 'Everyone has the right to freedom of thought, conscience and religion; *this right includes freedom to change his religion or belief*' (my emphasis).

the concept of race) that govern how an individual should live his or her life. Fifthly, international human rights law distinguishes between race and religion on the basis that the evils of racial and religious discrimination are prohibited under separate international documents.[128] And finally, statistics from the most recent national census appear to cast doubt on the view that there is always an obvious link between a citizen's religion and their race. A vociferous advocate for the creation of an offence of incitement to religious hatred has claimed that such legislation is necessary to thwart the activities of 'those who dislike people who do not fit into their *white* perception of how Britain should be.'[129] Yet there is evidence to suggest that this attempt to link race and religion is flawed. For example, whilst three quarters of Muslims in Britain are from a South Asian ethnic background, a not insignificant eleven per cent of Britain's Muslims are 'white.'[130] Similarly, the perception that Christianity is only a religion for 'white' people is contradicted by the fact that seventy-one per cent of black people in Britain describe themselves as Christians,[131] while the notion that Buddhism is primarily a religion for Chinese people is rebutted by the fact that only twenty-five per cent of the nation's Buddhists are Chinese, with white people comprising the largest ethnic group (at thirty-eight per cent) of Buddhists in Britain.[132] Thus, it is argued that the theoretical premise underpinning the Racial and Religious Hatred Bill, that there is a necessary correlation between one's race and one's religion, is questionable.

□ *The dubious assumption that the* ECHR *is a valuable safeguard for religious speech*

Government ministers have made much of the fact that an offence of incitement to hatred on religious grounds is not a threat to free speech

128 For example, even though it was originally envisaged that racial and religious discrimination would be governed by a single document, today racial discrimination is outlawed by the International Convention on the Elimination of All Forms of Racial Discrimination (1966), while religious discrimination is prohibited by the less influential Declaration on the Elimination of All Forms of Intolerance and of Discrimination Based on Religion or Belief (1981).

129 See Chris Bryant, Hansard, HC, col. 1114 (7 December 2004); (my italics in the quotation above).

130 See National Statistics Online <http://www.statistics.gov.uk/>.

131 Ibid.

132 Ibid.

because of the important safeguards that are enshrined under Article 10 of the European Convention on Human Rights.[133] However, it is important to enter a significant caveat in this regard. Whilst the European Court of Human Rights has boldly defended aspects of free speech,[134] especially freedom of the press,[135] its track record in the area of religious speech is much less impressive. The shortcomings of its approach were graphically illustrated in the recent decision of *Murphy* v. *Ireland*.[136] In *Murphy*, the European Court held that an Irish law imposing a total ban on the broadcasting of religious advertisements was compatible with the Convention, and that the restrictions imposed on a proposed radio advert about 'evidence of the resurrection' were justified.[137]

In giving judgment, the European Court ignored Murphy's protestations that the advertisement was a manifestation of his religious belief and focussed almost exclusively on the issues relating to freedom of expression under Article 10 of the ECHR.[138] In ascertaining the compatibility of

---

133 For example, see Charles Clarke, Hansard, HC, cols 671, 673, 675, 679 (21 June 2005) and Paul Goggins, Hansard, HC, cols 631 and 646 (11 July 2005).

134 See *Handyside* v. *UK* (1976) 1 EHRR 737.

135 For example, see *Sunday Times* v. *UK* (1979) 2 EHRR 245 and *Jersild* v. *Denmark* (1995) 19 EHRR 407.

136 *Murphy* v. *Ireland* (2004) 38 EHRR 13.

137 Murphy's radio advert was banned under § 10(3) of Ireland's Radio and Television Act 1988. The text of Murphy's advertisement was as follows: 'What think ye of Christ? Would you, like Peter, only say that he is the son of the living God? Have you ever exposed yourself to the historical facts about Christ? The Irish Faith Centre are presenting for Easter week an hour-long video by Dr Jean Scott, PhD, on the evidence of the resurrection from Monday 10 to Saturday 15 April every night at 8.30 and Easter Sunday at 11.30 AM and also live by satellite at 7.30 pm.'

138 Art. 9(1) provides that 'Everyone has the right to freedom of thought, conscience and religion; this right includes freedom to change his religion or belief and freedom, either alone or in community with others and in public or private, to manifest his religion or belief, in worship, teaching, practice and observance.'

Art. 9(2) provides that 'Freedom to manifest one's religion or beliefs shall be subject only to such limitations as are prescribed by law and are necessary in a democratic society in the interests of public safety, for the protection of public order, health or morals, or for the protection of the rights and freedoms of others.'

Art. 10(1) provides that 'Everyone has the right to freedom of expression. This right shall include freedom to hold opinions and to receive and impart information and ideas without interference by public authority and regardless of frontiers. This Article shall not prevent States from requiring the licensing of broadcasting, television or cinema enterprises.'

Art. 10(2) provides that 'The exercise of these freedoms, since it carries with it

the Irish broadcasting restrictions with Article 10(2), the European Court held that the ban on religious advertisements had been 'prescribed by law' (as per § 10(3) of Ireland's Radio and Television Act 1988) and that its introduction had been motivated by a 'legitimate aim' (i.e. the need to maintain 'public order' and the 'protection of the rights and freedoms of others'). But the decision in *Murphy* ultimately turned on whether the curbs on religious advertising were 'necessary in a democratic society', as required by Article 10(2). Applying its usual test (whether there was a 'pressing social need' for the ban that was 'proportionate to the legitimate aim pursued'[139]), the Court held that Murphy's advertisement 'might be considered offensive' to many in Ireland because of that nation's long history of religious conflict.[140]

At first glance the European Court's decision, that the Irish restrictions on religious advertising were a justifiable restriction on freedom of expression, seems plausible. However, on a closer inspection, doubt can be cast on this view for at least three reasons. First, the advertisement in *Murphy* was innocuous, and few belonging to either of Ireland's Protestant or Catholic traditions would have been offended by its reference to 'evidence of the resurrection' or its claim that Christ is the 'son of the living God'.[141] Secondly, in accepting the Irish government's arguments about the risk of sectarian division, the European Court failed to take account of the many positive changes that have taken place in the north of Ireland since the Good-Friday agreement. And thirdly, it is ironic that one of the few issues on which there has been unanimous agreement in recent years between members of the Northern Ireland

---

duties and responsibilities, may be subject to such formalities, conditions, restrictions or penalties as are prescribed by law and are necessary in a democratic society, in the interests of national security, territorial integrity or public safety, for the prevention of disorder or crime, for the protection of health or morals, for the protection of the reputation or rights of others, for preventing the disclosure of information received in confidence, or for maintaining the authority and impartiality of the judiciary'.

139 *Murphy* v. *Ireland* (2004) 38 EHRR 13, para.68.

140 Ibid., para. 73.

141 Had the argument been made (and it wasn't) that the ban was necessary to avoid risking offence to non-Christian groups – say, in the light of the claims about Christ, Irish Muslims – the curbs on free expression would have been easier to justify. Yet it is hard to see how Murphy's advert could have led to conflict between the two main 'Christian' traditions in Ireland, a conflict (by implication) it was meant to prevent.

Assembly has been a campaign for the introduction of Christian radio.[142] Thus, the European Court's ready acceptance of the Irish government's claim that Murphy's proposed adverts would exacerbate sectarian conflict is illustrative of the Court's latent suspicion of *religious* speech.

The Court's ruling in *Murphy* stands in marked contrast to its ruling in *VgT Verein gegen Tierfabriken* v. *Switzerland.*[143] In the latter case an animal-rights group complained that its anti-meat advertisement, which drew attention to the conditions under which pigs are raised, had been banned under Swiss legislation that prohibits political advertising on national television. In contrast to *Murphy,* the European Court ruled that the imposition of a blanket ban on the broadcasting of political advertising was contrary to Article 10. The two contrasting rulings graphically illustrate the European Court's implicit assumption that there is a difference between political and religious speech.[144] Unlike political speech, which is seen as contributing positively to a democratic society, there appears to be a perception that religious speech is of less intrinsic value because of its unique capacity to cause offence and provoke public disorder.[145] Such considerations will therefore doubtlessly be a matter of some concern to those who are wary of the influence of the Racial and Religious Hatred Bill on free speech but assume that the ECHR will be a potentially valuable safeguard for their rights.

CONCLUSION

In making the case for the creation of an offence of incitement to hatred on religious grounds, government ministers have emphasised that the enactment of the Racial and Religious Hatred Bill will be relatively benign. However, to characterise legal reform in this area as little more than the

142 <www.ni-assembly.gov.uk/record/000613.htm>.

143 *VgT Verein gegen Tierfabriken* v. *Switzerland* (2002) 34 EHRR 4.

144 For an excellent analysis of the case law in this area see A. Geddis, 'You Can't Say God on the Radio: Freedom of Expression, Religious Advertising and the Broadcast Media After *Murphy* v. *Ireland*', *European Human Rights Law Review*, (2004) 181–92.

145 Even with the enactment of the Human Rights Act 1998, there is evidence that British judges are wary of what might be termed 'religious speech'. For example, in *Hammond* v. *DPP* (2004) EWHC 69 (Admin.), an evangelical Christian preacher who had publicly attacked homosexuality was convicted, under § 5 of the Public Order Act 1986, for using 'threatening, abusive or insulting words or behaviour' likely to cause 'harassment, alarm or distress' to others nearby.

closing of a legal 'loophole' is surely a dangerous over-simplification.[146] Notwithstanding the fact that prosecutions are likely to be rare,[147] there is a real risk that the enactment of the Racial and Religious Hatred Bill may jeopardise community relations. Indeed, far from just 'plugging a gap in the law',[148] the creation of an offence of incitement to hatred on religious grounds may well open the floodgates for demands for comparable legislation from other communities (gay men, lesbians, transgenders) whose members are regularly subject to hateful attacks.[149]

The practical challenge of extending the current offence of incitement to racial hatred to the area of religion should also not be underestimated. For example, in enforcing the law, police officers will be required, often at short notice, to make difficult and controversial decisions. In addition, the Attorney General will have the unenviable task of distinguishing between a robust attack on the shortcomings of another's faith and forms of expression that constitute incitement to hatred on religious grounds. And in turn, the courts will have to grapple with nebulous terms such as 'incitement', 'hatred' and 'religious belief'. In seeking to assuage the fears of those who are concerned about the impact of the Racial and Religious Hatred Bill on free speech, Home Office Minister Paul Goggins has characterised the proposed new law as being tantamount to the drawing of 'a line in the sand'.[150] But lines in the sand are seldom rigid, and they can be easily redrawn or swept aside. Thus, in spite of ministerial assurances to the contrary, a number of significant challenges lie ahead; once the Racial and Religious Hatred Act 2005 is in force, the proverbial 'devil' will be 'found in the detail'.

---

146 See the comments of Caroline Flint, Hansard, HC, col. 1136 (7 Dec. 2004) and Baroness Scotland, Hansard, HL, col. 1646 (20 Dec. 2004).

147 Lord Goldsmith, the Attorney General, Hansard, HL, col. WA 5 (31 Jan. 2005).

148 Charles Clarke, Hansard, HC, col. 678 (21 June 2005).

149 For example, see B. Townley, 'Support Grows for Anti-Gay Hate Protection' <http://uk.gay.com/headlines/8699>. Indeed, there have been calls for the creation of a 'general offence of incitement to hatred that encompasses all aspects of life': Celia Barlow, Hansard, HC, col. 674 (21 June 2005).

150 *The Times* (10 June 2005).

CHAPTER 14

Theoretical and Institutional Framework: The Soft Spot where Human Rights End and God Begins

Frederik Harhoff

Human rights and religion appear to be interrelated not only materially, in the sense that they address the same matter, i.e. the substance of a good life, but also normatively, in the sense that they exercise a mutual influence on one another. From each side, therefore, there is a prolific inspiration and spread of ideas into the other, but the transition of norms has at the same time a radical effect on the nature of the conversed norms, because they operate differently in different environments; they become subject to different standards of interpretation and applicability. This alteration of the operability of norms is frequently overlooked in the discourse over religion and human rights, but it is certainly relevant to the abstract question of whether 'God believes in human rights', because it affects the framework within which we can meaningfully discuss the relationship between religion and human rights. This chapter seeks to explore the impact of the normative interaction between human rights and religion.

The border area in which this traffic of notions takes place is what I have called 'the soft spot where human rights end and God begins'. By choosing this title, I have also suggested a structural hierarchy between religion and human rights, by which religion is the overarching, superior concept, while human rights forms a much narrower concept within a particular (legal) context. To begin with, I shall speak of religion as *faith*, which is the mental activity of resorting to visions beyond reasoning and linguistic explanation for the purpose of providing meaning in life. *Belief*, in contrast, is what people actually believe in – God, Mohammed, and so on – according to their individual conviction and contingent upon time and place. Faith, in other words, is the unchanging way in which people believe, manifested in the questions they ask, the engagement they vest

Frederik Harhoff is Senior Legal Officer, UN International Criminal Tribunal for the Former Yugoslavia. The views expressed in this article are personal to the author and do not in any way represent the Tribunal or the UN.

in rituals and the tales they trust. In this sense, faith is what is common to all religious denominations: the bustle of believing. I shall commence, then, by introducing a few initial observations on the similarities and differences between the two regimes.

Common to human rights and religion, obviously, is their *normative* function of supplying standards of good behaviour for mankind. Human rights as well as religion both seek to promote order in our perception of the world: they offer guidance, meaning, values and direction of action in relations between men, wherever choices are possible. Both realms set out principles to enable us to distinguish right from wrong, and both include norms governing the social and moral relations between human beings. Both are founded in moral values.

Yet human rights and religion are also very different because they emerge from very different origins and operate by very different methods. Human rights, as a legal concept, is a system of individual and enforceable rights and duties, while religion is a system of faith. Human rights prescribe peace and order by connecting one individual with the next ('All men are equal'), while religion helps to absolve man from his inadequacies by connecting him with the Creator.

Human rights, above all, are secular, created by human determination and founded in what is understood as common reason. Human rights provide no explanation or answer to the questions about the origins of life or the relations between man and nature, although these questions are indirectly relevant also to human rights. They have no established liturgy or places of worship, nor do they employ any clergy to perform the rituals. And human rights are universal in the sense that they – or at least a core of them – apply indifferently and equally to all mankind irrespectively of religious creed or cultural background.

Religion, in contrast, is rooted in particular tales about the creation of life, and it is metaphysical by its very nature. Religious beliefs or convictions, however, are divisive in the sense that every conviction applies to its believers only, introducing differences and distance between Christians, Muslims, Jews, Buddhists and Hindus, etc.; it is inherently 'them' and 'us'. Each religious tradition, in essence, is mutually exclusive of the others and therefore cannot logically acknowledge a universal freedom of religion – even if it associates itself with democracy. The universality claim by human rights, thus, defies religion's insistence on inter-religious difference and diversity, although in one conviction – the Second Vatican Council in 1962 – it was finally acknowledged that there does exist a right to freedom of religious belief and practice. Human rights claim to protect a fundamental freedom of creed, but not all religious convictions appear to be equally protective of fundamental human rights.

If we look further into at the *functional* origin of human rights and religion, it is obvious that while the former are embedded in the history of the modern State and were originally designed as an instrument to protect the individual against abuse of public power, the latter is of a much older origin and came about as tales to explain the very genesis and ethics of life on earth; subsequently it provided divine legitimacy and authority to the princes and the organs of the State. We have seen many wars fought over religious convictions but so far only few over human rights – with NATO's intervention in Kosova in 1999 as the prime example.[1] Before the emergence of the modern States and the reformist separation of State and Church in the fifteenth and sixteenth centuries, each religious tradition used to be the single and central provider of moral values and determinations of right and wrong within its geographical sphere of influence, but this function has partly been assumed by human rights enshrined in the constitutions of many modern-day secular States. The implications of this ostensible vindication by States of the role of the guardian of moral values are vast, among other reasons because it implies a stronger role for short-term political interests. This renders human rights vulnerable to political seizure, obviously, but it also allows for continuous challenge, discourse and review, by which human rights may avoid the danger of becoming ideologically petrified.

Nevertheless, the fact remains that religious doctrine has played an important role in the development of human rights, not only as a source of normative inspiration, but also as a resource for innovation. In his contribution on 'The Functions of Religion', James Nafziger joins Oppenheim in the view that although much of modern international law did grow out of Christian civilisation, there are also significant examples

1 Armed interventions to bring an end to violations of humanitarian law, the so-called 'humanitarian interventions', have been subject to much legal debate, and their lawfulness is still uncertain. In most cases, the purpose has been a combination of protection of the intervening powers' own citizens and a general concern for the protection of fundamental human rights of the other.

of non-Western religious influence on international law, such as *extradition* of criminals (from Egypt and China); the practice of *asylum* (from Greece); the principle of *self-determination* (from Hinduism); and the *non-litigatory methods for resolving disputes* (from Confucian ideology).[2] Whether human rights have played a similar role the other way around as a doctrinal source of stimulation in religion is perhaps less obvious; one such feature which human rights could perhaps offer to religion is their *universality*, which may eventually provide a transformative and global framework for unified interpretation by each religious tradition of their sacred texts in a manner that is consistent with fundamental (human) rights. There is, in addition, a strong potential for ideological cross-fertilisation of values and concepts from religious traditions to human rights in view of the fact that the latter have developed as legal rights for the individual *without* any corresponding duties or obligations on the individual (because the obligations are mainly addressed to the State). Although this has been somewhat modified by judicial interpretation in both the European Court of Human Rights and in domestic courts to the effect that individuals can indeed be held accountable for violating the human rights of other individuals, human rights have essentially remained a matter of protection of the individual by the State. The individual, in other words, holds rights which are enforceable against the State, which in turn has the duties to protect those rights. This has brought about an indolent, consumerist or demanding attitude in some circles towards human rights, because individual beneficiaries can just passively claim all sorts of benefits from the State under the veil of human rights protection – without having to contribute anything in return to the public or the community. While this is not true for all parts of society, the sense of reciprocal responsibility towards society, the charitable impulse to care for the other and to offer something in return for the common good, is definitely a feature which human rights should pick up from religion; from an ideological point of view, we should boost human rights with 'human duties'. However, the limits of this chapter do not allow me to venture further into this question. For now, I shall concen-

2 See James A. R. Nafziger, 'The Functions of Religion in the International Legal System', in Mark Janis and Carolyn Evans (eds), *Religion and International Law* (Leiden: Martinus Nijhoff, 1999), 162.

trate on the qualitative impacts on any religious value or standard when it is integrated in a legal framework and transformed into a legal norm.

Unlike religious norms, human rights are legislative products and subject to judicial interpretation. The domestic process of law-making involves political agendas specific to history, culture and language; even on the international level, negotiations of human rights treaties are as much the result of finding common ground in the political concerns of the governments in power (anyone who has been involved in international negotiations of human rights instruments can corroborate this suggestion). Once adopted, however, human rights norms are given concrete substance and developed by public institutions who apply the norms in practice, by domestic or international NGOs and the media who monitor their observance, by scholars who expose the norms to theoretical analysis, and notably by courts who interpret the norms. The entire legal theoretical framework for judicial interpretation applies to this process, including the choice between dogmatic or hermeneutical interpretation, inductive or deductive methods, *lex superior* or *lex posterior* qualifications and so on. Testing a legal norm in the judicial laboratory of a courtroom, furthermore, comes about in an environment which is extremely rigid and offers no real dialogue between two opposing parties, except for the exchange of selective and strictly legal arguments. Moral discourse, religious assertions or other non-legal viewpoints, thus, are generally inadmissible premises in the process of judicial reasoning. The entire exercise is kept well within the public perception of the legal profession, which carefully selects the legally relevant factors and dismisses everything else. Like members of any other profession, lawyers are trained to spot the objective legal elements in a given course of events and disregard other factors which, in the lawyer's eye, are without legal significance. A medical doctor would most likely perceive different factors in the same event, and a priest yet other features.

Altogether, this provides a very particular but also very active and dynamic environment for legal clarification and political monitoring, in which a number of questions are raised and important challenges made. Do human rights, for instance, entail only rights or do they also impose legal duties? If so, are such duties binding only upon government agencies or do they also apply to private individuals, companies or other non-State actors? Do Human Rights take priority over, say, environmental or religious norms? In my opinion, the transformation of a religious norm into a legal norm will in most cases impact so strongly on the contents of the norm that it quickly emancipates from its religious origin. This is not to say, of course, that the norm completely changes its meaning, but, as a result of its entrenchment in law, the conditions for its practical application become so particular to the legal regime that the norm in question can no longer function in its original religious context in its legal outfit, or can only do so with strict limitations. Legalised concepts, in other words, acquire features and qualities that render them unsuitable in their original milieu.

Let me take a few examples to illustrate my point. Without going into any discussion of whether *respect for the sanctity of the individual human being* was originally a religious concept that spilled over into human rights, or whether it emerged in human rights as a result of Enlightenment or both, no doubt remains that the right to individual integrity is today a human rights norm. This norm is manifested, *inter alia*, as a right to equal recognition as a person before the law (Articles 6 and 7 of the UN Universal Declaration of Human Rights), without distinction of any kind, such as race, colour, sex, language, religion, political or other opinion, national or social origin, property, birth or other status (Article 2 of the Universal Declaration). From a religious point of view, the right to equal recognition as a subject of law, to own property and to seek and obtain legal protection thereof is clear and unequivocal. Yet in most countries this right is curtailed in any number of ways through municipal laws requiring a certain age or a certain degree of wealth or status or a particular nationality or even the male sex as a condition for enjoying this fundamental right. Another example is the assurance in Article 9 of the Universal Declaration that no one shall be subject to arbitrary arrest, detention or exile; post-September 11 practices in many countries reveal an appalling departure from the gist of this fundamental freedom. What originally appeared as simple and straightforward religious norms, in other words, may quickly transform into something very different once they are entrenched into law. This is not to say that there may not be good reasons to justify these legal qualifications; my point is that we cannot always speak of religious norms and human rights on the same footing because they belong to different regimes. Any discourse on cross-border fertilisation of ideas and concepts between the two regimes must include proper consideration of the particular terms of conceptualisation, interpretation and reasoning that apply in each regime. The norms and values which appear to be common to religion and human rights, in other words, exist in a polycentric environment in which they may acquire different and possibly irreconcilable meanings.

These observations lead to my concluding remarks about the principal question this volume's title poses: does God believe in human rights? The question, of course, is absurd because the object of belief does not itself believe in anything outside its own scope. Be that as it may, the true core of this question is really whether religion takes primacy over human rights or vice versa in case of a clash between the two. If, for the sake of the discourse, God were really to believe in human rights, He (assuming He is a Man!) would be bound to submit to the human rights norm, because that is exactly what *belief* requires. If He does not, on the other hand, He is free to impose his own ruling in the matter at hand and will disregard the opposing human rights norm. Now, whether religion takes precedence over human rights, or the other way around, depends in my submission entirely on the situation and the nature of the conflicting norms; I do not adhere to any universal solution to this dilemma. The only approach I can point to in this respect is for each camp to show enough flexibility and willingness to engage in an unprejudiced discourse for the purpose of reconciling the conflicting views and concerns expressed by each party. This is the only way in which the religious traditions may embrace binding human rights, and human rights may entail human duties.

Thus the most intelligent answer to the question of whether or not God believes in human rights is, *Yes, of course He doesn't!*

CONTRIBUTORS

PETER CUMPER IS a Senior Lecturer in the Faculty of Law in the University of Leicester, UK, where he teaches Constitutional and Administrative Law, Human Rights Law, and Law and Religion. He has published on various subjects within the field of human rights and in a number of journals including *Public Law, Legal Studies, European Human Rights Law Review, Emory International Law Review,* and *Journal of Social Welfare and Family Law.* He is the joint editor of *Minority Rights in the 'New' Europe* (Kluwer, 1999).

DR DENNIS DE JONG currently serves as Advisor on Human Rights and Peacebuilding in the Human Rights and Peacebuilding Department of the Netherlands Ministry of Foreign Affairs. Within this position, one of his assignments is the freedom of religion or belief. Dr de Jong also serves as a member of the OSCE Advisory Panel on Freedom of Religion or Belief. He obtained his doctorate in international law in 2000. This has been published as *The Freedom of Thought, Conscience and Religion or Belief in the United Nations (1946–1992)* (Intersentia and Hart, 2000).

PROFESSOR MALCOLM D. EVANS, OBE, is Professor of Public International Law and currently Dean of the Faculty of Social Sciences and Law at the University of Bristol, UK. He is a member of the OSCE Advisory Council of Freedom of Religion or Belief; the International Law Association Committee on Human Rights Law and Practice; the UK FCO Panel of Advisors on Torture; and a member of the Board of Management of the Association for the Prevention of Torture. His principle publications include *Religious Liberty and International Law in Europe* (CUP, 1997), *Preventing Torture* (OUP, 1998), *Protecting Prisoners* (OUP, 1999), *Combating Torture in Europe* (Strasbourg: Council of Europe Press, 2001) and (ed.) *International Law* (OUP, 2003, 2006).

PROFESSOR CONOR GEARTY serves as the Rausing Director of the Centre for the Study of Human Rights, and Professor of Human Rights Law at the London School of Economics, UK. He has published widely on terrorism, civil liberties and human rights. His publications include *Terror* (Faber, 1990); (with K. D. Ewing) *Freedom under Thatcher* (Oxford Paperbacks, 1990); *The Struggle for Civil Liberties* (OUP, 2000); and *Principles of Human Rights Adjudication* (OUP, 2004, 2005). His most recent book, *Can Human Rights Survive?* is published by Cambridge University Press. Professor Gearty is a barrister and was a founder member of Matrix Chambers from where he continues to practice. He has served as adviser to judges, practitioners and public authorities on the implications of the UK Human Rights Act, and lectures widely on human rights.

DR NAZILA GHANEA is Senior Lecturer in International Law and Human Rights at the University of London, Institute of Commonwealth Studies. She is editor of the international academic journal *Religion and Human Rights*. Her research is primarily in the areas of freedom of religion or belief, minority rights, the UN human rights machinery and human rights in the Middle East.

Her publications include *Human Rights, the UN and the Bahá'ís in Iran* (Kluwer Law, 2003); the edited collection (with A. Xanthaki) *Minorities, Peoples and Self-Determination* (Nijhoff, 2005) and *The Challenge of Religious Discrimination at the Dawn of the New Millennium* (Nijhoff, 2003); and journal articles in the *ICLQ* and *Human Rights Quarterly*. Nazila will be taking up a University Lectureship at the University of Oxford in late 2006.

DR FREDERIK HARHOFF is an Associate Professor in International and EU Law at the Faculty of Law, University of Copenhagen, Denmark. He served as Head of the Legal Section at the Chambers of the International Criminal Tribunal for Rwanda from 1996 to 1998. His specialist areas and extensive publications are in the following areas: public international law, international law of the sea, international humanitarian law, the law of war crimes, the law of armed conflicts, international human rights, the right of self-determination for indigenous peoples, and the international law of environmental protection. His journal articles in English have been published in the *Nordic Journal of International Law*, *Duke Journal of Comparative and International Law, International Review of the Red Cross, Canadian Yearbook of International Law* and the *Encyclopedia of Public International Law.*

THE RT REVD THE LORD HARRIES OF PENTREGARTH, DD FKC FRSL. Richard Harries was Bishop of Oxford from 1987 to June 2006. Before that he was Dean of King's College, London. He has been a parish priest and a lecturer in Christian Doctrine and Ethics. He is a Fellow of King's College, London and of the Royal Society of Literature. The Bishop's twenty-two books include *Art and the Beauty of God* (Mowbrays, 1993), chosen as a book of the year by Anthony Burgess in *The Observer, The Passion in Art* (Ashgate, 2004) and *Praying the Eucharist* (SPCK, 2004). The Bishop was Chairman of the Council of Christians and Jews 1992–2001 and is a founder member of the Abrahamic Group in Oxford, bringing Jews, Muslims and Christians together for serious theological dialogue. His biography by John Peart Binns, *A Heart in the Head,* is to be published by Continuum in 2007.

THE VEN. DR MICHAEL IPGRAVE is Archdeacon of Southwark, with pastoral and administrative oversight of forty Anglican churches in the multi-cultural and multi-faith communities of South London. He previously served as Inter-Faith Relations Adviser to the Archbishops' Council of the Church of England and Secretary of the Churches Commission on Inter-Faith Relations. He has written widely on the practice and theology of inter-faith relations. His publications include (ed.) *Bearing the Word: Prophecy in the Biblical and Quranic Perspective* (Church House Pub., 2005), *Scriptures In Dialogue: Christians and Muslims Studying The Bible and the Quran Together* (Church House Pub., 2004), *Trinity and Inter-Faith Dialogue: Plenitude and Plurality* (Peter Lang, 2003), *The Road Ahead: A Christian–Muslim Dialogue* (Church House Pub., 2002) and *Religious Discrimination: A Christian Response* (CTBI, 2001).

JOHN BARNABAS (BARNEY) LEITH has degrees in Sociology and in Social Psychology and Philosophy. After leaving teaching he established and directed a centre for alcoholism counselling and subsequently moved into publishing and design.

In 1993 Barney was elected to the UK Bahá'í community's national governing council, the National Spiritual Assembly. He served as its

Secretary (1998–2005) and is currently its Secretary for External Affairs, directing the National Assembly's relations with government and parliament, with other NGOs and with the diplomatic world.

He is a member of the UK government's Faith Community's Consultative Council; chairs two national multi-faith bodies in the UK: the Religion and Belief Consultative Group on Equality, Diversity and Human Rights, and the Faith-Based Regeneration Network; and is a trustee of the Inter-Faith Network for the UK.

MELANIE PHILLIPS is a British journalist and author best known for her controversial column in the *Daily Mail.* Awarded the Orwell Prize for journalism in 1996, she is the author of *All Must Have Prizes* (Warner, 1998), an acclaimed study of Britain's educational and moral crisis which provoked the fury of educationists and the delight and relief of parents. Her ideas have influenced politicians in both government and opposition, who follow her battles in the culture wars. Styled a conservative by her opponents, she prefers to think of herself as defending authentic liberal values against the attempt to destroy Western culture from within. Her other publications include *The Sex-Change Society* (Social Market Foundation, 1999), *America's Social Revolution* (Civitas, 2001) and *The Ascent of Woman* (Little Brown, 2003).

JAVAID REHMAN is Professor of International Human Rights Law, Brunel University, UK. He has held teaching posts at the Universities of Hull, Leeds and Ulster and visiting professorships at several institutions including Emory University Law School and the Law College University of Peshawar, Pakistan. His publications include *Islamic State Practices, International Law and the Threat from Terrorism* (Hart, 2005); *International Human Rights Law* (Longman, 2003); (with S. S. Ali) *Indigenous Peoples and Ethnic Minorities of Pakistan* (Routledge/Curzon, 2001) and *The Weaknesses in the International Protection of Minority Rights* (Kluwer Law, 2000). He is also the author of over fifty refereed articles on issues of human rights, religion and international law.

ROGER RUSTON is a freelance theologian who has worked closely on the Dominican Justice and Peace Commission, and for the Christendom Trust. He is the Christendom Trust Research Fellow at the Centre for Law and Religion at Cardiff University, Wales, UK. He was Lecturer in

Ethics and Moral Theology in the Dominican School of Theology at the University of Oxford, and Lecturer in Christian Ethics in the Department of Theology and Religious Studies at the University of Bristol. He is a member of the Commission for International Justice and Peace. He is the author of a number of publications, including *Human Rights and the Image of God* (SCM, 2004), which appraises the Catholic church's attitude to human rights over the past century.

PROFESSOR AVROM SHERR qualified as a solicitor in commercial litigation and has taught at the Universities of Warwick, Liverpool and London. He has been at the Institute of Advanced Legal Studies since 1995 as founding Woolf Professor of Legal Education, and as Director since 2004.

Professor Sherr's main areas of interest have been the development of legal education, the sociology of the legal profession, ethics in professional work and the provision of legal services. He has written in the area of freedom of protest, on discrimination relating to AIDS/HIV and on welfare rights provision within health care.

He was a member of the Lord Chancellor's Advisory Committee on Legal Education and Conduct, and of the Race Relations and Equal Opportunities Committees of the Law Society of England and Wales.

DR NORMAN SOLOMON was Fellow in Modern Jewish Thought at the Oxford Centre for Hebrew and Jewish Studies until his retirement in 2001. He was previously Director of the Centre for the Study of Judaism and Jewish/Christian Relations at the Selly Oak Colleges, Birmingham. He has served as rabbi of Orthodox congregations in Manchester, Liverpool, London and Birmingham.

He is a past president of the British Association for Jewish Studies; Vice President of the World Congress of Faiths; and a Patron of the International Interfaith Centre. His publications include *Judaism and World Religion* (Macmillan, 1991), *The Analytic Movement: Hayyim Soloveitchik and his School* (Scholars Press, 1993), *A Very Short Introduction to Judaism* (OUP, 1996), and *Historical Dictionary of Judaism* (Scarecrow Press, 1998).

ALAN STEPHENS was born in Swansea, South Wales. He read law at University College London, and was called to the Bar at the Middle

Temple. He was on the board of editors of the *Netherlands Yearbook of International Law* (1975–84), and is currently on the board of editors of *Religion and Human Rights*, an international journal. He has been a panellist at the annual meeting of the American Society of International Law. From 1984 until his retirement in 2002, he was publisher, and later publishing director, of Kluwer Law International/Martinus Nijhoff Publishers. In recent years he has initiated research projects with, *inter alia*, the International Bar Association, the Raoul Wallenberg Institute and the Hague Institute for the Internationalisation of Law. He is Director of Research of the Clemens Nathan Research Centre.

RAPHAEL WALDEN was educated at Balliol College, Oxford, and at the London School of Economics. He is an English solicitor and member of the Israeli bar. He joined the Israeli Foreign Ministry in 1974, where he held the posts of Director of the Treaty Division, Director of the International Law Division, Counsellor at the Israel Embassy in Copenhagen, Deputy Chief of the Mission to the UN in Geneva, and finally Ambassador to Eritrea. Since retirement from the Ministry in 2000, he has been adviser to the Consultative Council of Jewish Organisations and Director of the Clemens Nathan Research Centre. His publications include the co-edited collections *Racism and Human Rights* (Nijhoff, 2004) and *For the Sake of Humanity* (Nijhoff, 2006).

PAUL WELLER is Professor of Inter-Religious Relations at the University of Derby, where he is Senior Research Fellow and Head of Research and Commercial Development in the Faculty of Education, Health and Sciences. He is editor of *Religions in the UK: Directory 2001–3* (Multi-Faith Centre, University of Derby, 2001) as well as of its two previous editions (1997, 1993), and is currently working on a 2007 update. His publications include *Time for a Change: Reconfiguring Religion, State and Society* (T & T Clark, 2005); with Alice Feldman and Kingsley Purdam, *Religious Discrimination in England and Wales* (Research Development Statistics Directorate, The Home Office, 2001); and, with Jim Beckford, Richard Gale, David Owen and Ceri Peach, *Review of the Evidence Base on Faith Communities* (Office of the Deputy Prime Minister, 2006) <http://www.communities.gov.uk/index.asp?id=1165319>.

Studies in Religion, Secular Beliefs and Human Rights

This Series is designed to shed light on issues of current concern in the field of religion, law and human rights.

ISSN 1871-7829

1. Whiting, A. and C. Evans (Eds), *Mixed Blessings*. Laws, Religions, and Women's Rights in the Asia-Pacific Region. ISBN 978-90-04-15141-3. 2006.
2. Lerner, N., *Religion, Secular Beliefs and Human Rights*. 25 Years After the 1981 Declaration. ISBN 978-90-04-15209-0. 2006.
3. Bayefsky, A.F. and A. Waldman, *State Support for Religious Education*. Canada versus the United Nations. ISBN 978-90-04-14980-9. 2006.
4. Shah, N.A., *Women, the Koran and International Human Rights Law*. The Experience of Pakistan. ISBN 978-90-04-15237-3. 2006.
5. Ghanea, N., A. Stephens, R. Walden (Eds), *Does God Believe in Human Rights?* Essays on Religion and Human Rights. ISBN 978-90-04-15254-0. 2007.
6. Rehman, J. and S.C. Breau (Eds), *Religion, Human Rights and International Law*. A Critical Examination of Islamic State Pratices. ISBN 978-90-04-15826-9. 2007.

www.ingramcontent.com/pod-product-compliance
Lightning Source LLC
LaVergne TN
LVHW010631300926
849162LV00001B/129